British Literature

A HISTORICAL OVERVIEW

Volume B

British Literature

A HISTORICAL OVERVIEW

Volume B

GENERAL EDITORS

Joseph Black, University of Massachusetts
Leonard Conolly, Trent University
Kate Flint, Rutgers University
Isobel Grundy, University of Alberta
Don LePan, Broadview Press
Roy Liuzza, University of Tennessee
Jerome J. McGann, University of Virginia
Anne Lake Prescott, Barnard College
Barry V. Qualls, Rutgers University
Claire Waters, University of California, Davis

with

Laura Cardiff
Emily Bernhard Jackson
Janice Schroeder
Yevgeniya Traps

broadview press

Library and Archives Canada Cataloguing in Publication

British literature ; a historical overview / general editors, Joseph
Black ... [et al.].
Includes bibliographical references and index.
ISBN 978-1-55481-001-7 (v. 1).—ISBN 978-1-55481-002-4 (v. 2)

1. English literature—History and criticism. I. Black, Joseph, 1962-
PR83.B74 2010   820.9   C2010-902477-X

Broadview Press is an independent, international publishing house, incorporated in 1985.

We welcome comments and suggestions regarding any aspect of our publications—please feel free to contact us at the addresses below or at broadview@broadviewpress.com.

North America	PO Box 1243, Peterborough, Ontario, Canada K9J 7H5
	2215 Kenmore Ave., Buffalo, New York, USA 14207
	Tel: (705) 743-8990; Fax: (705) 743-8353
	email: customerservice@broadviewpress.com
UK, Europe, Central Asia,	Eurospan Group, 3 Henrietta St., London WC2E 8LU, UK
Middle East, Africa, India,	Tel: 44 (0) 1767 604972; Fax: 44 (0) 1767 601640
and Southeast Asia	email: eurospan@turpin-distribution.com
Australia and New Zealand	NewSouth Books, c/o TL Distribution
	15-23 Helles Ave., Moorebank, NSW, Australia 2170
	Tel: (02) 8778 9999; Fax: (02) 8778 9944
	email: orders@tldistribution.com.au

www.broadviewpress.com

Broadview Press acknowledges the financial support of the Government of Canada through the Canada Book Fund for our publishing activities.

Developmental Editor	Jennifer McCue
Textual Editors	Eileen Eckert, Colleen Franklin, & Morgan Rooney
Design Coordinator	Eileen Eckert

This book is printed on paper containing 100% post-consumer fibre.

PRINTED IN CANADA

CONTENTS

PREFACE

This book and its companion emerge out of an anthology—but they are very much books for those who don't like anthologies. The anthology in question is *The Broadview Anthology of British Literature*, which first appeared in 2006. Both the full six-volume anthology and the two-volume concise version that followed have been highly popular as texts for a wide variety of courses in British literature. The introductions to the anthology's six volumes, which together provide an overview of the full sweep of the subject, have been particularly well received. Even many who say they would never teach from an anthology have praised the introductions as providing a wealth of helpful background information for those new to the subject—information that is often difficult for a professor to find time to cover in lectures during the short span of a university course. It is above all for those academics—and for their students—that we at Broadview are publishing these two volumes. We hope, too, that the volumes will be interesting and helpful for general readers.

"Writing by Committee"

One of the first things that readers may be struck by when opening these volumes is the number of people listed on the title page. In addition to the names of the ten general editors, the names of four individuals who have made particularly significant contributions to the drafting of the period introductions appear on the title page. Why so many? When we began in the early years of this century to plan a new anthology of British literature, we immediately recognized the degree to which the expansion of English Studies as a discipline had made the task of assembling and editing an anthology that fully and vibrantly reflects the ways in which the British literary tradition is studied and taught an extraordinarily daunting one. We could see that the sheer amount of work involved would be enormous—and so too would be the amount of expertise that we would need to call on. And so we charted a new course in the preparation of *The Broadview Anthology of British Literature*. Rather than dividing up the work among a relatively small number of academics, we involved a large number of contributors in the process, and encouraged a high degree of collaboration at every level. First and foremost were (and are) the distinguished academics who have served as general editors for the project, but literally hundreds of people have been involved at various stages in researching, drafting text, reviewing material, editing material, choosing illustrations, and finally carrying out the work of designing and typesetting the volumes. That approach allowed us to draw on a diverse range of talent and to prepare an ambitious work with unusual speed. It also facilitated the maintenance of a high degree of consistency. For this two-volume overview, as with the anthology itself, material has been reviewed and revised not only in-house at Broadview, but also by outside editors, by a variety of academics with an extraordinarily diverse range of backgrounds and academic specialities, and by our general editors. The aim has been to ensure accuracy and to make sure that the same standards be applied throughout to matters such as balance (of the social, the political, and the economic with the literary), tone of writing, and accessibility to the student or general reader. We once heard tell of a representative of one of our competitors deriding this approach as "writing by committee," as if that could be taken as evidence that the work was of inferior quality. The fact is, though, that for certain large projects a "writing-by-committee" approach can work extremely well. We would not for a moment be so bold as to suggest that the current project meets the standards of that prepared in the name of King James, but we are very proud of having also worked as a large group in a collaborative fashion. Readers will judge for themselves whether the result helps to illuminate the history of British literature.

"Women's Place"

A central element of the broadening of the canon of British literature in recent generations has of course been a great increase in the attention paid to texts by women writers. As one might expect from a publisher that has played an important role in making neglected works by women writers widely available, this overview follows that trend. But it also reflects this broadening in other ways. In many accounts, women writers have tended to be set somewhat apart, referenced in introductions only in relation to issues of gender, and too often treated as important only for the fact of their being women writers. We have strenuously resisted such segregation; while women writers are of course discussed in relation to gender issues, their works are also discussed alongside those by men in a wide variety of other contexts.

"British," "English," "Irish," "Scottish," Welsh," "Other"

The broadening of English Studies, in conjunction with the expansion and subsequent contraction of British power and influence around the world, has considerably complicated the issue of exactly how inclusive works such as anthologies and literary histories should be. Like its competitors from Norton and Longman, *The Broadview Anthology of British Literature* is significantly more inclusive than its title suggests, including a number of non-British writers whose works connect in important ways with the traditions of British literature. So too with these two overview volumes. We have endeavored to make clear the fluid and multilingual reality of the medieval period through discussions not only of works in Old and Middle English but also, where other cultures interacted with the nascent "English" language and "British" culture, works in Latin, in French, and in Welsh. In later periods the word "British" becomes deeply problematic in different respects, but on balance we have preferred it to the only obvious alternative, "English." There are several objections to the latter in this context. Perhaps most obviously, "English" excludes authors or texts not only from Ireland but also from Scotland and from Wales, both of which retain to this day cultures quite distinct from that of the English. "English literature," of course, may also be taken to mean "literature written in English," but since the anthology does not cover *all* literature written in English (most obviously, excluding American literature), the ambiguity would not in this case be helpful.

The question of whether to touch on Irish writers in a work of this sort presents a related but even more tangled set of issues. At the beginning of the period covered in this overview we find works such as the Book of Kells, which may have been created in what is now England, in what is now Scotland, in what is now Ireland—or in some combination of these. Through most of the seventeenth, eighteenth, and nineteenth centuries almost the whole of Ireland was under British control—for the most part unwillingly. Not far into the twentieth century, Ireland was partitioned, with Northern Ireland becoming a part of Great Britain, and the Republic of Ireland declared independent of Britain (on December 6, 1921). Less than two months earlier, James Joyce had completed *Ulysses*, which was first published as a complete work the following year (in Paris, not in Britain). It would be obviously absurd to regard Joyce as a British writer up to just before the publication of *Ulysses*, and an Irish writer thereafter. And arguably he and other Irish writers should never be regarded as British, whatever the politics of the day. If on no other grounds than their overwhelming influence on and connection to the body of literature written in Britain, we have included discussions of Ireland and of Irish writers throughout this work. We have also endeavored to give a real sense of how the histories and the cultures of England, Ireland, Scotland, and Wales, much as they interact with one another, are also distinct.

Also included in these volumes are discussions of writers from areas that are far removed geographically from the British Isles but that are or have been British possessions. Writers who came of age in an independent United States, on the other hand, are not discussed, unless (like T.S. Eliot) they subsequently relocated in Britain and became important British literary figures. Surrounding such issues are of course substantial gray areas. One might well argue, for example, that Henry James merits inclusion in an overview of British literature, or that W.H. Auden and Thom Gunn are more American poets than British ones. But the chosen subject matter of James's work has traditionally been considered to mark him as having remained an American writer, despite having spent almost two-thirds of his life in England. And both Auden and Gunn so clearly made a mark in Britain before crossing the Atlantic that it would seem odd to exclude them from these pages on the grounds of their having lived the greater part of their adult lives in America.

The History of Language and of Print Culture

For the past generation or more, English Studies has tended increasingly to integrate the study of literature with such topics as the spread of literacy, the development of copyright laws, the growth of book publishing—in short, with the study of print culture—and these two volumes are in that respect very much in accord with recent trends. Perhaps less common these days is the integration of the study of literature with the study of the history of the English language, but the latter is an area we see as being of direct and vital relevance; we thus include a section on the history of the language as part of each of the introductions.

Other Materials

A chart of monarchs and prime ministers is provided within these pages, while a range of other adjunct materials may be accessed through *The Broadview Anthology of British Literature* website, <www.broadviewpress.com/BABL>. Chronological charts are provided for each of the time periods. "British Money" provides a thumbnail sketch of the world of pounds, shillings, and pence, together with a handy guide to estimating the current equivalents of monetary values of other eras. And "Sounds of British Literature" provides readings that may help to make the sounds of British literature—from Chaucer to Robert Burns and beyond—more accessible to the reader.

Introduction to
the Age of Romanticism

Perhaps the spirit and ethos of the Romantic era and its creative output are nowhere better captured than in the evolution of clothing during the period. When the artistic, literary, and political changes that are usually associated with Romanticism began in the 1780s, the heavy and elaborate costumes of the eighteenth century still prevailed, constricting their wearers into a rigid formality and mirroring contemporaneous social and aesthetic structures. In the heady years surrounding the French Revolution, when the possibility of

Ball dress, c. 1800.

Morning dress, c. 1800.

greater freedom seemed within reach, these stiff garments gave way to loose, flowing dresses for women, clothes cut from muslins and patterned cottons that had been rendered relatively inexpensive by increasing British imperial control in the East and by technological advances in weaving in Britain itself. During the same period, local militiamen, sporting magnificent military uniforms, demonstrated Britain's growing national pride, all the while masking persistent fear of French invasion. By the time the Romantic period drew to a close in the mid-1830s, these looser fashions and glittering uniforms had themselves been superseded by the tightly laced corsets, salt-and-pepper trousers, and bell skirts heavily supported by hoops and petticoats that are now inextricably associated with English Victorianism.

As the combination of freedom and militarism expressed by Romantic fashions suggests, the fifty years between the French Revolution and the reign of Queen Victoria were neither historically simple nor culturally straightforward. Despite its seeming cohesiveness and unity, the Romantic period was a complex nexus of revolution and conservatism, of bold iconoclasm and hidebound conventionality. Revolutions played a central role in shaping the Romantic period—and continue to shape our perceptions of it. The form and structure of the British Romantic era, as well as the very concept of "Romanticism," have changed radically in recent decades. What in the mid-twentieth century was seen as a literary period centered on five or six major poets—all male—and a select number of prose writers—also all male—has gradually come to be seen as an era made up of writers and thinkers of different genders,

Richard Dighton, George "Beau" Brummell, *1805. Brummell, the leading "dandy" of the age, brought into fashion a new style of dress coat, pantaloons, and black evening dress for men. Brummell was fastidious about cleanliness as well as clothing, but denounced perfume for men and any form of showy display.*

beliefs, and social backgrounds. Whereas familiarity with British Romantic poetry once meant having read only William Blake, William Wordsworth, Samuel Taylor Coleridge, Lord Byron, Percy Bysshe Shelley, and John Keats (collectively known as "The Big Six"), today, the voices of Mary Robinson, Anna Laetitia Barbauld, Felicia Hemans, and Letitia Landon—all respected and popular in their day but largely unstudied until recently—are seen as integral to a proper understanding of the period's verse. So too with Romantic non-fiction, which was once seen as consisting of the prose of Coleridge, Charles Lamb, and William Hazlitt, but now encompasses the proto-feminist writing of Mary Wollstonecraft, the didactic prose of Hannah More and Maria Edgeworth, and the natural sketches and observations of Dorothy Wordsworth. The prose fiction of the period (aside from a nod or two acknowledging Jane Austen and Sir Walter Scott) was once given short shrift; the drama was, generally, neglected. At this moment, Mary Shelley's novels—particularly *Frankenstein* (1818) and *The Last Man* (1826)—receive at least as much critical attention as do the works of her husband Percy Shelley, with *Frankenstein* probably being read more widely than any other single work of the Romantic period; Austen's works are now seen to hold a central position in the history of the novel; and the work of other writers of fiction—from William Godwin to Mary Hays, Amelia Opie, Mary Robinson, and Charlotte Smith—has been much more fully and more favorably assessed. In the study of drama, a similar, if less marked, shift has occurred, with the importance of the work of Hannah Cowley, Elizabeth Inchbald and Joanna Baillie, as well as that of Percy Shelley and of Byron, being newly recognized.

If recent decades have brought a substantial shift in the emphasis placed on various authors in the study of the Romantic period, they have also brought a shift in the way the period as a whole is perceived. Whereas Romantic literature in English was once discussed far more with reference to nature and to the imagination than it was with reference to politics or to ideology, a broader perspective is now almost universally acknowledged as essential to a more comprehensive sense of the period. Not everything has changed however; it is still almost universally accepted that the Romantic mind-set and the literary works it produced were shaped, above all, by the French Revolution and the Industrial Revolution.

For Romanticism, the French Revolution was epoch-making. When the Bastille fell on 14 July 1789 and the French National Assembly issued its democratic, anti-monarchical *Declaration of the Rights of Man and Citizen* on August 27 of the same year, it seemed to the people of Great Britain, a mere 12 miles across the Channel, that a new dawn was on the horizon. For liberals and for many authors, artists, and intellectuals this dawn was a rosy one, promising not only greater equality and better government in France itself, but also the beginning of a thoroughgoing transformation of the world. Mary Robinson's "Ainsi Va Le Monde" (1791) provides a vivid sense of the degree to which a fervent faith in and enthusiasm for freedom knew no bounds in the breasts of many writers of the time:

> Hark! "Freedom" echoes thro' the vaulted skies.
> The goddess speaks! O mark the blest decree,—
> Tyrants Shall Fall—Triumphant Man Be Free!

Wordsworth, present in France during the early days of the Revolution, famously wrote of it later, "Bliss was it in that dawn to be alive!" while his friend and fellow poet Robert Southey recalled that "a visionary world seemed to open … [N]othing was dreamt of but regeneration of the human race." Mary Wollstonecraft, who had recently published *A Vindication of the Rights of Woman*, moved to Paris in 1792, inspired by revolutionary idealism. The Revolution became a central Romantic metaphor, as well as a central psychological influence, on the first generation of Romantic writers.

The younger generation too, particularly Byron and Shelley, were stirred by revolutionary fervor. What these poets hoped for, however was a continuation of the *spirit* of the French Revolution. For, in actuality, Wordsworth's new dawn soon darkened into a terrible thunderstorm and a rain of blood. In August of 1792, the leaders of the Revolution overthrew the French monarchy, and, a month later, a Parisian mob massacred more than a thousand prisoners whom they believed to be Royalist conspirators. Extremist Jacobins[1] now prevailed over more moderate Girondins,[2] and the Revolution turned into the

---

1   The term was used throughout the Romantic period to denote those in sympathy with the radical, revolutionary ideals associated with the French Revolution. Those opposing the Revolution were termed "anti-Jacobins." The ideological differences between the radical Jacobins and the conservative anti-Jacobins were often played out in the novels of the late eighteenth and early nineteenth century.

2   A loosely affiliated coalition of moderate republicans, the Girondins controlled the French Legislative Assembly from late 1791 to late 1792, when they were ousted by more

Reign of Terror (1793–94). In January 1793, King Louis XVI went to the guillotine; Marie Antoinette followed him in October. France declared war on Britain in 1793, and Britain quickly reciprocated the declaration. As the terror progressed under the guidance of Maximilien Robespierre, thousands of aristocrats, clergy, and alleged opponents of the Revolution were guillotined including, eventually, Robespierre himself. In 1794, France offered to support any and all revolutions abroad, proceeding to invade its neighbors. In 1799, Napoleon had himself named First Consul for life, and, in 1804, he crowned himself Emperor. When he invaded the Iberian Peninsula in 1807, Britain intervened to aid the Spanish and Portuguese. The Napoleonic Wars, as these military conflicts came to be known, did not end until Napoleon was thoroughly routed at the Battle of Waterloo in 1815.

What had begun as a movement for democracy, then, had become a military dictatorship. Looking back from a distance of 24 years, Byron wrote, in *Childe Haroldé's Pilgrimmage* (1812–18), that the French made themselves a fearful monument:

> The wreck of old opinions ...
> ... the veil they rent
> And what behind it lay all earth shall view.
> But good with ill they also overthrew,
> Leaving but ruins, wherewith to rebuild
> Upon the same foundation, and renew
> Dungeons and thrones ...

The Revolution's promise of freedom died in a frenzy of oppression, destruction, violence, and imperialism, and many of Britain's intellectuals watched in horror, gradually turning from bold liberalism to a cautious conservatism they saw as both pragmatic and necessary. To use the political terminology that first developed out of the seating arrangements in the French National Constituent Assembly in 1789, they moved from the left of center to the right of center; Wordsworth, Coleridge, and Southey, all radical thinkers in their youth, were firm conservatives by the end of their lives. Others—such as Barbauld—remained politically on the left but became disillusioned, both by the course that

---

radical politicians. Many Girondin leaders were summarily executed during the Reign of Terror.

revolution had taken in France and by the failure of the British to embrace the principles of freedom. Barbauld surveyed what seemed to her a decadent and oppressive England in "Eighteen Hundred and Eleven" (1812)—"The worm is in thy core, thy glories pass away"—and Shelley despaired in "England in 1819" (composed in 1819, but not published until 1839) at "Rulers who neither see nor feel nor know, / But leechlike to their fainting country cling."

The British government's response to the developments in France had been swift and repressive. In 1794, the right of habeas corpus—which required the state to show legitimate cause for imprisonment and to carry out trials in a timely manner—was suspended. As a result, those accused of crimes could be held for an indefinite period. In 1795, Parliament passed the Treasonable Practices Act, which made criticism of the government a crime; in the same year, it passed an act that limited the size of public meetings and the places in which they could be held. The Combination Acts of 1799 and 1800 forbade workers to associate for the purposes of collective bargaining. To enforce all these restrictive measures, the government set loose a herd of spies, many of whom acted as *agents provocateurs*, infiltrating liberal and radical groups and prompting them to commit criminal acts they otherwise might not have committed. In at least

William Heath, The Battle of Waterloo *(detail), 1815. British infantrymen to the right are firing into the ranks of the French cavalry. The full battle involved approximately 75,000 French troops under Napoleon; the Duke of Wellington commanded an allied force of well over 100,000. The casualties totaled over 50,000—60 per cent of them French.*

one important case, that of the Cato Street Conspiracy of 1820—a scheme to murder cabinet ministers and stage a government *coup*—these government agents first urged on and then exposed conspirators who were punished with hanging or with transportation to Australia. In Scotland and Ireland, authoritarianism could be even more severe, particularly since rebellion there required no instigating. In 1798, the United Irishmen, led by Theobald Wolfe Tone and Lord Edward Fitzgerald and assisted by French forces, attempted a country-wide uprising to achieve complete Irish independence. The rebellion ended in failure, and the oppression of the Irish under British rule became more strongly entrenched than ever.

T.W. Huffram, Theobald Wolfe Tone, *date unknown. Tone is shown in French uniform.*

If the French Revolution and the 22 years of war with France that followed produced ruinous government authoritarianism, they also acted to create for the first time a widespread and shared sense among British citizens that England, Wales, Scotland and, to a lesser extent, Ireland, formed one cohesive nation: Great Britain. Scotland had been linked to England by the Union of 1707, while union with Ireland, which had been firmly under English control since the time of Cromwell, was made official with the Act of Union in 1800. The wars with France allowed the English people to see themselves as leading a larger body defending liberty and freedom (even if that liberty and freedom

James Gillray, United Irishmen in Training, *1798. The famous English caricaturist here portrays the Irish as cruel buffoons; they are assaulting a British uniform stuffed with straw.*

were now, ironically, defined by a conservative authoritarian mind-set). At the same time, the wars raised very real threats of invasion—there were scares in 1778, 1796–98, and 1803, and Wales was actually invaded in 1797. The threats from without acted to foster cohesion within. Foreign travel was out of the question for all but the very rich or the very brave, and this forced the British to turn inward and discover their own country instead. Sir Walter Scott's collection of folk-songs and ballads, *Minstrelsy of the Scottish Border* (1802–03), Thomas Moore's *Irish Melodies* (1807–34), and Felicia Hemans's *Welsh Melodies* (1822) gave their readers a sense of the nation's rich past, both celebrating the blend of cultures that went into making up Great Britain. Regional poets, such as Robert Burns and John Clare, gave proud voice to those cultures, so that the individual nations which made up the one great nation were simultaneously celebrated for their respective traditions and recognized as within the British fold. Long poetical works such as John Thelwall's *The Hope of Albion; or Edwin of Northumbria* (1801) expanded the sense of an epic British mythology, while collections such as Hemans's *Tales and Historic Scenes* (1819), a celebration of military valor, fostered a sense of pride in present-day accomplishments.

The sense of a larger Britain served as further confirmation of the English belief that their country was particularly, even divinely, favored. Such notions were perhaps given their most memorable, if also most ambivalent, expression in the opening to William Blake's "Preface" to *Milton* (1804), in which ancient England is linked with Christ:

> And did those feet in ancient time
> Walk upon England's mountain's green?
> And was the Holy Lamb of God
> On England's pleasant pastures seen?
> And did the countenance divine
> Shine forth upon our clouded hills?[1]

Although Blake leaves it up to his reader to determine whether the answers to these rhetorical questions are yes or no, the stanza that follows explicitly figures England as a land worthy of being the new Jerusalem (if only sometime in the future):

---

1   The opening two stanzas of the "Preface" (a total of 16 lines) were set to music by Charles H.H. Parry in 1916; under the title "Jerusalem," these verses have become an unofficial national anthem for the English.

I will not cease from mental fight,
Nor shall my sword sleep in my hand,
Till we have built Jerusalem
In England's green and pleasant land.

Between these invocations of the divine in Britain, however, Blake inserts an insidious question, one that began to plague English writers and citizens more and more as the Romantic period progressed: "was Jerusalem builded here / Among these dark Satanic mills?" The phrase "dark Satanic mills" has become the most famous description of the force at the center of the Industrial Revolution. Even as the French Revolution changed the consciousness of the British people, this other revolution in their own country had as much impact on them as did any conflagration abroad.

In the sixteenth and seventeenth centuries, the British Isles, and England in particular, had begun undergoing extensive changes in economic structure. The pace of change increased dramatically as the eighteenth century progressed. From being a largely rural nation with a largely agricultural economy, Britain became an urban nation with an economy based in manufacturing. James Watt's refinement of the steam engine and James Hargreaves's invention of the

Thomas Girtin, Westminster from Lambeth, *c. 1800. Girtin's watercolor was one of a series of sketches for a panorama of London (now lost).*

Spinning Jenny (a machine that allowed cotton to be woven on several spindles simultaneously) were only the most famous of a host of changes that produced a boom in industrialization. Factories sprang up in what had once been countryside, and the populations of towns and cities, particularly those associated with manufacture, swelled. At the beginning of the 1770s, about a quarter of England's population lived in urban centers, but by 1801 that proportion had risen to one-third, and by the 1840s half of the English population resided in cities. In 1750, the total English population was roughly 5.5 million; by the time of the first census in 1800, it had grown to 8 million, while the population of Scotland and Ireland totaled more than 6.5 million. By 1831, the total population of Great Britain was thus approximately 14 million. This increase fueled the Industrial Revolution from both ends, supplying more consumers eager to acquire goods and more able bodies to work in factories that produced those goods.

Industrialization also contributed to an important shift in the country's social structure. The paradigm of classes and ranks that placed the nobility at the top with everyone else keeping to their places beneath had begun to change as early as the seventeenth century, with those involved in business and commerce growing wealthy enough to exert power of their own. The process was greatly accelerated in the late eighteenth and early nineteenth centuries as more and more factory owners and other men of business—and they were exclusively male—amassed larger and larger fortunes. Still, the road that led from newly acquired wealth to social acceptance remained a long and circuitous one. An inherited fortune stemming from longstanding ownership of large amounts of land—and the rents thereby produced—remained the most respectable form of wealth. To possess a good deal of money as a result not of belonging to the "landed gentry" but rather of having amassed it through commercial activity was considered

Illustration of an early locomotive engine, 1808.

more than faintly disreputable. It might take two or three generations before the taint of anyone in the family having been "in trade" (a term applied to industrialists as much as to tradesmen) was removed, and the source of the family fortune forgotten. The social nuances involved in such transitions were vividly captured in the novels of Jane Austen; here, for example, is her description of the Bingley sisters in *Pride and Prejudice* (1813):

> They were rather handsome, had been educated in one of the first private seminaries in town, had a fortune of twenty thousand pounds, were in the habit of spending more than they ought, and of associating with people of rank; and were therefore in every respect entitled to think well of themselves, and meanly of others. They were of a respectable family in the north of England; a circumstance more deeply impressed on their memories than that their brother's fortune and their own had been acquired by trade.

Fine gradations of respectability were attached to every occupation, with social position often at odds with financial circumstances. Members of the clergy and their families, for instance, though sometimes impecunious, were generally respected; whether members of the gentry or born into the working class,

George and I.R. Cruikshank, Sporting a Toe at Almacks, *1821. Many clubs were restricted to men; Almack's was an exclusive London club controlled by a group of society women. During "the season" a fashionable ball was held at Almack's every week.*

they often moved in elevated social circles. Physicians, defined as those medical men who had a degree from a university, could sometimes move in the "best circles" in a community, although apothecaries and surgeons, who gained their knowledge through apprenticeship, could not.

The Romantic literary world reflected the increased social mobility possible during the period. John Keats, for example, was the son of a stable keeper who had increased his financial standing by marrying the daughter of the stable owner. Keats trained as a surgeon-apothecary (a job that combined the duties of a present-day pharmacist, general practitioner, and surgeon), but, at the age of 18, he came into an inheritance and was able to devote himself entirely to literature. He wrote to a friend that he thought he would "be among the English poets" after his death, and, as it turned out, no social barriers could prevent that from occurring. Similarly, Samuel Taylor Coleridge, a parson's son who attended a London charity school as a child, ended his life lauded and respected as "The Sage of Highgate."

The Industrial Revolution may have increased social mobility; it certainly allowed goods to be produced more efficiently. But it also devastated large portions of England's underclasses, the agricultural laborers and peasants who had benefited, however slightly, from the land-based economy that was passing away. In Wordsworth's "Tintern Abbey" (1798), the reference to "vagrant dwellers in the houseless woods" describes a very real phenomenon. In the late eighteenth and early nineteenth centuries, a series of Enclosure Acts resulted in the continued conversion of formerly common land into large, privately held farms.[1] To be fair, enclosures did often result in an increase in agricultural production, but they also often spelled ruin for thousands of small farmers. Large landholders benefited from their enlarged acreage, but many of those who had heretofore been able to eke out a living from a tiny patch of land and sell their modest surpluses now lost all ability to support themselves. These smallholders and their families were forced either to labor for others for meager wages, to migrate to the city and enter the manufacturing workforce, or to turn to begging or thievery. Poor harvests in 1794–95, 1799–1800, and 1810–11 worsened the

---

1   The process of enclosure was not new; it had been occurring since the late Middle Ages, in response to population pressures and as Britain was transformed first into a largely mercantile economy and then into an industrial society.

plight of the rural poor even further. The proliferation of vandals, vagrants, and beggars in the writing of this era thus reflected a growing social reality.

The leading literary figures of the day were, for the most part, sympathetic to the plight of the poor in a time of growing inequity, but, beyond that, they held widely divergent attitudes concerning these developments, and concerning the commoners themselves. Anna Laetitia Barbauld was one writer who sought to ameliorate the inequities that had become so characteristic of English life; she condemned the power relations involved, harshly criticizing the privileged, and took a view of commoners that saw them as prey to vice as a result of the circumstances in which they had been placed through economic hardship and lack of education. As she wrote in *Thoughts on the Inequality of Conditions* (1800),

> Power enables the indolent and the useless not only to retain, but to add to their possessions, by taking from the industrious the natural reward of their labour, and applying it to their own use.… It is not sufficiently considered how many virtues depend upon comfort, and cleanliness, and decent apparel. Destroy dirt and misery, and you will destroy at once a great many vices.

It is the approach of William Wordsworth, however, that has more often been taken to characterize British Romanticism. That approach posits nature as central to human experience—nature in its simpler or wilder forms, not distorted by human artifice. Wordsworth was interested not only in "the beautiful and permanent forms of nature" but also in the ways in which human passions are excited by these forms; he describes "the mind" (rather than nature) as "My haunt, and the main region of my song." He was vitally interested, too, in the minds of those whom he saw as most closely connected to the natural world. If Barbauld's focus was very largely on the struggle to ameliorate conditions for the poor, Wordsworth's was more on the worth inherent in the hearts and minds of rural common folk—and on the associated poetic value. In the same year as Barbauld wrote her *Thoughts on the Inequality of Conditions*, Wordsworth expressed his ideals in the 1800 "Preface" to *Lyrical Ballads*:

> Humble and rustic life was generally chosen, because, in that condition, the essential passions of the heart find a better soil in which they can attain their maturity, are less under restraint, and speak a plainer and more emphatic language; because in that condition of life our elementary feelings coexist in a state of greater simplicity.…

Poems such as *Lyrical Ballads*, such as "Michael," "The Ruined Cottage," "Idiot Boy" and "Resolution and Independence," represent Wordsworth's attempt to put those ideals into practice. In "Resolution and Independence," the poet encounters an old, poor, itinerant leech-gatherer, ending the poem by admiring "In that decrepit Man so firm a mind." Whereas Barbauld regarded theft as a justifiable response to the oppression of extreme poverty in an iniquitous social system, Wordsworth pays homage to the old leech-gatherer for earning an "honest maintenance" despite the "many hardships" he must endure.

If the rural working-poor fared badly during these years, life for the workers in the cities and the unemployed-poor was just as bad. In 1815, at the instigation of large land holders, who stood to benefit from high prices for grain, the government passed the Corn Laws to institute a substantial tariff on imports of grain from foreign countries, making such imports much more expensive.[1] The tariff was effective in protecting British grain producers; at the same time, it inflated the price of bread and other foodstuffs for the consumer. The poor in the cities suffered particularly, and, from 1815 until the Corn Laws were finally repealed in 1845, they remained a lightning rod for political dissent.

Had conditions for the urban poor been better in other respects, the Corn Laws might have had less impact. The British government, however, assured by Adam Smith's highly influential work of economic philosophy, *The Wealth of Nations* (1777), that the best way to encourage national economic success was to leave businesses free to grow without hindrance, for the most part adopted a laissez-faire[2] approach to regulating treatment of employees and working conditions during this period. In practice, "laissez-faire" ultimately meant shifts of as much as fifteen hours at a stretch, often for very young children. Wages were kept as low as manufacturers could manage and injuries were common; children were the preferred workers for clearing jams in mechanized looms, for example, and the frequent result was the loss of the tiny fingers and hands that made them ideal for the job. Workers' health was often ruined by unsanitary working and living conditions—employers often owned not only the factories, but the slums in which their workers lived—and by unfettered pollution.

---

1   In Britain, "corn" denotes grain, most commonly wheat; what North Americans call "corn" is referred to in Britain as "maize."

2   "Let do" (French). See also the note on p. 68.

It is often assumed that the worst extremes of the Industrial Revolution in Britain occurred during the Victorian era, but, by the time Victoria came to the throne, Parliament had already been pressed to take a succession of measures to restrict the abuse of children: the largely ineffectual Health and Morals of Apprentices Act (1802), the Regulation of Cotton Mills and Factories Act (1819), and the Act to Regulate the Labour of Children and Young Persons in the Mills and Factories of the United Kingdom (1833). Even after the passage of this last, children as young as nine could be forced to work nine-hour days, and thirteen-year-olds to work twelve-hour days; still, this represented a degree of improvement from the late eighteenth and early nineteenth centuries. Robert Blincoe, for example, an orphan raised in a London workhouse and transported in 1799, at the age of seven, to work in the Lowdham Mill near Nottingham, described his life at the mill to John Brown in 1829:

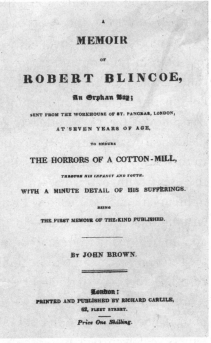

Blincoe heard the burring sound [of the machinery] before he reached the portals and smelt the fumes of the oil with which the axles of twenty-thousand wheels and spindles were bathed the moment he entered the doors. The noise appalled him, and the stench seemed intolerable. It was the custom at Lowdham Mills, as it is in most water mills, to make the apprentices work up lost time [i.e., time when the machines had been unable to run during regular working hours], by working over hours.... When children of seven years of age had to work fourteen hours every day in the week, Sundays excepted, any addition was severely felt.... Almost from the first hour [Blincoe] entered the Mill, till he arrived at a state of manhood, it was one continual round of cruel and arbitrary punishment.... I asked him if he could state the average number of times in which he might safely say he

Title page, A Memoir of Robert Blincoe, *first published in 1828, re-issued in 1832. Demonstrations in 1832 and 1833 for factory reform frequently cited the evidence of factory conditions that he had provided, and Blincoe testified before the Royal Commission that investigated the issue of child labor in 1833.*

had suffered corporal punishment in a week. His answer invariably was, that his punishments were so various and so frequent, it was impossible to state with anything approaching to accuracy.... Supper consisted of milk-porridge, of a very blue complexion [together with] bread partly made of rye—very black, and so soft they could scarcely swallow it, as it stuck like bird-lime to their teeth.

If the government addressed such outrages only with reluctance—sometimes Parliamentary committees looking into allegations would not hear any direct testimony from the workers—many citizens found them harder to ignore. Demonstrations of popular dissatisfaction were frequent and took various forms. Luddites, followers of the imaginary "General Ned Ludd," attacked and broke machinery during the years 1811–16, sometimes to force concessions from their employers but sometimes simply to express their dissatisfaction with creeping mechanization. After the bad harvests and the passage of the Corn Laws in 1815, food riots occurred across the country. Coercion Acts were passed in 1817 to try to stifle dissent, but they provoked strong antagonism, and both in London and in parts of Scotland some republican groups advocated revolution. Throughout the 1820s, farm workers staged violent protests, culminating in mass barn-burnings in 1830. Perhaps the most famous popular uprising was the 1819 gathering of nearly 100,000 mill workers at St. Peter's Field, near Manchester. A peaceful demonstration that ended with an address to the crowd by Henry Hunt,[1] this gathering so alarmed the local gentry that they sent drunken, armed militiamen to break it up and arrest Hunt. The militiamen attacked the crowd with their sabers when it jeered them, and the ensuing melee left 11 dead—including one trampled child—and more than 400 injured, many from saber wounds.

"Peterloo," as it came to be dubbed by the radical press, in reference to the British victory at Waterloo four years earlier, was a seminal event in nineteenth-century politics and economics. Parliament did nothing to relieve the sufferings of these poor or the hundreds of thousands like them, instead strengthening its repressive powers by passing the Six Acts at the end of 1819. These Acts made it a crime to demonstrate; gave magistrates the power to enter private homes to search for weapons; outlawed meetings of more than 50 people unless all those attending a meeting were residents of the parish in which the meeting

---

1   Known as the "Orator," Hunt (1773–1835) was a radical speaker and agitator, renowned for his advocacy of Parliamentary reform and the abolition of the Corn Laws.

was held, thus effectively curtailing any kind of large gatherings; tightened the guidelines on what could be considered blasphemous or treasonous libel; and raised the newspaper tax, thereby cutting the circulation of formerly inexpensive radical newspapers.[1]

Political Parties and Royal Allegiances

For most of this period, the upheavals among the lower classes found little reflection in the English government, where the Tories held sway from 1783–1830, with only one short interruption. The Tories were the conservative party: they saw themselves as upholders of law and tradition, determined to preserve the prevailing political and social order. From 1793 to 1801, and again from 1804 to 1806, the Tories—and the country—were led by Prime Minister William Pitt, whose fiscal restraint and willingness to suppress political protest (sometimes with open brutality) made him a hero to some and a villain to many others. After Pitt died in office in 1806, certainly of overwork and probably of alcoholism—his last words were either, "Oh, my country! how I leave my country!" or "I think I could eat one of Bellamy's veal pies," depending on the source—the Tories continued in power, on their own or in coalition, until 1830.

The Whigs, who remained the party of opposition during this time, presented themselves against the Tories as advocates of greater civil and religious liberty. In reality, neither party would have been called "Liberals" or "Democrats" by today's standards, but the Whigs did advocate the abolition of the slave trade, Catholic emancipation (which would allow greater political participation to Catholics, heretofore barred from a role in government), and Parliamentary reform. From 1782–1806, the leader of the Whigs was the charismatic Charles James Fox, gambler, gourmand, and political colossus, whose political machinations made him as many enemies as friends. Not until 1806, a year after Fox's death, would the Whigs participate in government—and then for only a relatively short period, as part of a coalition. They would not gain power in their own right until 1830. They were then at last able to pass the Reform Act

---

1   The Six Acts ultimately proved repugnant to certain members of the liberal Whig party— who subsequently became politically powerful—and led to the liberal Reform Act of 1832. Thus, the eventual result of the massacre was a measure of relief from the extraordinarily repressive measures it had spawned.

of 1832 (also known as the Great Reform Act), which extended voting rights to a broader spectrum of propertied males,[1] redistributed Parliamentary seats, and brought significantly fairer political representation.

While the politicians plotted and schemed, the British royal family suffered its own difficulties. George III, who had ascended the throne in 1760, embodied Toryism both politically and personally; traditionalist, ponderous, and domestic, he produced a large family, embraced conservative politics, and allegedly liked to wander the countryside incognito, chatting with farmers. In 1788, however, he suffered a bout of mental illness that lasted until early 1789. This illness, now believed to be the result of the hereditary blood disease porphyria, reappeared in 1810, leaving him permanently insane. In 1811, when it became apparent that the King would not recover, his eldest son was declared Regent.

Left: Sir Thomas Lawrence, Caroline Amelia Elizabeth of Brunswick, *1804 (detail). Right: Sir Thomas Lawrence,* The Prince Regent in Profile, *c. 1814. The Prince knighted Lawrence, the leading English portraitist of the day, in 1815, saying that he was "proud in conferring a mark of favor on one who had raised the character of British art in the estimation of all Europe."*

---

1   The changes are estimated to have altered the composition of the electorate to approximately one in seven males from fewer than one in ten.

Monarchs of the House of Hanover traditionally clashed with their eldest sons, and George III and the Prince, who would become George IV, were no different. Bred to wait for his father to die, growing ever fatter (at the end of his life he weighed more than 300 pounds), the Regent was a stark contrast to his thrifty father. In 1787, when he was 25, his debts totaled more than £160,000 (equivalent to about £8,000,000 today). He lived with a Roman Catholic mistress whom he later married, secretly and unconstitutionally, before abandoning her for a series of other mistresses. Later, to secure relief from debts, he married his cousin Caroline of Brunswick, a woman he found so instantly and completely loathsome that his first words upon seeing her were, "I am not well; pray get me a glass of brandy." Although they did manage to produce one daughter, Charlotte, who later died in childbirth, the Prince and his wife never lived together, and his attempt to divorce her after his accession in 1820 was one of the great scandals of the period.

George IV was not without redeeming virtues; notably, he was a keen patron of the arts, particularly architecture. In addition to a magnificent pavilion in Brighton, he and his architects built Trafalgar Square, modified and improved Buckingham House into Buckingham Palace, and created parks, streets, and crescents throughout London. He was an enthusiastic reader and promoter of literature, as well as a generous patron of the sciences, establishing several fellowships and prizes. Nonetheless, the Prince became a figure of increasing public contempt. Leigh Hunt described him as "a libertine head over heels in debt and disgrace, a despiser of domestic ties"; Percy Shelley called him, in prose, an "overgrown bantling [infant]," and, in poetry, "the dregs of [his] dull race." When he died in 1830, *The Times* wrote, "There never was an individual less regretted by his fellow creatures than this dead King."

Imperial Expansion

Even as Britain was experiencing its own internal power struggles and upheavals, the nation was expanding its presence around the globe. Throughout the first half of the nineteenth century, Britain was well on its way to forging the Empire that would reach full flower in the Victorian period. The East India Company, founded by a group of London merchants in 1600, controlled most of eastern India by 1765, and thereafter continued to extend their administrative and governmental control over the sub-continent. British interest in

China began in the late eighteenth century, when Britain began to import the tea that would soon become a staple of the British table, and rose throughout the 1800s. Increased contact with—and domination of—various parts of the Far East led to increased fascination with its cultures, a fascination widely reflected in literature. "Eastern" influence pervades the prose and poetry of this period, from William Beckford's novel *The History of the Caliph Vathek* (1786), to Byron's *Eastern Tales* (1813–14), to Percy Shelley's *Alastor* (1816), where the protagonist makes his way

> through Arabie
> And Persia, and the wild Carmanian waste,
> And o'er the aerial mountains which pour down
> Indus and Oxus from their icy caves,
> In joy and exultation [he] held his icy way,
> Till in the vale of Cashmire …
> … he stretched
> His languid limbs.

Wearing her India cotton frock, sipping her tea from Canton, coffee from Yemen, or chocolate from Mexico, the English consumer of the Romantic period felt the influence of imperial expansion everywhere, from the commodities she purchased to the pages she turned.

But if the British Empire brought rewards to the nation's citizens, it all too often entailed exploitation and horror in the colonies themselves. Chief amongst these was the slavery that fueled the economy of the British West Indies. The mass of sugar required to sweeten Britain's tea, coffee, and chocolate was cultivated, cut, and processed on these islands by slaves who worked under inhuman conditions until they literally wore out—at which point their white masters simply purchased fresh replacements. Over the course of the eighteenth century, British slavers transported some three million slaves to the West Indies and other agricultural colonies; the economic success of the port towns Bristol and Liverpool was based in large part on the important part they played in the English slave trade—and the trade in sugar from plantations that relied on slave labor.[1]

---

1   At the start of the American Revolution, British imports from the largest sugar plantation center, Jamaica, were worth five times more than British imports from the Thirteen Colonies.

James Gillray, Fashionable Contrasts, or the Duchess' Little Shoe Yielding to the Magnitude of the Duke's Foot, *1792. At the time, the press had been fawning over Princess Frederica Charlotte Ulrica Catherina, who had just married Frederick Augustus, Duke of York; the daintiness of her feet had been particularly praised.*

James Gillray, The Plum Pudding in Danger, *1805. Napoleon and British Prime Minister William Pitt are shown carving up the globe, with Napoleon skewering Europe and Pitt helping himself to the ocean. (1805 saw both the Battle of Trafalgar, at which the British under Lord Nelson established dominance at sea; and the Battle of Austerlitz, at which Napoleon defeated Russian and Austrian armies to cement his control of the continent.)*

Arguably the strongest resistance to slavery in the West Indies came from the slaves themselves. The British invaded the formerly French island of Saint-Dominique in 1793 in order to aid in the suppression of a slave uprising led by Toussaint L'Ouverture but withdrew five years later, having sent more troops to the West Indies over that period than they had sent to America during the War of Independence. When a subsequent effort by Napoleon also failed and the former slaves founded the Republic of Haiti in 1804, the message that emancipation was inevitable had registered widely in Britain.

Emancipation was also spurred by a widespread and effective protest movement within Britain. Between 1787, when protests first began, and 1791, abolitionists gathered 500 petitions against slavery from across Britain. In all some 400,000 signatures were collected; this was Britain's first large-scale petition campaign. The abolitionist movement attracted support from Evangelicals, from Whig politicians, and from radicals, and has been described as the first British political movement in the modern sense. The leading figures in the movement were abolitionists Thomas Clarkson, Granville Sharp, and William Wilberforce, but it also drew considerable support from the poets of the day,

Sir Charles D'Oyly, The Emporium of Taylor & Co. in Calcutta, *c. 1825–28.*

Henry Fuseli, The Nightmare, *1790–91. The Swiss-born artist Fuseli (1741–1825) moved to England in 1779, and soon became one of the leading artistic figures of the day. Beginning in 1781, Fuseli painted several different versions of* The Nightmare *for which he became famous; it remains an iconic image of the Gothic sensibility, and of Romantic interest in what we now term "the unconscious." Fuseli moved in London's artistic and intellectual circles through the 1790s, and was briefly involved romantically with Mary Wollstonecraft before her marriage to William Godwin.*

William Blake, The Sun Standing at his Eastern Gate, *illustration to John Milton's* L'Allegro.

William Blake, The Sick Rose, *from Songs of Experience, 1794.*

Phillipe Jaques de Loutherbourgh, Coalbrookdale By Night, 1801. The small Shropshire town of Coalbrookdale has been sometimes described as the birthplace of the Industrial Revolution. Located in a gorge on the River Severn, it was the site of the first ironworks that used the modern method of smelting with coke rather than charcoal (an innovation of Joseph Darby in 1709). Together with the adjacent towns of Madeley, Ironbridge, Jackfield, and Coalport, Coalbrookdale was part of an early industrial powerhouse; at the end of the eighteenth century it had a greater concentration of furnaces and forges than anywhere else in the world. Darby's son Abraham also constructed the world's first iron bridge nearby in 1779; the bridge and much of the old ironworks remain today, and the Ironbridge Gorge has been declared a World Heritage Site.

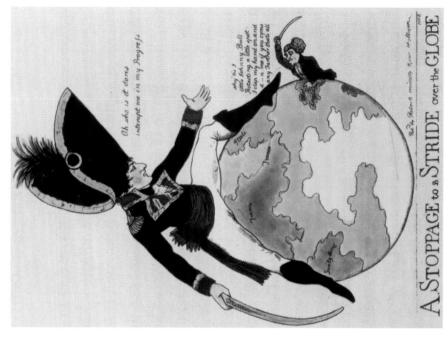

Artist unknown, A Stoppage to a Stride over the Globe, *1803.*

Jean-Jacques David, Bonaparte, *1798.*

Thomas Phillips, George Gordon, Lord Byron, *1814. Byron is wearing clothing of a sort native to the region of Epirus (then part of Albania, now part of northern Greece); he had bought this outfit while traveling through the area in 1809.*

Elizabeth Levenson-Gower, Mountain Landscape, c. 1830. Levenson-Gower published two volumes based on her watercolor images of Scottish landscapes, the first a collection of etchings, Views of Orkney and the North-Eastern Coast of Scotland (1807), and the second a volume of twenty aquatints, Views on the Northern and Western Coasts of Sutherland (1833). The artist intended that various of the wide Sutherland images be joined together to form 360-degree scenic panoramas.

J.M.W. Turner, The Burning of the Houses of Parliament, *1835. In the 1830s it became Turner's practice to send unfinished work (often with only rough underpainting completed) to the Royal Academy in advance of its annual exhibition. During the period devoted (in the case of other artists) to the varnishing of already-completed work, Turner would complete the painting itself, often watched by a sizeable crowd. An eyewitness, E.V. Rippingille, described Turner completing* The Burning of the Houses of Parliament *in 1835:*

For [the] three hours I was there ... he never ceased to work, or even once looked or turned from the wall in which his picture was hung. A small box of colors, a few very small brushes, and a vial or two, were at his feet ... In one part of the mysterious proceedings Turner, who worked almost entirely with his palette knife, was observed to be rolling and spreading a half-transparent stuff over his picture, the size of a figure in length and thickness. As Callcott was looking on I ventured to say ... "What is that he is plastering his picture with?" to which enquiry it was replied, "should be sorry to be the man to ask him" ... Presently the work was finished: Turner gathered his tools together, put them into and shut the box, and then with his face still turned to the wall, and at the same distance from it, went sidelong off, without speaking a word to anybody ... Maclise, who stood near, remarked, "There, that's masterly, he does not stop to look at his work; he knows it is done, and he is off!"

J.M.W. Turner, Slavers Throwing Overboard the Dead and Dying—Typhoon coming on,
*1840. Turner's painting depicts a 1781 incident in which Captain Luke Collingwood of the slave
ship "Zong," with his ship running short of water and other supplies when it had been blown off-
course during a severe storm, ordered that all sick and dying slaves be thrown overboard; 133 were
killed as a result. Insurance ws a factor in Collingwood's decision; compensation could be claimed
for property lost or jettisoned in storms, but not for slaves killed by disease or other natural causes.
The incident became widely publicized and spurred support for the abolitionist movement. In the
ensuing legal case the court upheld the insurance company's financial liability; no criminal charges
were brought against the captain. In the wtentieth century the incident became the basis for several
literary works, including a long poem by David Dabydeen and a novel by Fred D'Aguiar.*

among them William Cowper, Hannah More, William Blake, Mary Robinson, Anna Laetitia Barbauld, and Anne Cromarty Yearsley (whose *A Poem on the Inhumanity of the Slave Trade* [1788] inveighed against the very business that supported her home town of Bristol).

Central to the literature of the abolitionist movement were books written by former slaves, such as Olaudah Equiano and Mary Prince, which laid out plainly the horrors of a slave's life and openly sought sympathy and fellow-feeling from readers. In his autobiography, *The Interesting Narrative of the Life of Olaudah Equiano* (1786), Equiano described conditions both in West Indies and in America. As he observed with telling effect, the system bred degradation for "free negroes" as well as for slaves:

> I have often seen slaves, particularly those who were meagre, in different islands, put into scales and weighed; and then sold from three pence to six pence to nine pence a pound. My master, however, whose humanity was shocked at this mode, used to sell by the lump. And at or after a sale it was not uncommon to see negroes taken from their wives, wives taken from their husbands, and children from their parents, and sent off to other islands, and wherever else their merciless lords chose, and probably never more during life to see each other! …

> [Free negroes] live in constant alarm for their liberty; and even this is but nominal, for they are universally insulted and plundered without the possibility of redress; for such is the equity of West Indian laws, that no free negro's evidence will be admitted in their courts of justice.

Such accounts, coupled with a determined and prolonged campaign and with the effects of the growth of the Asian sugar trade, led to the abolition of the slave trade in 1806–07, and (following another uprising, this time in Jamaica in 1831–32) to an act in 1833 that provided for the full abolition of slavery. The persecution of blacks by whites, however, continued both in the West Indies and throughout the British Empire.

Noticeably absent from the list of abolitionist writers are several of the leading names of English Romantic poetry. Wordsworth,[1] Coleridge, Byron,

---

1   In *The Prelude*, Wordsworth admits that in the 1790s "this particular strife had wanted power / To rivet my affections." He did write two sonnets (one to Clarkson, one to Toussaint L'Ouverture) in 1807, the year in which abolition of the slave trade was accomplished.

Shelley, and Keats were in general all sympathetic to the aims of the abolitionist movement, and Coleridge in particular spoke out strongly both against slavery itself and against the maintenance of the slave trade, memorably writing that "a slave is a person perverted into a thing," and slavery not so much "a deviation from justice as an absolute subversion of all morality." It has been plausibly suggested that some major works of Romantic poetry (notably Coleridge's "The Rime of the Ancient Mariner" [1798] and Keats's "Lamia" [1819]) may usefully be read in relation to the slave trade. But directly pressing for the abolition of slavery through verse in the manner of Cowper, Robinson, and Yearsley was never a significant part of these poets' agendas.

The Romantic Mind and Its Literary Productions

It is not surprising that in a world overwhelmingly concerned with change, revolution, and freedom the makers of literature should be similarly preoccupied; as has already been discussed, the French Revolution and its aftermath lent vital force to the Romantic impulse. That force, though, was not exerted on all the literary minds in the Romantic era with equal force or in quite the same direction. For several of the leading figures of English Romanticism, the freedom that animated the poetic imagination was only tangentially related to the collectivist enterprise that the revolution in France had represented. Instead, it was very much an *individual* freedom; the freeing of the individual mind and the individual soul took pride of place. Subjective experience and the role that it played in the individual's response to and experience of reality are dominant themes in the works of the Romantics. Wordsworth's "Ode: Intimations of Immortality" (1807) surveys what becomes of the "heaven-born freedom" with which every individual who enters the world is born. Percy Shelley's *Mont Blanc* (1817) is an extended exploration of power and creativity, and Keats's various Odes continually express their author's fascination with the connection between physical experience and the individual human imagination. In Byron's work, subjectivity, creativity, and epistemological questing all find expression in a series of heroes for whom the power of the will is a central concern. The question of what it means to be an individual looms large in the works of all these authors.

Nature became a fulcrum in the balancing of subjective and objective in the Romantic construction of reality, and most of the period's leading writers were particularly preoccupied with the relationship between the natural world and the individual mind. Percy Shelley appealed to the wind, "Make me thy lyre, even as the forest is," and, in "Tintern Abbey," Wordsworth recognized nature as

> The anchor of my purest thoughts, the nurse
> The guide, the guardian of my heart, and soul
> Of all my moral being.

This commingling of self and nature was, at least in part, an expression of the late eighteenth- and early nineteenth-century tendency to see the natural world in opposition to the human world. In the same poem, for example, Wordsworth describes himself as coming to nature

> more like a man
> Flying from something that he dreads than one
> Who sought the thing he loved.

Less frequently did poets of the Romantic period comment on the relationship between humans and nature as an objective reality. The focus was much more often on what non-human nature had to offer to the individual human soul than on how humans in aggregate were reshaping the natural world. Barbauld was unusual in observing and commenting on the latter clearly; in her grim survey of England in "Eighteen Hundred and Eleven," she described how

> Science and Art urge on the useful toil,
> New mould a climate and create the soil, ...
> On yielding Nature urge their new demands,
> And ask not gifts but tribute at her hands.

Such clear-eyed observations of human manipulation of nature were few and far between.

The importance of the subjective sense of reality to the Romantic imagination also comes out clearly in the widespread fascination with the visions experienced in dreams, in nightmares, and other altered states. The question Keats poses at the end of "Ode to a Nightingale" (1819)—"Was it a vision, or a waking dream?"—is of a sort that occurs frequently in the literature of Romanticism. Among the many works of the period that touch on this theme are Coleridge's fragment "Kubla Khan" (which he claimed came to him during a drug-induced sleep); Keats's visionary *The Fall of Hyperion: A Dream*; Mary

Joseph Severn, Percy Bysshe Shelley *(detail), 1845.*

Shelley's *Frankenstein* (the story of which came to her in a dream, and in which Victor Frankenstein acquires the habit of taking "every night a small quantity of laudanum" in order to "gain the rest necessary for the preservation of life"); and De Quincey's *Confessions of an English Opium Eater*.

In the work of female writers of the period, interest in the individual and the mind often took different forms from those that engaged the interest of male writers. Many were concerned with education: Hannah More produced a series of Cheap Repository Tracts designed to enlighten the poor, while Maria Edgeworth gained fame as a children's writer and educationalist. Mary Wollestonecraft authored not only her famous *Vindication of the Rights of Woman*, but also *Thoughts on the Education of Daughters* (1787) and *The Female Reader* (1772). The Romantic period abounded in outspoken female writers who engaged with the issues of their day and sought to make a difference in their world. In their own time, however, such authors were often derided as "Bluestockings," unnatural women who revealed their prudishness through their interest in intellectual pursuits. In their own day, the writings of these authors made little, if any, difference to the social, legal, and economic position of women, who remained little more than property in the eyes of the law for many more years. But over the longer term their impact was considerable; Wollstonecraft and the Bluestockings laid the intellectual foundations for the social and political progress of women that would slowly be achieved over the next 200 years and more.

It would be a mistake to think of the female writers of the Romantic period as solely concerned with women's rights and with the stereotypical "female arenas" of education and religion, however. Much of the writing by women in this period is as rich, strong, and plaintive as anything produced by their male counterparts. Mary Robinson, for example—famous first as an actress and mistress of the Prince of Wales, then as a successful poet and novelist—earned the admiration of both Wordsworth and Coleridge (who called her "an undoubted genius") and preceded them in the writing of poetry concerned with the poor and disenfranchised. In her *Elegiac Sonnets* (1784), Charlotte Smith displayed all the power, control, and skill at incisive self-examination that has come to be associated with the male Romantics. Poet Felicia Hemans rivaled (indeed, perhaps surpassed) Byron in popularity. Playwright Joanna Baillie, famous for producing works that, as she put it, "delineate the progress of the higher passions in the human breast," was considered by Walter Scott to be "the best dramatic writer since the days of Shakespeare."

One area of common ground for almost all Romantic writers, male and female, was a strong interest in the "Imagination," the creative power by which an individual took the raw material of the physical world and transformed it into art. Although "Imagination" was recognized as being distinct from religious inspiration, descriptions of imaginative or poetic power often took on strong religious overtones, as in Blake's assertion that "One Power alone makes a Poet: Imagination, the Divine Vision." Coleridge, Blake, and Wordsworth were all deeply invested in the notion of the poet as *vates*, or prophet. And the imagination was seen as invested with moral as well as prophetic power. Like earlier ages (though unlike our own), the Romantics saw the realms of the aesthetic and the moral as being closely bound up with each other. But whereas earlier ages had tended to see literature as expressing truths emanating from elsewhere and the ethical element of literature as inhering in its ability to illustrate virtues and vices and point out moral lessons, the leading Romantics tended to locate the moral element, not only of literature but of life itself, in the imagination and tended to see the imagination as embodying truth as well as morality. "The great instrument of moral good," wrote Shelley in his *Defense of Poetry* (1821), "is the imagination," while Keats proclaimed that "what the imagination seizes as beauty must be the truth."[1] More broadly, a belief took root among poets—the great male Romantic poets in particular—that the aesthetic and imaginative truths of poetry were possessed of a transcendent status, a status that placed such insights above the historical or scientific truths of the ordinary world.

Another opposition that animates the literature of the Romantic period is that between sense and sensibility—a tension with parallels to that between reason and emotion in the intellectual landscape of any age, but also one possessing elements particular to the late eighteenth and early nineteenth centuries. In this era, the terms "sentiment," "sentimentality," "sentimentalism," and "sensibility" were all widely used (and to some extent overlapped in meaning),

---

1   Keats's notion of the value of "negative capability—that is, when a man is capable of being in uncertainties, mysteries, doubts, without any irritable reaching after fact and reason"—destabilizes in interesting ways the connections that he and other Romantics drew between morality and the imagination and between the imagination and truth.

but none more so than "sensibility." The concept of "sensibility" entailed strong emotional responsiveness, with life and literary work animated by powerful feeling. Indeed, "sensibility" was frequently associated with emotional excess: when Jane Austen describes Marianne's "excess of sensibility" in *Sense and Sensibility* (1811), she is using the notion of sensibility in ways that would have been familiar to any late eighteenth- or early nineteenth-century reader:

> She was sensible and clever; but eager in every thing; her sorrows, her joys, could have no moderation. She was generous, amiable, interesting: she was every thing but prudent. The resemblance between her and her mother was strikingly great. Elinor saw, with concern, the excess of her sister's sensibility; but by Mrs. Dashwood it was valued and cherished.

It may well be that most educated Britons of the period privileged sense over sensibility in very much the way that Austen appears to do. But it is also true that the feelings associated with the Romantic sensibility—above all, as they were expressed in poetry—became the defining passions of the age. What is more, the poetry of sensibility carried intellectual as well as aesthetic force; for a considerable period, it stood in the vanguard of the movement for social and political change.

That is not to say that the distinction separating poets of sensibility from the rest was entirely clear; far from it. Rather in the way that competing factions today will sometimes each accuse the other of being controlled by their emotions rather than their reason, many in the late eighteenth century tried to situate sensibility in a natural alliance with political views they opposed. Anti-Jacobins suggested there was a natural affinity between the supposed excesses of sensibility and those of political radicalism, while radicals often portrayed sensibility as associated with reactionary political views. In truth, the language of sensibility was used by both sides.

Still another pair of oppositions that occur throughout the literature of the Romantic period are the natural and the artificial and the original and the imitative. If "artificial" is taken simply to mean "human-made," of course, the distinction between the natural and the artificial is purely a matter of physical process. But "artificial" and "natural" as matters of taste and of style have more fluid meanings. As the culture of sentiment and of sensibility grew over the course of the eighteenth century, "artificial" came to be used less and less frequently to mean "displaying special art or skill" and more and more frequently to mean "contrived, shaped in a way not spontaneous or natural," or even "not expressive of reality." The divide between natural and artificial was felt to connect with that between "novelty" of thought and expression—"originality," we would call it—and the "servility" of the stale or overly imitative. Whereas the neoclassical poets had proudly imitated classical models, often devoting themselves to translations of classical works into English poetry, Romantic writers—and the leading Romantic poets in particular—had little interest in seeing the work of earlier eras as models to be imitated. They might admire the poets of earlier eras, they might be inspired by them—by Shakespeare and by Milton above all—they might aspire to similar glory, but they had no interest in taking the same path to glory. If not entirely for the first time, then certainly to an unprecedented degree, originality came in the Romantic period to be seen as a criterion of poetic achievement. Even at the beginning of the period we find judgments on poetic worth being made largely on the grounds of the originality the verse displays. A 1791 assessment of a volume of Robinson's poetry, for example, sets up an opposition between the original and the natural—two qualities often assumed to normally accompany each other:

> The attempt at originality is in all pursuits laudable. Invention is a noble attribute of the mind. But the danger is, lest, by pursuing it too intensely, we deviate so far from ease and nature, that the real object of Poetry, that of touching the heart, be lost.

A more familiar set of oppositions involving the natural and the artificial, the "original" and the imitative, is put forward by William Hazlitt in his *The Spirit of the Age* (1825), as he assesses, at the end of the Romantic period, the place of Wordsworth in the poetry and the intellectual life of the age:

> His popular, inartificial style gets rid (at a blow) of all the trappings of verse, of all the high places of poetry: "the cloud-capt towers, the solemn temples, the gorgeous palaces," are swept to the ground.... All the traditions of learning, all the superstitions of age, are obliterated and effaced. We begin *de novo* on a *tabula rasa* of poetry.... He chooses to have his subject a foil to his invention, to owe nothing but to himself.... Taught by political opinions to say to the vain pomp and glory of the world, "I hate ye," seeing the path of classical and artificial poetry blocked up by the cumbrous ornaments of style and turgid commonplaces, so that nothing more could be achieved in that direction but by the most

ridiculous bombast or the tamest servility, he has … struck into the sequestered vale of humble life, sought out the muse among sheep-cotes and hamlets, and the peasant's mountain-haunts, has discarded all the tinsel pageantry of verse, and endeavored (not in vain) to … add the charm of novelty to the familiar.

In passages such as this one, we may see the paradigms according to which the literature of the Romantic period is still largely seen being articulated even before the period had ended. On the one side are the natural, the spontaneous, the original, fresh and new; on the other, the artificial, the studied, the imitative, the tired, and traditional. On the one side, imagination and sensibility; on the other, excessive rationalism. On the one side, a passion for freedom, especially, aesthetic freedom and freedom of the spirit; on the other, restraint, reaction, oppression. On the one side, in short, the Romantic; on the other, the classical, the neoclassical, the conservative.

If these sets of oppositions often bear some correspondence to reality, it is important to recognize that the correspondences are just as often loose and unreliable. Romantic literature—the Romantic period itself—is filled with unexpected parallels, with surprising evolutions, with unexpected paradoxes, with outright contradictions. The Della Cruscans[1] and their followers, for example, have often been taken to task for the supposed artificiality of their verse. Wordsworth, usually seen as the great poet of a natural world set apart from the oppressive workings of the human-made world of cities and factories, wrote, in 1833, that "Steamboats, Viaducts, and Railways … Nature doth embrace / Her lawful offspring in Man's art." Coleridge, who in the early 1790s felt strongly the attractions of sensibility and planned to establish a community in Pennsylvania founded on revolutionary democratic ideals, became in later life as dismissive of sensibility as he was of revolutionary fervor. Byron, the paradigmatic Romantic figure, professed to reject many of the impulses at the core of the Romantic movement; in "To Romance" (1807), he vows to leave the realms of romance "for those of truth":

Romance! disgusted with deceit,
Far from thy motley court I fly,

---

1   The Della Cruscans were poets of sensibility, who, in the late 1780s and early 1790s, took the lead in exuberantly embracing revolutionary freedom in the wake of the French Revolution.

Where Affectation holds her seat,
And sickly Sensibility…

Keats, for his part, is perhaps at his most enthusiastic when he exclaims not over nature or freedom but over the experience of classical literature ("On First Looking into Chapman's Homer" [1816]) and classical art ("On Seeing the Elgin Marbles" [1817], "Ode on a Grecian Urn" [1819]). The distinctions made in the attempt to define the essence of the Romantic, in short, often become elusive or indistinct when it comes to particulars; indeed, such divisions can be downright misleading. Throughout most of the nineteenth and twentieth centuries, literary critics and theorists tended to accept very much at face value the Romantics' self-representations of the nature and importance of their work; more recently, these self-representations have been frequently problematized and widely challenged.

There have been few challenges, however, to the view that this was a period of revolutionary developments—or to the notion that at the center of those developments (so far as English literature is concerned) was an extraordinary body of verse. Looking back, in 1832, Letitia Landon was among those who identified poetry as a particular locus of change:

> Already there is a wide gulf between the last century and the present. In religion, in philosophy, in politics, in manners, there has passed a great change; but in none has been worked a greater change than in poetry, whether as regards the art itself, or the general feeling towards it.

Poetic ambition was in itself central to the spirit of Romanticism. When they spoke of the confident outpouring of Romantic verse, Romantic poets did not hesitate to compare their own work to that of the great poets of the past—and to feel themselves capable of such greatness. "I would sooner fail than not be among the greatest," wrote Keats.

The tendencies of our own age, when poetry is usually taken in small doses and the lyric mode predominates, sometimes lead modern readers to place far less emphasis than did the Romantics themselves on their longer works. The shorter poems of the Romantic canon (among them Blake's "The Tyger" [1794], Wordsworth's "Ode: Intimations of Immortality," Coleridge's "Dejection: An Ode" [1802], Byron's "She Walks in Beauty" [1814], Shelley's "To a Skylark" [1820], and Keats's odes and sonnets) are justly celebrated, and Wordsworth and Coleridge's *Lyrical Ballads* is rightly seen as the era's most significant single volume of literature. But even as these works retain pride of place, it is important to give full notice too to the vast range of the ambitions of the Romantic poets—ambitions that found their fullest expression in extended poetic work. Blake's long prophetic poems charted new territory for English verse, both in the poetry itself and in his unique marriage of the verbal and the visual. Robinson's more substantial works include the long sonnet sequence *Sapho and Phaon* (1796) and the series of longer poems on related themes that were eventually published as the sequence *The Progress of Liberty* (1806). Over the course of some 50 years, Wordsworth reworked his poetic autobiography, *The Prelude*, into an 8,000-line epic. Coleridge's narrative poems "The Rime of the Ancient Mariner" and "Christabel" (1800) are works of modest extent by comparison with these—but still long by modern standards. Byron gave extraordinary new life to the epic romance with *Childe Harold*, broke new ground poetically with what he termed the "epic satire" of *Don Juan* (1824), and wrote seven full-length poetic dramas. Shelley's long works encompass not only the complex allegorical drama *Prometheus Unbound* (1820) but also the poems "The Mask of Anarchy" (1819) and "Adonais"[1] (1821) and the poetic drama *The Cenci* (1819). Keats's *Endymion* (1818) is another memorable work of epic proportions. And, though Keats abandoned both the original epic-length version of his *Hyperion* (1819) and the later *The Fall of Hyperion: A Dream* (1821), what remains of both also constitutes a very substantial poetic achievement. Charlotte Smith's monumental poem of history, nature, and the self, "Beachy Head" (1807), is a landmark in early nineteenth-century poetry, while George Crabbe's *The Borough* (1810) memorialized village life in meticulous detail. Felicia Hemans remains best known for her short poems "Casabianca" (1826) and "The Homes of England" (1827), but her most significant works are the poetic drama *The Siege of Valencia* (1823) and the 19 poems that together comprise *Records of Woman* (1828).

The ambitions of the Romantic poets extended, too, to poetic theory and criticism; to a heretofore unprecedented degree, the leading poets of the time were also the leading critics and theorists. Wordsworth's "Preface" to the *Lyrical Ballads*, in its various versions, Shelley's *A Defense of Poetry*, Coleridge's scattered but enormously influential body of literary theory and criticism, and the

---

1   Subtitled "An Elegy on the Death of John Keats," the poem is a pastoral elegy, written by Shelley upon hearing of Keats's death.

critical insights of Keats's letters, have all long been regarded as central documents in the literature of Romanticism. But other leading writers too wrote perceptively and extensively about literature—among them Barbauld, Landon, and Elizabeth Inchbald.

The novel, dramatic writing, and the essay all flourished alongside poetry in the Romantic period, even if these genres were not accorded the same degree of respect as poetry. Barbauld commented wryly on the situation of the novel in 1810:

> A collection of novels has a better chance of giving pleasure than of commanding respect. Books of this description are condemned to the grave and despised by the fastidious; but their leaves are seldom found unopened, and they occupy the parlour and the dressing-room while productions of higher name are often gathering dust upon the shelf.

Though such laments reflected the perception of the novel fairly accurately, the novel nonetheless became increasingly popular, and the changes and innovations to the form arising during the Romantic period continue to reverberate and resonate to this very day.

The Romantic era saw the decline of that mainstay of eighteenth-century prose, the epistolary novel, and the development and proliferation of other forms of fiction. James Hogg produced one of the great masterpieces of psychological literature, *The Private Memoirs and Confessions of a Justified Sinner* (1824). Historical novels—especially those celebrating nationhood—became increasingly popular, among them Maria Edgeworth's *Castle Rackrent* (1800), Sydney Owenson's *The Wild Irish Girl* (1806), and Jane Porter's *The Scottish Chiefs* (1810). It was Sir Walter Scott, however, who took the genre of the historical novel and made it his own. Perhaps the most influential fiction writer of the Romantic period, Scott single-handedly reshaped notions not just of "the historical novel" but of the novel itself. After beginning his career as a highly successful poet, he switched to long fiction in 1814 and produced a succession of extraordinarily popular novels, including *Waverley* (1814), *Rob Roy* (1817), and *Ivanhoe* (1819), the first modern bestsellers. Using his works to explore the ongoing political struggles of the time—the clash between traditionalism and progress, the tempting attractions of an idealized past that is really a cover for abuse and exploitation, the struggles and missteps that characterize the creation of a just society—Scott at the same time created vivid, entirely engrossing

J.M.W. Turner, Melrose Abbey, *1822. The lines in the lower left corner are (slightly misquoted) from Canto 2 of Sir Walter Scott's long poem* The Lay of the Last Minstrel *(1805): "If thou would'st view fair Melrose aright, / Go visit it by the pale moonlight."*

characters. Indeed, one hallmark of his writing is his ability to use these fully realized individuals to give human expression to broad social and political issues.

Scott produced more than 25 full length novels, as well as a number of other works. His use of dialect and his decision to set his works almost exclusively in Scotland validated the language and folklore of regional and marginalized people at a time when "British" was increasingly equated with "English." His use of editorial personae, interlocutors, mediated (sometimes twice-mediated) story presentation, and complexly constructed authorial selves raise questions about the natures of authority and authorship, the difficulty of interpretation, and the concept of truth itself. Scott not only largely created the now well-known version of "Scotland" as a land of kilts and clans, with fierce rivalries fought out against a backdrop of misty mountains and purple heather, filled with eccentric but kind-hearted peasants, he also anticipated or pioneered many of the devices associated with modern and post-modern literature.

Many novels of the period, including Scott's, had roots in an earlier form of long prose fiction, the romance. Whereas "romance novel" today denotes a form of pulp fiction focused on romantic love as wish-fulfillment, the tradition of romance literature has its roots in medieval tales of the supernatural, of chivalry, and of courtly love, in which a sense of the extraordinary or the fantastic continually colors the narrative. The genre of romance made its influence felt in several different sorts of literary work in the Romantic era, but none more so than the Gothic. Gothic novels of the late eighteenth and early nineteenth centuries typically investigate human responses to supernatural occurrences, or those things known to be "impossible," thanks to the advances of science and natural history. These novels tend to feature stereotypical characters and to take place in worlds temporally or geographically distant from England. The surrounding landscape is often highly symbolic, reflecting the psychological world of the characters, and the heroine's plight—and the protagonist was almost without fail a heroine—is usually rendered in often highly expressive rhetoric, full of rhapsodic feeling. The structure of the Gothic novel frequently corresponds to the political and social tensions that result from the integration of long-ago, remotely historical time—preserved in ancient castles or abbeys—into an otherwise modern world. The Gothic setting of Charlotte Smith's

Emmeline, the Orphan of the Castle (1788), for example, allows for the exploration of social concerns such as English laws of primogeniture[1] and women's social status and identity within the frame of a courtship novel. Her novel illustrates the ways in which the frightening, distorted world of the Gothic could also serve as a forum for social commentary—as it also does in William Godwin's *Caleb Williams* (1794) and in Eliza Fenwick's *Secresy* (1795). Gothic novels such as Matthew Lewis's *The Monk* (1796), Charlotte Dacre's *Zofloya, or The Moor* (1806), Charles Maturin's *Melmoth the Wanderer* (1820), and Anne Radcliffe's series of highly successful Gothic novels, including *The Romance of the Forest* (1791) and *The Mysteries of Udolpho* (1794), welcomed their readers into a world marked by sexual perversity, threatened female virtue, and grotesque sights and experiences. Concerned with revealing what lay repressed or hidden behind the mask of middle-class conformity, the Gothic also often veered into savagery and melodrama, tendencies captured perfectly in the following exchange from *The Vampyre* (1819), by John Polidori, in which a mysterious villain extracts a promise from his traveling companion:

> "Swear!" cried the dying man raising himself with exultant violence. "Swear by all your soul reveres, by all your nature fears, swear that for a year and a day you will not impart your knowledge of my crimes or death to any living being in any way, whatever may happen, or whatever you may see."—His eyes seemed bursting from their sockets; "I swear!" said Aubrey; he sunk laughing upon his pillow, and breathed no more.

If the heightened atmosphere of the Gothic novel often veers toward imaginative excess, it can also foster literary art of the highest order—as *Frankenstein*, Mary Shelley's famous first novel, amply demonstrates. The story of a "monster" who turns against his creator Victor Frankenstein, *Frankenstein* is, on one level, a gripping tale of adventure, written with apparent simplicity. But it is also a text that brings together virtually all the great themes of the era: freedom and oppression; science and nature; society and the individual; knowledge and power; gender and sexuality; dream and reality; creation and destruction; self-deception and self-discovery; death and life; God and the universe.

If one strand of the tradition of romance literature runs through the evolution of the Gothic novel, a very different strand runs through the development

---

1   The common-law right of the first-born son to inherit the entire estate, to the exclusion of younger siblings.

of the courtship novel in the Romantic period. From Frances Burney's *Camilla*
(1796) to Elizabeth Susan Ferrier's *The Inheritance* (1824), the pages of Romantic fiction are filled with young people who are misguided, thwarted, and,
ultimately, united in love. It seems no exaggeration to say that no author of the
period was as successful with the courtship genre as was Jane Austen. Between
1811 and 1817, her six major novels were published, all of them warmly engaging yet sharply observant and often satirical, telling of courtship, social class,
and domestic life. Much as her novels do not engage directly or obviously with
the large issues of her age, Austen reveals a shrewd awareness of both politics
and economics, particularly as they concern women; her novels emphasize the
limited possibilities open to women during the period in which she wrote. But
within this limited frame, Austen provides a vividly three-dimensional picture
of the shaping of female character, of the inner world of the emotions as much
as the outer world of social behavior. Austen's heroines are preoccupied with
wooing, marriage, and the minutiae of income, entailment,[1] and other details of domestic and marital economy, precisely because these dominated and
defined the lives of women of the period, while her concentration on "3 or 4
Families in a country village" (as she famously remarked to her niece) draws
attention to the geographical and physical constraints imposed on middle- and
upper-class women during this time. Even the happy endings that have de-
lighted generations of Austenites are undercut by the obvious and acknowledged fictionality of the novels—emphasized through authorial asides, direct
appeals to the reader, and other devices—by means of which Austen suggests
that all happy endings may be mere fictions.

  Austen was a skilled stylist, as well a keen-eyed social critic, bringing to
her novels an unprecedented range of novelistic technique. With *Lady Susan*
(an early novella, written around 1794, but not published until 1871), she
proved herself adept at epistolary narrative; with *Sense and Sensibility*, *Pride
and Prejudice* and *Emma* (1815), she brought new flexibility to the use of the
third-person narrative voice, demonstrating perfect pitch in a variety of ironic
tones, and pioneering the technique now known as free indirect discourse.
In this mode of narration, the apparently independent third-person narrative
voice temporarily assumes the viewpoint of one or more of the characters—or

---

1   Legal provisions specifying that a property may not be sold or otherwise disposed of by
     the owner, as it must pass to the owner's (male) heirs upon his death.

indeed of an entire social class, as is the case with the famous opening to *Pride and Prejudice*: "It is a truth universally acknowledged, that a single man in possession of a good fortune, must be in want of a wife." In her tone, Austen is at a great remove from the leading poets of the Romantic period, but in the importance she places on the exercise of moral imagination—both by her characters and through her own narrative style—she is very much at one with the age.

Other Romantic novels sought to reflect the social and political concerns of the world around them in fiction more fully and more directly than did either most Gothic novels or most courtship novels; a number of writers used the novel as a means of challenging prevailing beliefs and mores. Maria Edgeworth's series of Irish novels—*Castle Rackrent* (1800), *Ennui* (1809), *The Absentee* (1812), and *Ormond* (1817)—explored the colonial relationship between England and Ireland. William Godwin's *Caleb Williams* (1794) sought to reveal, in the author's words, the "perfidiousness exercised by the powerful members of the community against those who are more privileged than themselves." Hogg's *Private Memoirs* was a powerful indictment of the smug superiority that could be engendered by religious zeal. And Mary Hays's *The Victim of Prejudice* (1799), a passionate tale of a young woman who dares to resist the pressure put upon her to marry the man who has raped her, was among those novels that spoke powerfully of injustice in a male-dominated society. Conservative voices also spoke out loudly through the medium of prose fiction; important anti-Jacobin novels of the period include Jane West's *A Tale of the Times* (1799), Elizabeth Hamilton's *Memoirs of Modern Philosophers* (1800), and Charles Lucas's *The Infernal Quixote* (1801). And a number of novelists used the novel as a means of making politically pointed connections with other parts of the world, whether to cast a critical eye on the course of European imperialism—as in Sydney Owenson's *The Missionary* (1811)—or to criticize aspects of British society by presenting them through the view of an outsider—as in Hamilton's *Translations of the Letters of a Hindoo Rajah* (1796).

While the novel prospered and evolved, so too did the genre of non-fictional prose. With the rise of the periodical (see "The Business of Literature" section below) came the rise of first critical and then more general essays, designed to engage, enlighten, and entertain the reader. William Hazlitt, originally intended for the Church and later an aspiring painter and philosopher, turned his hand to writing and became the most trenchant cultural critic of his time. His works include dramatic, literary, and art criticism, as well as political journalism, general essays, and his famous collection of pieces on important figures of the eighteenth century and the Romantic period, *The Spirit of the Age* (1824). His friend Charles Lamb rivaled Hazlitt's renown as an essayist, although his style was very different. Where Hazlitt used plain language and popular modes of construction to express his points cleanly and carefully, Lamb cultivated a more genteel style, rich in allusions and puns, with the resulting prose emerging as both thoughtful and rhetorically complex. Together, the two played a central role in the development of the essay during the Romantic period, but they were far from the only practitioners of the art. From Francis Jeffrey, whose pieces in the *Edinburgh Review* made literary criticism an exercise in stylish perspicacity, to Thomas De Quincey, whose psychological probing anticipates Freud, Romantic essay writers came in all shapes and sizes.

In the field of drama, the Romantic period is traditionally seen as an era of great "closet dramas."[1] And, given that the period produced both Byron's powerful verse drama, *Manfred* (1816–17), his iconoclastic meditation on sin and damnation, *Cain* (1822), and Shelley's mythographic masterpiece, *Prometheus Unbound*, its reputation as a breeding ground for rich, multi-layered private theatricals may fairly be said to be well deserved. Other serious plays failed on the stage but were widely read and highly praised as literature. Chief among these was Joanna Baillie's series of tragedies, collectively entitled *Plays on the Passions* (1798–1812); depicting the passions "in their rise and progress in the heart" was Baillie's intent, and she believed that such drama could have a moral purpose, though she made no transcendent claims for the moral value of the imagination. Drama, in her view, "improves us by the knowledge we acquire of our own minds, from the natural desire we have to look into the thoughts, and observe the behavior of others." Baillie's explorations in psychology harked back to Enlightenment concepts, but her plays also engaged powerfully with the issues of her own day, primarily the question of women's rights.

In Byron's view, the distaste many serious writers felt for the public theater in this period was entirely justified:

---

1   Plays written not for the stage but for private performance—in a private room or "closet"— or to be read.

When I first entered upon theatrical affairs, I had some idea of writing for the [play]house myself, but soon became a convert to Pope's opinion of that subject. Who would condescend to the drudgery of the stage, and enslave himself to the humours, the caprices, the taste or tastelessness, of the age? Besides, one must write for particular actors, have them continually in one's eye, sacrifice character to the personating of it, cringe to some favorite of the public, neither give him too many nor too few lines to spout …

Baillie was rather more charitable, attributing the low tolerance of audiences for serious drama to an escapism born of a desire to find refuge from the "commercial hurricane" of the age—and locating a good deal of the problem in the poor acoustics and lighting of the theaters of the day:

The Public have now to choose between what we shall suppose are well-written and well-acted plays, the words of which are not heard, or heard but imperfectly by two-thirds of the audience, while the finer and more pleasing traits of the acting are by a still greater proportion lost altogether; and splendid pantomime, or pieces whose chief object is to produce striking scenic effect, which can be seen and comprehended by the whole.

As both Byron's and Baillie's comments indicate, the theater in this period was, in some sense at least, thriving. People thronged to the theaters, where they saw plays by such popular and prolific playwrights as Hannah Cowley and Elizabeth Inchbald, as well as successful dramas such as Samuel Taylor Coleridge's *Remorse* (1812) and Charles Maturin's *Bertram* (1816). The Stage Licensing Act of 1737 meant that, in London, only two theaters, Covent Garden and Drury Lane (and, in the summer, the Haymarket) were permitted to present "legitimate" drama, but this in no way limited theatrical production. Stage entertainments of all sorts were held in venues from pubs to tents. In cities and provinces outside London, theaters sprang up to meet the demands of an increasing audience: a survey completed in 1804 counted 280 playhouses throughout the nation. The Licensing Act also required the texts of plays to be submitted to the Lord Chamberlain for censorship before performance. As a result, many works intended for the stage were forced into the closet; perhaps the most famous example is Shelley's *The Cenci*, which features not only father-daughter incest but also parricide. Many, however, were not, and a roll call of drama produced between 1780 and 1834 features everything from light comedy to melodramatic tragedy and from pantomimes to operas, as well as spectacles that featured impressive special effects.

The Business of Literature

The thriving literary scene of the period is intimately tied to developments in the worlds of book publishing, book selling, and book marketing. The most influential of these was the rise of the periodical. By the 1760s, there were more than 30 periodicals in London alone, including monthly journals, quarterly magazines, collections of reviews and essays, all designed to inform and stimulate their readers. This boom in the periodical press meant increased employment for those who sought to become men and women of letters; the demand for articles often outweighed the supply. For readers and publishers, it meant an ever-growing number of publications in which reviews of the latest books might appear. Published books were expensive—a three-volume novel could cost a total of nine shillings, roughly $40 today—but reviews often printed long extracts, and thus readers could experience the book through the review. Such extracts were also, of course, excellent advertisements for the books under review.

At the same time as the number of periodicals increased, so did ways of obtaining books. Between 1740 and 1790, the number of outlets nearly doubled. Most obviously, books could be bought: well-established bookshops

Thomas Rowlandson, Dr. Syntax and a Bookseller, *1812*.

flourished in cities all over the nation. In provincial towns and villages, where bookselling was not profitable on its own, literature was often sold side by side with stationery, patent medicines, and even groceries. Because the cost of books put them outside the means of many readers, however, some booksellers began to lend volumes to customers for a small fee, thus initiating the circulating library. A patron would pay a yearly fee, enabling him to borrow books as he pleased.

J. Bluck, after Augustus Charles Pugin, Ackermann's Art Library *(detail), c. 1812–15. Rudolf Ackermann (1764–1834) moved to London from his native Germany and opened a print shop in London on the Strand in 1795, selling books and artist supplies as well as prints, and exhibiting paintings. He later also began to publish color-plate books, the most notable of which was* The Microcosm of London, *a three-volume set with 104 hand-colored aquatint plates by various artists (including Thomas Rowlandson and Augustus Pugin), published between 1808 and 1811.*

Although both circulating and subscription libraries offered a good value, they still lay outside the financial resources of those below the lower middle classes. For these readers, there were other alternatives. Pedlars and hawkers sold street literature that included ballads, sermons, and tracts. Those who could not afford library subscriptions but who wished to read something more than broadsheet ballads or pamphlets often formed book clubs in which a number of people contributed money to buy a single book, which they would then share. After all had read the book, it might well be sold to a local booksell-er, with the proceeds put toward the price of a new one. Slightly more formally, in numerous towns and villages, the local male elite came together to select and discuss books and pamphlets, usually on a controversial topic of the day. This literature, too, was sold on, often by means of an auction among members at the end of the year.

Perhaps as a result of these efforts in group reading, or perhaps simply be-cause people enjoyed it, reading aloud remained a feature of the Romantic era. The fiction and the non-fiction of the period abounds in scenes of communal reading, and the visions that come down to us range from Countess Granville's admission that when her husband read *Don Juan* to her "I roared till I could neither hear nor see" to Henry Austen's description of his sister Jane as one who "read aloud with very great taste and effect. Her own works, probably, were never heard to such advantage as from her own mouth." Writers of the Ro-mantic period were not very far removed from a time when illiteracy was more common than literacy, a time when literature was still an oral art. It is worth bearing in mind that many of them wrote texts intended to be read aloud, and many of their works gain luster from being heard.

"Romantic"

Of the six periods into which the history of British literature has long been conventionally divided, the era of Romanticism is by far the briefest, extending over less than 40 years. Arguably it is also the most intense, particularly during the years 1789–1815: the era not only of the French Revolution and the Napo-leonic Wars but also of the era's most tumultuous literary developments—and most lasting literary achievements.

This was unquestionably an age of contradiction. It was a period in which political consciousness spread through society in unprecedented ways, with a great growth in collective awareness not only among those whose hearts resonated with revolutionary developments on the continent but also amongst workers, the disenfranchised poor, women, and anti-slavery activists. It was also a time of unprecedented growth in awareness of humans as individuals, of a rights-based political individualism, and of the Romantic individualism of the soul.

Applying a broad title to any literary or historical period is always risky. As much as any group of authors and thinkers may at first appear to have in common, deeper examination tends to reveal complexities and complications. Literature, like history, does not occur in isolation. One idea bleeds into another: revolutions are often old ideas returning under new names; factions develop, and their members deny that they are in any way related to the members of other factions. In its own time, Romanticism—a label never used by any of its writers, but rather first applied by the Victorians looking back on the period—was very frequently a house divided. "Lakers"[1] like Wordsworth and Southey denounced the "Satanic School"[2] of Shelley and Byron, who in turn produced vicious satires of these elders. "The Cockney School"[3] of Londoners Leigh Hunt and John Keats was derided by critics of the day, while writers now long ignored, such as Felicia Hemans, Samuel Rogers, and Thomas Moore, were lauded for their skill and rewarded with tremendous popularity. The Romantic era gains richness and interest if we view it not as a perfect stream but rather more accurately as a thick murmuring torrent of powerful voices that chorused and clashed, that simultaneously sought and struggled. These mingled tones together make up the voice of a movement that changed English literature.

---

1   The Lake Poets were so known because they resided in the Lake District of northwest England; the three most famous Lake Poets were Wordsworth, Coleridge, and Southey. The name "the Lake School of Poetry" was first used—derisively—in the *Edinburgh Review*.

2   The name was first used by Southey in *A Vision of Judgment* (1821), as a condemnation of writers, Byron and Shelley foremost among them, whose literary output was "characterized by a Satanic spirit of pride and audacious impiety."

3   The term first appeared in negative reviews of Hunt's poetry in *Blackwood's Magazine* in 1817. John Scott, the editor of *The Statesman*, a literary journal founded by Hunt, died in a duel fought over the contemptuous "Cockney" designation.

A Changing Language

Of all the places in which the political clashes of the Romantic period made themselves felt, perhaps the most surprising was in the arena of linguistics. Concern with questions of nationalism and political loyalties reached into the very language of Britain. From 1750 onward, the book market was flooded with pronunciation guides, a deluge inspired by the belief that standardized pronunciation would foster a sense of national unity. In this case, "standard" pronunciation meant the speech of educated urban dwellers. Even as many adhered to the essentially Tory belief that this supposedly standard speech was superior, there grew up a precisely opposite point of view, largely expressed by radical publishers and writers, that in the everyday speech of the common people one might find all that was best and most true about England: honesty, frankness, and English liberty given verbal form. In his *Classical Dictionary of the Vulgar Tongue* (1785), Francis Grose transcribed and celebrated the speech of commoners in their many regional variations, and, in 1818, the radical William Cobbett published his *Grammar of the English Language*, a book which explicitly treated language as a political matter. Cobbett took issue with the "false grammar" that he saw as having been put forward by eighteenth-century "authorities" such as Samuel Johnson, and attacked the grammatical slips as well as the privileged position of kings and nobles in a chapter entitled "Errors and Nonsense in a King's Speech." He addressed his work to the less privileged classes, who he believed should be enabled to participate in political discussions—"to assert with effect the rights and liberties of [their] country." As Cobbett saw it, "tyranny has no enemy so formidable as the pen."

Evidence of the Romantic celebration of "common language" can be found throughout the literature of the period. It accounts in part for the huge popularity of Robert Burns—a poet whose greatest effects come from his mixing of standard English with his native Scots dialect. But it finds its most famous expression in the "Preface" to the 1800 edition of *Lyrical Ballads*. There, Wordsworth writes that

> "men" in "low and rustic life" hourly communicate with the best objects from which the best part of language is originally derived; and because, from their rank in society and the sameness and narrow circle of intercourse, being less under the influence of social vanity they convey their feelings and notions in simple and unelaborated expressions. Accordingly, such language, rising out of

repeated experience and regular feelings, is a more permanent, and far more philosophical language …

Still, it is important to note that, Wordsworth's opinions on this point represented a minority view, and the Romantic belief in the "philosophical language" of "low and rustic life" was altogether short-lived, becoming less and less widely held. Fifteen years later, one finds Wordsworth's collaborator on *Lyrical Ballads*, Coleridge, writing that

> The best part of human language, properly so called, is derived from reflection on the acts of the mind itself. It is formed by a voluntary appropriation of fixed symbols to internal acts, to processes and results of imagination, the greater part of which have no place in the consciousness of the uneducated man.…

As the Romantic period slid into the Victorian and the vogue for rustic or uneducated authors passed away, so the point of view represented in Coleridge's remark came to dominate, and "standard" educated English became more and more widely accepted as an ideal to which all should aspire. However, even as the varieties of English were to some extent dissolving into the forms of standard English over the course of this period, many regional variations persisted, and the forms of standard English itself were far from unchanging.

In pronunciation, the most significant change in "standard British English" was the disappearance of the /r/ sound before many consonants, and before a pause, so that in words such as "harm" or "person," for example, the "r" has since the late eighteenth century been flattened into the smooth "hahm" or "pehson" associated with modern "standard English" pronunciation. Interesting geographical variations have developed over this change, however. In Scotland and in Ireland, as in Canada and most of the United States, the "r" has continued to be sounded in such contexts; these varieties of English are referred to by linguists as "rhotic." In Australia, New Zealand, and South Africa, on the other hand, as well as in some parts of the United States, for instance in Massachusetts and some other parts of New England, non-rhotic forms have come to predominate in much the same way as they have in England.

As the rhymes of English poetry reveal, there were also changes in the sounding of some vowels in the late eighteenth century. In the early eighteenth century, for example, Alexander Pope rhymed "tea" with "obey"; other rhymes suggest that "sea" was pronounced in a manner closer to "say" than to "see." By

1797, however, Coleridge could rhyme "sea" with "free;" and by the end of the Romantic period the older pronunciations of such words had almost certainly died out.

Eighteenth century habits of capitalization and punctuation were also largely abandoned during this period. Capitalization and typography had generally been considered the business of the compositor rather than that of the author, and the tendency in the early and mid-eighteenth century had been to capitalize (or sometimes italicize) a wide range of nouns. By the end of the century, patterns of usage were coming to approximate the conventions of modern English.

Paragraphing remained less strongly conventionalized than it is now—many writers tended to start new paragraphs very infrequently—and the conventions for writing direct speech were still unstable, with the practice of using double quotation marks surrounding the exact words spoken starting to become common at the end of the eighteenth century. The practice of using single rather than double quotation marks did not become common in Britain until later in the nineteenth century and did not become entirely standardized as British usage until the twentieth century.

INTRODUCTION TO
THE VICTORIAN ERA

The word "Victorian" conjures up a series of images that both accurately describe and misrepresent the literature and culture of the last two thirds of the nineteenth century in Britain. Stiff collars and stiff upper lips, draped table legs, exceedingly long novels, and gritty urban squalor have become the iconic images of Victorian Britain. But these images reveal only one dimension of what is a much more complex picture. While it is certainly the case that Victorians tended to place a high value on such qualities as honor, duty, moral seriousness, and sexual propriety—at least officially—it is a mistake to assume that most were humorless or repressed. And while many of the best-known Victorian novels run to many hundreds of pages, we need to remember that Victorian audiences tended to read these in weekly or monthly installments, or in shorter volumes. Although brutal factory conditions, pitiful wages; and crowded cities impoverished many millions of people, the Victorian period also saw the passage of progressive labor laws, unprecedented wealth creation for some, and the first public sewage systems in Britain. And though "Victorian" still suggests "repressed" to many readers, historians and literary scholars alike have increasingly shown that discourses about sexuality developed and proliferated throughout the period, not least in its literary output.

Franz Xavier Winterhalter, Queen Victoria, *1842.*

In fact, it may be fair to say that there was never a single "Victorian mindset" or "Victorian value system" but rather a range of them, and that these shifted throughout the century. Indeed, there is no real consensus about when the Victorian era began and ended. Some point to the passage of the Reform Bill of

1832 as the dawn of a new era, others to the abolition of slavery in the British Empire in 1833. Still others argue for the unity of a longer period,[1] beginning perhaps with the end of the Napoleonic Wars in 1815 and ending with the outbreak of World War I in 1914. Perhaps the obvious choice is to date the period as starting with Victoria's ascension to the throne in 1837 and concluding with her death in 1901, but the identification of the period so entirely with her reign is ultimately arbitrary and tells us little about the Victorian era.

Photographer unknown, Queen Victoria, *c. 1897. A picture of Albert is in the background.*

Although a great deal of overlap can be found between the Romantic and Victorian periods, most scholars agree that the 1830s was a pivotal decade, marked by the transition of the monarchy from William IV to Victoria and by the spread of a spirit of political and social reform that would characterize the next several decades. During the 1850s and 1860s, Britain emerged from a depressed economy and experienced a level of political and social stability that made these decades the most prosperous of the century, and the mid-Victorian period is now often regarded as a kind of high-water mark for Victorian culture, particularly because the 1870s and 1880s saw some decline in the strength of the economy and in Britain's imperial dominance abroad, despite its continued acquisition of colonial possessions. These decades were also marked by the glimmerings of social change, a wave that culminated in

---

1   Some historians have suggested that the period's beginning should perhaps be dated even earlier, with the seeds of "Victorianism" being planted as early as the late eighteenth century, with the reemergence of Evangelicalism and the Methodist revival. The religious movement countered the ideals of the Enlightenment and may thus be said to mark the conclusion of the primary movement of the eighteenth century.

the fin-de-siècle spirit of the 1890s, which saw many challenges to the values and conventions of the preceding decades in literature, politics, and everyday life.

A Growing Power

During Victoria's reign, Britain was the richest nation and the most powerful empire on the globe, with unchallenged military supremacy until the latter decades of the century and an imperial reach that covered one-quarter of the earth's surface by 1897.[1] As the world's first industrialized country, Britain experienced both the benefits and the horrors of enormous growth throughout the nineteenth century. The census of 1801 put the population of the country at 11 million people; at century's end that number had increased by almost 300 per cent to 37 million. Just as striking was the movement of this population, from 75 per cent rural distribution in the early decades to nearly the same percentage residing in urban districts by the end of the century. Northern industrial cities grew particularly fast: Manchester, a town of no more than 15,000 people in 1750, had grown to 75,000 by 1800, and to 125,000 by 1820; by 1850 its population was over 300,000. Between 1815 and 1914, more than 20 million people emigrated from Britain to other parts of

Fleet Street, London, c. 1890.

---

1   The scope of England's imperial holdings was memorably expressed in a popular saying of the period: "The sun never sets on the British empire." (A popular rejoinder to the sentiment was the saying that God did not trust the English in the dark.)

Left: Construction of the sewer beneath Fleet Street, London, early 1860s. By 1858 the stench of sewage from the Thames had become so overwhelming that the Houses of Parliament at Westminster found it impossible to meet; construction of a city-wide underground system of sewers, under the direction of Joseph Bazalgette, began the following year. Top right: Building the Holborn Viaduct across the Fleet valley (Illustrated Times, *18 September 1869). The viaduct, carrying both road and rail traffic, was a vast project carried out by the Corporation of the City of London between 1863 and 1869. Bottom right: Alfred Morgan,* An Omnibus Ride to Piccadilly Circus—Mr. Gladstone Travelling with Ordinary Passengers, *1885. The previous year Prime Minister William Gladstone's government had extended the franchise to working-class males, through the Reform Bill of 1884.*

the world, over half of them to the United States, but millions, too, to Australia and to Canada.

The shift from an agrarian to an industrial wage economy meant an increase in income for many people, creating a sector of the population that was neither rich nor poor and was increasingly termed "middle class." A spirit of entrepreneurship and market thinking—dominated by upwardly mobile males—gradually replaced what had once seemed an entrenched, unchangeable system of aristocratic patronage and paternalism in the world of business and trade. The Reform Bill of 1832 granted political representation in Parliament to certain sectors of the middle-class male population for the first time, although even with its passage, only one in six adult males could vote, and the suffrage was still linked to property ownership. Rail travel, the advent of the telegraph, daily newspapers, and the manufacture and import of goods via steamship from all over the globe collapsed time and space, and flooded the homes of the affluent with new luxuries and conveniences. The Great Exhibition of 1851, the first World's Fair, showcased Britain's industrial dominance with exhibits of new consumer goods and remarkable technologies; the event symbolized Britain's reputation as the "workshop of the world." Thus, for many the overall mood was positive, and Thomas Macaulay's confident assertions on the nation's progress in his bestselling *History of England* rang true for much of his audience.

Grinding Mills, Grinding Poverty

The paradox of the economic life of the time was summed up by Thomas Carlyle in 1843: "England is full of wealth," he wrote, "of multifarious produce, supply for human want in every kind; yet England is dying of inanition." For millions of people, low wages, unemployment, and fluctuations in trade created widespread misery in crowded industrial cities such as Manchester and Birmingham. According to one estimate, 70 per cent of the population at mid-century was considered poor. The New Poor Law,[1] passed in 1834, divided and categorized the poor as either "deserving" (the elderly and the physically infirm) or "undeserving" (the able-bodied but unemployed). The poor were now eligible to receive public assistance only in the notorious workhouses,

---

1   The "Old Poor Law" was passed during the reign of Queen Elizabeth I.

also known as the "Poor Law Bastilles,"[1] which often served to punish and stigmatize rather than relieve. In addition, inadequate housing and slum conditions led to frequent outbreaks of illness and disease. Between 1831 and 1866, four cholera epidemics killed more than 140,000 people, inaugurating Britain's first wide-scale public health movement. Scores of "Blue Books"—statistical investigations, surveys, and government reports on the condition of inner-city neighborhoods—culminated in the Public Health Acts of 1848 and the 1870s. Similarly, between 1802 and 1847, factories and mines producing iron, cotton, and coal, which had been unregulated, employing men, women, and children in conditions that were often dirty and dangerous, were made subject to a series of Factory Acts, designed to force employers to limit work hours—working 14 hours a day had been not uncommon—and prohibit the employment of children under the age of nine in certain industries.

In her poem, "The Cry of the Children" (1843), Elizabeth Barrett Browning drew attention to the problem of child labor, helping to create humanitarian awareness on the part of middle-class readers by asking "How long, O cruel nation, / Will you stand to move the world, on a child's heart."[2] Thomas Hood's "The Song of the Shirt" (1843) focused on the plight of the genteel but impoverished female needle-worker who toils alone in grim conditions for meager wages. Cast in the elevated and stylized "voices" of their victimized speakers, such poems were both wildly popular and highly sentimental, qualities that have until recently served to exclude them from serious study by scholars of English literature. Yet these poems did as much or more than government reports and statistical surveys to shed light on major social issues. So too did Carlyle's *Past and Present* (1843), which called England to responsibility for the many starving workers in the land of "plenty":

> We have more riches than any Nation ever had before: we have less good of them than any Nation had before.... We have forgotten everywhere that *Cash-payment* is not the sole relation of human beings; we think, nothing doubting, that it absolves and liquidates all other engagements.

1   The Paris fortress-prison was stormed on 14 July 1789, initiating the French Revolution.
2   Many of the poem's details were drawn from the 1842–43 Parliamentary commission report investigating the conditions of child employment in mines and factories. The report's author, R.H. Horne, was a close friend of the poet.

John Everett Millais, Ophelia *(1851–52). The drowning of Ophelia (from Shakespeare's* Hamlet*) was a frequent subject in Victorian painting; the best known representation is that of Millais. As the scene is described in Act 4, Scene 7 of the play, the mentally ill Ophelia comes to a stream "with fantastic garlands" of flowers. Distracted, she falls into the "weeping brook." For a while before she drowns, "her clothes spread wide" hold her up.*

Henry Wallis, Chatterton *(1856). The suicide of Thomas Chatterton (1752–70), of arsenic poisoning after years of living close to starvation as a struggling poet, captured the Victorian imagination even more strongly than it had the Romantic one. Wallis's painting was widely praised when exhibited in 1856 at the Royal Academy; John Ruskin described it in his notes on the exhibit as "faultless and wonderful."*

Thomas Jones Barker, The Secret of England's Greatness *(detail), c. 1863. Barker's painting depicts the Queen presenting a Bible. The recipient and the specific occasion remain unidentified; in the background are Elizabeth (Duchess of Wellington (who served as Mistress of the Robes to the Queen); Prince Albert; Lord Palmerston (then serving as Prime Minister); and Lord John Russell (then serving as Foreign Secretary). An engraving of the painting was published under the fuller title,* The Bible: The Secret of England's Greatness.

Franz Xavier Winterhalter, The Royal Family in 1846 *(detail), 1846.*

Ford Madox Brown, Work, *c. 1852–c. 1865. This famous painting (above), which took over twelve years to complete, brings together Victorians from an extraordinary range of backgrounds. The central group of excavators was the painting's starting point— the inspiration coming from the artist observing work on the construction of the London sewers. Less well-off members of society include the flower seller to the left and the motherless children in the foreground, cared for by an older sibling. To the right are two "brain-workers" admired by the artist, Rev. F.D. Maurice (founder of the Working Man's College, where Brown was an art instructor) and Thomas Carlyle. In the background members of the gentry on horseback observe the scene.*

George Clausen, The Stone Pickers, *1887*

William Holman Hunt, The Awakening Conscience, *1853–54. This canvas presents an elaborately coded story. In a letter to* The Times *of London, John Ruskin (signing himself as "The Author of Modern Painters") described the reaction of viewers—and elucidated the painting's intended significance: ". . . assuredly it is not understood. People gaze at it in a blank wonder, and leave it hopelessly; so that, although it is almost an insult to the painter to explain his thoughts in this instance, I cannot persuade myself to leave it thus misunderstood. The poor girl has been singing with her seducer; some chance words of the song "Oft in the stilly night" have struck upon the numbed places of her heart; she has started up in agony; he, not seeing her face, goes on singing, striking the keys carelessly with his gloved hand." As Ruskin discerned, the woman is evidently the mistress rather than the wife of the man; she wears a ring on every finger of her left hand except the fourth. The piece that has been played, "Oft in the stilly night," is a song in which a woman looks back to the innocence of her childhood. The doubling of the female figure through the use of the mirror suggests the possibility of a brighter future if she follows her awakened conscience and gives up the life of a "kept woman."*

G. W. Joy, General Gordon's Last Stand, *c. 1893. Gordon, who had held an administrative post in the Sudan in the 1870s (and played an important role during that period in ending the slave trade in the area), was sent again to the Sudan in 1884 on a mission to rescue garrisons of British troops that had been cut off after a rebellion by Mohammed Ahmad (known to the British as "the Mahdi"). Gordon's forces were besieged in Khartoum for ten months and finally overwhelmed, and he was killed during the battle (though almost certainly in the streets of the city, not as he is shown in Joy's iconic painting of the imagined scene). The incident became a* cause célèbre *in Britain, and there were many calls to avenge Gordon's death, but it was not until fourteen years later that the British under General Kitchener re-established British control of the Sudan.*

Trade Emblem, Amalgamated Society of Engineers, Machinists,
Millwrights, Smiths, and Pattern Makers, c. 1860.

Alfred Concanen, Modern Advertising: A Railway Station in 1874. *1874. This colored lithograph appeared as a fold-out frontispiece in the book* A History of Advertising from the Earliest Times.

(Left) John O'Connor, From Pentonville Road Looking West, *1884. In the background is St. Pancras, one of the greatest of Victorian railway stations. (Right) Advertisement, 1890s, "Cook's Tours in Scotland." Featured at lower left is the Firth of Forth Bridge (also known as the Forth Rail Bridge). The bridge, built in the wake of the collapse of the Firth of Tay Bridge, in which 75 lives had been lost, pioneered new techniques of cantilever construction; on its completion in 1890 it was by far the longest bridge in the world.*

Benjamin Duterrau, The Conciliation, *1840.*
The painting shows a Methodist lay preacher instructing native Tasmanians.

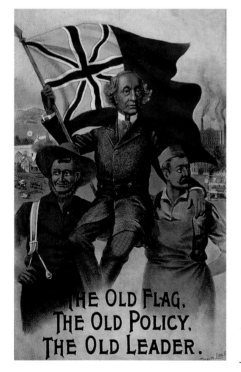

THE OLD FLAG,
THE OLD POLICY,
THE OLD LEADER.

Canadian election poster, 1891. The "Old Leader" was Sir John A. Macdonald, Canadian Prime Minister from 1867 to 1873 and again from 1878 to 1891. "The Old Policy" was Macdonald's NationalPolicy, under the terms of which industries in the Dominion would be protected by a tariff on imports from the United States, but "imperial preference" exempted goods from Britain and her possessions from any tariff.

Even as such voices spoke up in support of the destitute and the working class-es, over the course of the century, the voices of working-class people themselves were also increasingly heard. The 1828 publication of Robert Blincoe's *Memoir* of his appalling early life in the mills had a lasting impact; in addition to a di-rect effect on its readers, Blincoe's memoir provided much of the raw material for Frances Trollope's novel *Michael Armstrong: Factory Boy* (1840), and may also have inspired Charles Dickens's *Oliver Twist* (1838). Blincoe's memoir was followed by a number of other autobiographical narratives of working-class hardship; a particularly notable example of the genre was *A Narrative of the Experience and Sufferings of William Dodd* (1841). Ellen Johnson published a more wide-ranging memoir, *Autobiography of a Factory Girl* (1867), together

with her poems and songs. Another prominent working-class poetic voice was that of Ebenezer Elliott, the "Corn-Law Rhymer" from Yorkshire who became an active force first in the Chartist movement and then in the struggle to repeal the Corn Laws (both of which will be discussed in more detail below). In his *Corn-Law Rhymes* (1831) and in subsequent work Elliott attacked

> The deadly will that takes
> What labour ought to keep;
> It is the deadly power that makes
> Bread dear and labour cheap.

How to best respond to the force of this "deadly power" remained a matter of debate and speculation. If some emphasized the need to con-tinually press for political reform, others appealed emotionally for hearts to change; still others formu-lated new philosophical approaches

Thomas Iron Works, London, 1867.

to the underlying moral and socio-economic questions. Perhaps the most important of these approaches was Utilitarianism, a broad-reaching philosophy that had first been developed in the late eighteenth century, primarily by Jeremy Bentham, and that was expounded in a more careful, subtle, and thoroughgoing fashion by John Stuart Mill in the nineteenth.[1] Utilitarian thought began to shape governmental policy, including the New Poor Law, in the middle decades of the nineteenth century—and continues to be a shaping force in the social policy of most developed nations today. In its crude form, Utilitarianism holds—in the words of Bentham's 1776 "A Fragment on Government"—that "it is the greatest happiness of the greatest number that is the measure of right and wrong." In other words, the central guiding principle of

social morality should be the pursuit of that which is good for all members of society, with no one person or group's interests given special weight. But how does one calculate "the greatest happiness of the greatest number"? Can social, legal, economic, and political problems be resolved by a "moral arithmetic" that evaluates human pain and pleasure according to entirely rationalist principles? According to some crude versions of utilitarian philosophy—though certainly not that of Mill—the answer is yes; imagination, feeling, and individual desire are obsolete impediments to the operation of the "laws" of social improvement, which may be derived from empirical observation and calculation.

Hatting mill, Manchester, 1890s.

---

1   Mill first published *Utilitarianism*, his defense of the utilitarian philosophy in 1861, as a series of three articles in *Fraser's Magazine*. The essays appeared as a one-volume work in 1863.

Writers such as Elizabeth Barrett Browning, Dickens, Carlyle, and John Ruskin were intensely critical of Utilitarianism, taking its crudest forms as representative and regarding it as a morally and spiritually bankrupt response to the human condition. Dickens, in particular, caricatured utilitarian thinking with telling directness in his portrayal of Thomas Gradgrind in *Hard Times* (1854), his tenth novel, aimed at exposing the working conditions in English factories and initiating reform.[1] However, it may be fitting to understand the intensity of these writers' opposition to Utilitarianism in a larger context: for Mill, "the greatest number" included not only the poor white people of England but also brown and black people in poverty the world over; on the other hand, Dickens, Carlyle and Ruskin, for all their sympathy for the British poor, looked at those of other races, at best, with condescension and, at worst, with outright loathing. In any case, as the works of writers such as Dickens, Barrett Browning, and Elizabeth Gaskell amply demonstrated, opposition to the cruelties of poverty could be expressed—as plausibly and as powerfully—by means of emotional and aesthetic appeals through literature as it could by means of the philosophical arguments of the Utilitarians.[2]

Corn Laws, Potato Famine

As the powerful and privileged attempted to confront the range of social crises facing a newly industrialized nation, economic depression, unemployment, political instability in Europe, and a series of crop failures in the 1840s—a decade often dubbed the "Hungry Forties"—caused a disproportionate level of suffering for the poor. Artificial shortages of grain in the country inflated the price of bread beyond the reach of the working class, causing periodic bread riots and a discontented work force. These shortages were in part the result of the Corn Laws, which imposed heavy tariffs on imports of grain, and were intended to protect British agricultural interests and limit dependence on foreign supplies of cereal grains. The Corn Laws were repealed in 1846 under pressure

---

1   In a letter to his friend Charles Knight, Dickens accused the utilitarians of seeing "figures and averages, and nothing else."

2   Although the "social novel" had its origins in the eighteenth century, it was developed and popularized as a genre during the Victorian period.

NOTICE
TO
THE EARL OF CHARLEMONT'S TENANTRY.

IN consideration of the extensive failure in the POTATO CROP this Season, willing to bear his share in the general calamity, and anxious to relieve, as far as in him lies, his Poorer Tenants from an undue share of suffering under the Divine Will, LORD CHARLEMONT has directed that the following Scale of Reduction, in Payment of Rent, shall be adopted for this Year, upon his Estates in the COUNTIES of ARMAGH and TYRONE, viz. :—

25 per Cent. on Rents under £5	10 per Cent. on Rents under £20.
20 per Cent. on Rents under £10	5 per Cent. on Rents under £30.
15 per Cent. on Rents under £15	No Discount on Rents exceeding £30.

Notice of a rent abatement by an Irish landlord, 1846.

Evicted family, Glenbeigh, Ireland, 1888. In the 1880s an economic depression coincided with the election of a substantial number of Irish Home Rule Members of Parliament (under Charles Parnell's leadership), and with a campaign by the Land League to resist the practice of evicting impoverished tenant farmers unable to pay their rent.

from the Anti-Corn-Law League, an alliance of free-trade advocates and liberal, laissez-faire[1] trade reformers.

In the wake of the repeal of the Corn Laws, three successive crop failures in Ireland led to one of the worst humanitarian disasters of the century, the Irish potato famine of 1845–47. Prime Minister Robert Peel's government attempted to alleviate the situation by importing emergency shipments of grain from the United States in 1845, but when Peel's government was replaced by Lord John Russell's Whig administration in 1846, Russell in effect put a stop to emergency aid; the laissez-faire interests of Russell and his supporters led to the transfer of responsibility for famine relief to the inadequate jurisdiction of the Irish Poor Law. By 1847, between 850,000 and 1,500,000 Irish—from 10 to over 15 per cent of the population, depending on the estimate— had died of starvation; the English government policy toward Ireland, its nearest colonial possession, was in this instance one of such neglect that it may be said to have amounted to extraordinary cruelty.

---

1   From the French for "let do," the phrase "laissez-faire" came to be used in the late eighteenth century as a shorthand for the belief that government is best advised to intervene as little as possible in the workings of the economy. The term first appeared in English usage in George Whatley's *Principles of Trade* (1774), but it did not become popularized until James Mill's reference in an 1824 entry in *The Encyclopedia Britannica*.

Inevitably, hostility toward the English, and with it Irish nationalist sentiment, was greatly intensified by the potato famine. The seeds of the Irish independence movement had been effectively sown—and sown not only in Ireland but also in the United States, where hundreds of thousands of Irish emigrated during this period. As these immigrants prospered in America, they provided more and more support for the Fenian movement—which sprang up in the 1850s in support of Irish independence and launched attacks in the 1860s and 1870s, not only in England but also against British possessions in New Brunswick, Upper Canada, and Manitoba—and for subsequent political groups with similar aims. But the road to Irish independence was an extraordinarily rocky one: the Irish won the right to be represented in the British House of Commons, but their greatest Parliamentary spokesman, Charles Parnell,[1] after surviving dozens of scurrilous attempts to discredit him, was finally brought down when his affair with a divorced woman became a public scandal; British Prime Minister William Gladstone became a convert to the cause of Home Rule for the Irish and passed a bill authorizing it through the House of Commons in 1886, only to have the measure killed in the House of Lords; a similar bill in 1893 suffered the same fate; another bill to enact Home Rule was put aside with the outbreak of World War I in 1914. In the end, independence was only achieved after the violent struggles of the 1916 Easter Uprising and the War of Independence of 1919–22. Even then, the British retained possession of a substantial area in Northern Ireland.

"The Two Nations"

In the 1830s and 1840s, the human costs of the Industrial Revolution—what became known as the "Condition of England" question—were scrutinized by legislators, workers, and writers. Carlyle, Dickens, Gaskell, Harriet Martineau, Benjamin Disraeli, and Henry Mayhew documented the daily existence of poor and working people, and criticized the laws that were intended to address

---

1   Charles Stewart Parnell (1846–91) was the Irish Protestant founder and leader of the Irish Parliamentary Party and the leading champion of the Irish Home Rule Movement. The movement suffered a serious setback with the revelation of Parnell's affair with Katherine "Kitty" O'Shea, the wife of William O'Shea, another MP. The scandal caused many of Parnell's supporters to turn against him, and he died of a heart attack shortly after marrying Katherine in 1891.

Jabez Hughes, Benjamin Disraeli, *c. 1877. Disraeli, who led the Conservative Party from 1868 to 1880 (serving as Prime Minister briefly in 1868 and then again from 1874 to 1880), was seen as something of an exotic within the English establishment. Though he was baptized as an infant and remained a practicing Anglican throughout his life, Disraeli's parents were converted Jews; it is an interesting marker of the degree to which "Jew" was considered a racial rather than a religious category that he was not able to run for the House of Commons until the Parliament of 1858–59 had made it legal for Jews to enter Parliament. A fashionable figure, Disraeli was derided by his straitlaced rival, Liberal leader William Gladstone, as "Asiatic"—a word often used in Victorian times as a synonym for "indulgent and irresponsible." But Disraeli remained a popular figure with much of the general population as well as with much of the establishment—and with the Queen.*

their suffering. The "social problem novel" or "industrial novel," an important subgenre of Victorian fiction, drew attention to class conflict and the social ramifications of laissez-faire economic policies. Prominent examples include Charles Kingsley's *Alton Locke* (1850), Charles Dickens's *Hard Times*, and Elizabeth Gaskell's *Mary Barton* (1848) and *North and South* (1854–55).

In his 1845 novel *Sybil,* future Prime Minister Benjamin Disraeli coined the phrase "the Two Nations" to describe the disparity in Britain between rich and poor. Novelists felt that their work could provoke social reform by exposing their middle-class audiences to the plight of the working classes, who were often portrayed as either vulnerable and victimized by forces beyond their control, or as a violent, angry "mass"; intervention by those of goodwill from other social classes is often implicitly recommended in such fiction as a way of ameliorating the situation and bridging "the Two Nations." The middle-class narrator of Gaskell's novel *Mary Barton,* for example, adopts the role of mediator between Manchester's workers and their industrial "masters" in an attempt to foster understanding and prevent political insurrection.

Non-fiction writing may have been as important as that of any novelist in nurturing the seeds of social change. Henry Mayhew's interviews with working people and street folk for the *Morning Chronicle* newspaper opened a window for its readers onto the daily existence of an often voiceless underclass. It must be said, however, that Mayhew's reports contained no overt political commentary or reform agenda. Friedrich Engels, by contrast, in his chronicle of urban squalor *The Condition of the Working Class in England in 1844*, not only described the extraordinary scale of the human suffering he witnessed but also placed the blame squarely on the shoulders of a class system created by industrial capitalism: "Power lies in the hands of those who own, directly or indirectly, foodstuffs and the means of production. The poor, having no capital, inevitably bear the consequences of defeat in the struggle."[1]

It was not only middle-class writers and observers who were bringing attention to the great divide between Britain's rich and poor. Chartism, a movement that initiated a series of political campaigns in the 1830s and 1840s, was a concrete expression of the desire of working-class people to resist economic and social disparity and press for political reform. The People's Charter of 1838, from which the movement took its name, petitioned the government to adopt a range of key reforms, including annual elections, universal male suffrage, and the abolition of property qualifications for Members of Parliament and of the secret ballot. The mouthpiece of the Chartist movement was the *Northern Star* newspaper, one of many working-class periodicals that flourished in

The Six Points

OF THE

PEOPLE'S

CHARTER.

1. A VOTE for every man twenty-one years of age, of sound mind, and not undergoing punishment for crime.

2. THE BALLOT.—To protect the elector in the exercise of his vote.

3. No PROPERTY QUALIFICATION for Members of Parliament —thus enabling the constituencies to return the man of their choice, be he rich or poor.

4. PAYMENT OF MEMBERS, thus enabling an honest tradesman, working man, or other person, to serve a constituency, when taken from his business to attend to the interests of the country.

5. EQUAL CONSTITUENCIES, securing the same amount of representation for the same number of electors, instead of allowing small constituencies to swamp the votes of large ones.

6. ANNUAL PARLIAMENTS, thus presenting the most effectual check to bribery and intimidation, since though a constituency might be bought once in seven years (even with the ballot), no purse could buy a constituency (under a system of universal suffrage) in each ensuing twelvemonth; and since members, when elected for a year only, would not be able to defy and betray their constituents as now.

Chartist poster, 1838.

---

1   Engels's treatise, first published in Germany in 1845, was not translated into English until 1892.

the early decades of the nineteenth century. The Chartist petitions were signed by up to five million people and presented to Parliament by a coalition of workers in 1839, 1842, and 1848, but were rejected each time. A number of middle-class writers sympathetic to the claims of the working classes were nevertheless suspicious of the Chartist movement, particularly in light of the political revolutions taking place in continental Europe in the late 1840s. In his longing for the imagined social order of a feudal past, Carlyle denounced the "mad Chartisms" of the "anarchic multitude," comparing them to the events of the French Revolution and the Reign of Terror. With the defeat of the third petition, Chartism collapsed, but it had helped instigate a new level of class consciousness among ordinary people, and is now considered to be the first independent working-class movement in Britain.

In the 1880s and 1890s various socialist movements emerged, partly on the strength of Karl Marx's theories of capital, which he formulated under the dome of the British Library after moving to London in 1849. The Fabian Society was one of the most influential socialist organizations. Its membership was mainly drawn from the middle class and included such notables as George Bernard Shaw, Sidney Webb and Beatrice Potter Webb, Edith Nesbit, and Annie Besant. The Fabians' tactics were reformist rather than revolutionary; they advocated public ownership of utilities, affordable housing, improved wages, and greater access to higher education for all.

Trade unions and labor movements also grew gradually in scope and strength throughout the century, with the Trade Union Act of 1871 granting legal status to unions for the first time. Newly mobilized workers in the 1880s organized to mount a series of strikes with varying degrees of success. Two of the most highly publicized of these were the match-girls' strike in 1888 and the London dock workers' strike of 1889. Union membership doubled in these years, partly because of the success of these labor actions.

The match-girls' strike began after the dismissal of one of the workers at the Bryant and May Factory in Bow, London, in early July 1888, but its real causes lay in the terrible working conditions at the factory, including 14-hour workdays, poor pay and excessive fines, and severe health complications resulting from working with dangerotus materials. The strike attracted significant publicity, and factory owners were forced to concede to the strikers' demands for a better working environment.

The Match-Girl Strike Committee, 1888. The action was led by Annie Besant (who had initially become famous during her 1877 trial for obscenity —the charge being based on the distribution of her pamphlet offering practical advice on contraception).

The London Dock Strike began on August 14, 1889. At a Parliamentary hearing on the issue, the general manager at the Millwall Docks testified about the physical conditions of the workers, which led to the strike:

> The poor fellows are miserably clad, scarcely with a boot on their foot, in a most miserable state ... These are men who come to work in our docks who come on without having a bit of food in their stomachs, perhaps since the previous day; they have worked for an hour and have earned 5d.; their hunger will not allow them to continue: they take the 5d. in order that they may get food, perhaps the first food they have had for twenty-four hours.

The strike, which had succeeded in garnering strong middle-class support, ended in victory for the workers, whose principal demand had been for increased pay, and the establishment of unions for dock workers.

The Politics of Gender

Gender consciousness was central to Victorian England's political scene in a number of significant ways. At the beginning of the Victorian period, middle-class women were shut out of most remunerative employments and institutions of higher education, could not vote, and had few legal rights. By the end of the century, the situation did not, on the surface, look radically different—universal female suffrage, for example, was not achieved in Britain until 1928—but several key developments heralded the changes to come in the twentieth century.

The first major challenges by Victorian "strong-minded women" to patriarchal control were in the area of marriage law. The common-law doctrine of coverture ensured that a woman's legal identity was subsumed in that of her husband's upon marriage. In effect, the law of coverture regarded the husband and wife as "one person": the husband. This meant that upon marriage a husband had full control of his wife's personal property and any earnings she acquired during the marriage; he had absolute authority over their home and children; and he could legally use physical force to discipline the members of his family. If he deserted his wife, she could not sue for divorce and had no custody rights to their children. No viable legal mechanism was available to an average woman to contest her husband's decisions, since husband and wife were "one body" under the law.[1] The essayist Frances Power Cobbe was among the most effective in pointing out the illogic of such arrangements, as well as the terrible toll they exacted. In contemplating, for example, the situation of "the poor woman whose husband has robbed her earnings, who leaves her and her children to starve, and then goes unpunished because the law can only recognize the relation of husband and wife as ... one before the law," Cobbe observed in her provocative 1868 essay "Criminals, Idiots, Women, and Minors" that

> It is one of the numerous anomalies connected with women's affairs, that when
> they are under debate the same argument which would be held to determine

---

1   The tremendous pressures placed on women as a result of coverture are significant to the plot of a number of prominent Victorian novels, perhaps most notably Emily Brontë's *Wuthering Heights* (1847). In the novel, Heathcliff exploits marital coverture to usurp property as part of his plan for vengeance, repeatedly resorting to abuse and exploitation of the authority he is granted as husband.

other questions in one way is felt to settle theirs in another. If for instance it be proved of any other class of the community, that it is particularly liable to be injured, imposed upon, and tyrannized over (e.g., the children who work in factories), it is considered to follow as a matter of course that the law must step in for its protection. But it is the alleged *helplessness* of married women which, it is said, makes it indispensable to give all the support of the law, *not* to them, but to the stronger persons with whom they are unequally yoked.

Under pressure from organized networks of reformers, several major pieces of legislation, altering the status and position of married women, were enacted during the period. Perhaps the most economically significant of these was the Married Women's Property Act of 1870,[1] which finally allowed married women to legally own the money they earned and the property they inherited. In addition, the Matrimonial Causes Act of 1878 accorded some legal protection to female victims of domestic violence, and the Infant Custody Acts of 1839 and 1886 granted a woman custodial rights to her children. Although full equality within marriage was not realized in law until the twentieth century, the passage of the aforementioned legislation began to chip away at male patriarchal privilege and challenged the legal and religious "justifications" for women's oppression within the family.

In her 1851 essay "The Enfranchisement of Women" Harriet Taylor Mill addresses those "justifications" one by one, then proceeds to the heart of the matter: "The real question is, whether it is right and expedient that one half of the human race should pass through life in a state of forced subordination to the other half." *The Subjection of Women*[2] (1869), John Stuart Mill's famous extended essay on the topic, grew out of Taylor Mill's essay—the two worked largely collaboratively. "The Enfranchisement of Women" had set out

---

1   The Act's full title was "An Act to amend the law relating to the property of married women." Although the Act effectively overturned coverture by allowing women to legally claim their own earnings and property, serious loopholes made it possible to easily evade the law, particularly in regard to inheritance. An additional problem was posed by the fact that the Act was not retroactive, thereby limiting its usefulness for many women. The Act also made it a woman's legal duty to financially maintain her children from profits earned. That is, the Act effectively established both parents as responsible for the financial support of their children.

2   The essay was completed in 1861, but Mill waited to publish the work until he felt it would be more influential.

TAXATION WITHOUT REPRESENTATION.

POLITICAL CANDIDATE: "As your husband is dead, madam, and women do not vote. It is no use my staying."
TAX COLLECTOR: "As your husband is dead, madam, and women have to pay taxes, you will have to pay the tax instead of him."

Cartoon from Votes for Women III *(7 January 1910)*.

The movement to win the vote for women began in the 1850s, and articles and petitions on the issue appeared with increasing frequency thereafter. Many of the early arguments drew parallels with other efforts to extend the franchise; as Mary Margaret Dilke observed in an 1889 article, "it is really an interesting study to notice how every argument used to delay the enfranchisement of working men and farm labourers reappears to do duty against women. How often has the question been asked, 'What does Hodge know about finance and foreign policy, colonial affairs and commercial interests?'"

As the suffrage movement grew, differences of opinion developed over the appropriate level of militancy to adopt and over whether the movement should press for universal suffrage or only for certain categories of women to be allowed to vote. The granting of the vote eventually came in two stages, with certain classes of propertied women granted the right to vote in 1918 (the same year the vote was granted to all men of 21 years or more), and all women over the age of 21 finally being granted the franchise in 1928.

with utmost clarity the ideal that is still being striven for today: "the principle which regulates the existing social relations between the two sexes—the legal subordination of one sex to the other—is wrong in itself and now one of the chief hindrances to human improvement … it ought to be replaced by a principle of perfect equality, admitting no power or privilege on the one side, nor disability on the other."

The principles advocated by Cobbe, Taylor Mill, and Taylor were, of course, not only matters of law and politics; they pervaded every aspect of British life, from employment, to educational access, to a variety of cultural matters. The principle of "perfect equality" was far from being realized in any of these areas even at century's end. But, by 1900, some at least were beginning to feel that the slow movement toward acceptance of the principles of gender equality had become inexorable.

Empire

Victorian Britain's internal politics, enormous wealth, and its sense of national and global identity cannot be adequately understood in isolation from its imperial rule abroad. In an address at Oxford in 1870, the highly influential critic and social thinker John Ruskin urged England to "found colonies as fast and as far as she is able, … seizing every piece of fruitful waste ground she can set her foot on, and there teaching these her colonists that their first aim is to be to advance the power of England by land and sea." And under Victoria's reign such power did indeed grow steadily, with 18 major territories added to the British Empire, which already included India, Canada, Australia, New Zealand, and much of East Africa and the Caribbean.

If the Empire arose largely from the desire to increase trade and maximize commercial interests, it also increasingly took hold of the political and cultural imagination. The often brutal effects of colonial domination were rationalized by a pseudo-science purporting to demonstrate the inferiority of dark-skinned peoples and by a keenly felt, much-encouraged sense of racial and cultural superiority over other peoples. A paternalistic sense of responsibility for the peoples of the "inferior races" became known as the "white man's burden" in Rudyard Kipling's famous phrasing. Or, as evolutionary theorist Alfred Russel Wallace put it, "the relation of a civilized to an uncivilized race, over which it rules, is exactly that of parent to child, or generally adults to infants." In missionary

Edward Bulwer-Lytton, Viceroy of India, Calcutta, 1877.

work, travel and exploration, scientific writing, advertising, visual art, and literature, the culture and logic of imperial rule were formulated as part of the everyday "common sense" of the age.

Not everyone was in complete agreement about Britain's imperial policies and practices. Impassioned public debates about the moral and economic injustice of slavery had culminated in the abolition of the slave trade in 1807 and of slavery in all British possessions in 1833. Britain continued to rely on cheap imports of raw materials from its Caribbean colonies, however, and conditions for free workers were sometimes little better than they had been for slaves. Attention to British rule in the West Indies was renewed in 1865 during the controversy that attended Governor Edward Eyre's actions, when black Jamaicans attempted to liberate a black prisoner from a courthouse. Violent clashes between the rebels and white authorities resulted in martial law and the execution of 600 black Jamaicans. The opinions of two of the century's most respected public intellectuals—Thomas Carlyle and John Stuart Mill—represented the opposing poles of the public's response, with Carlyle supporting Eyre's imposition of a harsh law to restore order, and Mill calling for Eyre to be tried for murder.

The "Indian Mutiny" of 1857–58 presented a major challenge to British rule in India, which until that point was still largely under the control of the East India Company. Sepoys—Indian men employed as soldiers by the British—staged a rebellion at Meerut in early 1857, killing British officers. The violence spread throughout northern territories and to Delhi, with massacres of British men, women, and children taking place at Cawnpore and Lucknow. British reprisals were swift and bloody, leading to summary executions, looting, and massacres of Indian civilians. The Indian resistance was motivated by religious, cultural, and political opposition to British policies, and had a lasting impact on British rule in India. One especially significant change was the transfer of colonial governance from the East India Company to the Crown in 1858. In the meantime, the English press was filled with lurid reports of the violence, resulting in greater public fascination with India than ever before. Countless eyewitness accounts, sermons, plays, novels, and poems—some still being written 60 years after the events—expressed moral outrage about the insurgency. There were also those, including the soon-to-be Prime Minister Benjamin Disraeli, who tried to contextualize the violence by criticizihg Britain's exploitative attitudes and practices in India, but such dissenting voices remained very much a minority.

Famine victims, Madras, c. 1877. Famine was a recurrent reality in India throughout the nineteenth century, but the famine of the 1870s was particularly harsh. It gave rise to considerable controversy in Britain, with some (such as Florence Nightingale) pressing for investment in health, sanitation, and irrigation as well as short-term relief measures; others (in sympathy with the harsh approach taken by the Viceroy, Edward Bulwer-Lytton), saw such measures as too expensive or too "lenient."

Britain participated in few major wars during Victoria's reign; when it did, the results were often less than heroic. In the Crimean War of 1854–56, Britain joined Turkey and France in fighting Russian encroachment into the Middle East, but the war did little to change the balance of power in Europe; it nonetheless resulted in the deaths of 21,000 British troops, 16,000 of whom died of disease.[1] In the Anglo-Zulu War of 1878–79, the Zulus of southern Africa enjoyed considerable initial success against British forces before being subdued, and in the Anglo-Afghan War of 1878–80, the British suffered various reversals before achieving a tenuous hold over Afghanistan. The Boer War of 1899–1902, in South Africa, was fought between the British and the

---

1   When the deplorable conditions of the military's hospitals became public knowledge through reports in *The Times*, Florence Nightingale was dispatched to the Crimea to superintend Britain's female nurses.

Florence Nightingale in the Crimea, c. 1856.

Queen Victoria and her servant, Abdul Karim, 1893.

Boers[1] over gold and diamond fields. For the Boers, the war was part of a larger struggle to prevent the influence of foreign powers on agricultural lands they had claimed. A guerilla war ensued, and Britain's image as the greatest military power in the world suffered when the army was unable to defeat the vastly outnumbered Boers.

In England, popular support for the Empire reached its zenith in the 1880s and 1890s as Britain accelerated the pace of its drive to increase its imperial acquisitions to compete with other European powers and with the United States. Queen Victoria's Golden and Diamond Jubilees, during which she celebrated the fiftieth and sixtieth anniversaries of her sovereignty, provided grand occasions for the expression of national pride. As *The Times* crowed, Britain was "the mightiest and most beneficial Empire ever known in the annals of mankind." Much popular reading in these decades was devoted to a celebration of Empire, though warnings of its imminent demise were also increasingly sounded. Boys' adventure stories in such publications as *The Boy's Own Annual* featured tales of manly prowess in the service of Empire and promoted the values of honor, courage, and duty to Queen and country. Travel and exploration narratives were popular, too—particularly those that recounted the heroic journeys of such larger-than-life figures as Richard Burton and David Livingstone. Richard

---

1   White settlers of Dutch descent, also known as Afrikaaners.

Francis Burton (1821–90) was renowned for his travels throughout Asia and Africa and much celebrated for his mastery of foreign languages, of which he knew 29, by some counts. Perhaps his most famous exploit was traveling to Mecca in disguise, but he was also recognized for translating the complete *One Thousand and One Nights* from the Arabic and for bringing the *Kama Sutra* to publication in English. Although he served as a symbol of the Empire's might, Burton was a prominent critic of colonial policies. David Livingstone (1813–73) named Victoria Falls—perhaps the world's most impressive—in honor of the Queen. He was a national hero of sorts during the Victorian era, famed as a missionary, a scientist and explorer, an imperial reformer, who fought against slavery and advocated commercial empire. Speaking to students at Cambridge University in 1857, Livingstone declared,

> People talk of the sacrifice I have made in spending so much of my life in Africa. Can that be called a sacrifice which is simply paid back as a small part of a great debt owing to our God, which we can never repay? Is that a sacrifice which brings its own blest reward in healthful activity, the consciousness of doing good, peace of mind, and a bright hope of a glorious destiny hereafter? Away with the word in such a view and with such a thought! It is emphatically no sacrifice. Say rather it is a privilege.

Almost as popular as the narratives of Burton and Livingstone were travel journals by intrepid "lady explorers" such as Mary Kingsley and Isabella Bird, who unsettled conventional notions of Victorian femininity even as they satisfied the public taste for true stories with fictionalized elements. Kingsley (1862–1900) first traveled to Africa in order to complete research for a book left unfinished by her father at the time of his death. She lived with local tribes in Angola. Upon her return to England, she toured the country, giving lectures in which she criticized missionaries for their attempts to change the local people—earning her much censure from the Church of England. She also defended African customs, including polygamy. Her books about her experiences—*Travels in Africa* (1897) and *West African Studies* (1899)—were bestsellers. Bird (1831–1904) traveled extensively, visiting Australia, Hawaii, and Colorado—then the most recent state to join the United States—where she covered more than 800 miles in the Rocky Mountains. The letters she wrote to her sister during this time were published as the immensely popular *A Lady's Life in the Rocky Mountains* (1879).

Engraving by G. Durand, after a sketch by H.M. Stanley,
"The Meeting of Livingstone and Stanley in Central Africa" (from The Graphic, *3 August 1872).*

By 1869, it had been three years since the renowned missionary and explorer David Livingstone had embarked on an expedition in search of the source of the Nile River. American journalist Henry Morgan Stanley was commissioned in that year by a New York newspaper to find Livingstone; the story of the two finally meeting on the shores of Lake Tanganyika in 1871 became legendary. As Stanley described it,

"I ... would have embraced him, only, he being an Englishman, I did not know how he would receive me; so I did what cowardice and false pride suggested was the best thing—walked deliberately to him, took off my hat, and said, 'Dr. Livingstone, I presume?'

'Yes,' said he, with a kind smile, lifting his cap slightly."

The imperial romances of some authors were a symptom of the anxieties surrounding Britain's increasingly tenuous grip on its empire. Whereas early and mid-century Victorian fiction tended to imagine the Empire as a fairly static, unknown space to which characters can be exiled in the interests of narrative closure, late-century fiction often represented the Empire in darker, Gothic terms. Incorporating supernatural and psychological elements in their work, writers such as H. Rider Haggard, Arthur Conan Doyle, Rudyard Kipling, and Robert Louis Stevenson used colonial settings to explore themes of racial degeneration and human "savagery." In his 1899 novella, *Heart of*

Darkness, Joseph Conrad, a Polish émigré to England, drew on his experience as a merchant marine in his portrayal of imperial greed, exploitation, and corruption among ivory traders in the Congo. Even Kipling, called the "Laureate of Empire" for his energetic—and often jingoistic—portrayals of the glories of British imperialism, was not always unequivocal in his attitudes toward the Empire: in his 1897 poem "Recessional," he sounded a famous warning against imperial hubris: "Far-called, our navies melt away; / On dune and headland sinks the fire: / Lo, all our pomp of yesterday / Is one with Nineveh and Tyre!"[1]

Faith and Doubt

One of the most unsettling developments for average citizens during the Victorian period was the growing opposition to the authority of Christian faith and the established church. A rapidly changing social order, combined with the growing predominance of scientific rationalism and empiricist method, destabilized Christian certainty, creating a rising tide of secularism and religious skepticism. As critic J.A. Froude put it in 1841, "the very truths which have come forth have produced doubts ... this dazzle has too often ended in darkness."

The poet Arthur Hugh Clough was a central figure in the expression of the religious doubt of the age; in "Easter Day: Naples, 1849"—a poem whose title deliberately invokes the most sacred of days for Christians only to subvert the day's holiness—his verse conveys a strong sense of the passion that could accompany such feelings:

> My heart was hot within me; till at last
> My brain was lightened when my tongue had said—
> Christ is not risen!
> Christ is not risen, no—
> He lies and moulders low.

---

1   Nineveh, called an "exceeding great city" in the Book of Jonah, was the center of worship of the goddess Ishtar in Assyria; it was captured and razed in 612 BCE, signaling the end of the Assyrian Empire. Tyre—the largest and most important Phoenician city—was sacked by Alexander the Great during his campaign against Persia in 332 BCE.

Biblical scholars in England and Europe in the early decades of the century had begun to question the Scriptures as a source of literal truth and to present the figure of Jesus Christ as a mortal rather than a divine being. The German "higher critics" of the Bible—especially D.F. Strauss in his *Das Leben Jesu* (translated by George Eliot, 1844–46)[1]—were influential in this "scientific" discussion of biblical texts. Leading Victorian thinkers such as Carlyle, Eliot, and Martineau wrote of personal religious crises, and wrestled publicly with doubts about the value and meaning of Christian belief. As Matthew Arnold wrote in 1880, "There is not a creed which is not shaken, nor an accredited dogma which is not shown to be questionable, not a received tradition which does not threaten to dissolve." In the climate of uncertainty as to whether the divine could be knowable, Carlyle's arrival, in *Sartor Resartus* (1833–34), at an affirmation of "natural supernaturalism" offers a telling statement of the almost desperate determination to find the divine in both nature and other human beings.

Traditional religious belief received its greatest challenge in the Victorian period from the evidence of the fossil record and Darwinian explanations of the origins of the universe and human beings' place within it. Charles Darwin's theories of evolution and natural selection in *On the Origin of Species* (1859) and *The Descent of Man* (1871) rejected the Christian idea that human beings had been created in God's image and were thus of a different order than the rest of the natural world. In *Descent*, Darwin provoked and challenged his audience by declaring, "He who is not content to look, like a savage, at the phenomena of nature as disconnected, cannot any longer believe that man is the work of a separate act of creation."[2]

---

1   David Friedrich Strauss (1808–74) shocked and outraged Christian Europe with his depiction of the "historical Jesus." *Das Leben Jesu*, or *The Life of Jesus, Critically Examined*, caused a scandal with its insistence on the need to understand the miraculous events depicted in the Gospels as "mythical" in character. Eventually, Strauss's views came to dominate the new epoch of scriptural study, focused on textual interpretation.

2   Much recent debate has focused on the question of Darwin's own Christian faith. His *Autobiography* (completed in 1876, but first published in 1887, five years after his death) and letters suggest Darwin's growing agnosticism. In the *Autobiography*, Darwin recalls "In my Journal I wrote that whilst standing in the midst of the grandeur of a Brazilian forest, 'it is not possible to give an adequate idea of the higher feelings of wonder, admiration, and devotion, which fill and elevate the mind.' I well remember my conviction that there

And religious controversy and doubt extended further still. Not only were the divinity of Christ, the literal truth of the Bible, and the processes of creation at issue, so too was the very existence of a creator or divine being. One of Darwin's strongest supporters, the scientist Thomas Henry Huxley, coined the term "agnostic" in 1869 at a party held in connection with the forming of the Metaphysical Society, a learned society that met regularly for over a decade to discuss theological issues, and whose members also included Tennyson, Ruskin, and Gladstone. The term agnostic named a person of a sort unimaginable in most earlier ages—one who neither believes nor disbelieves in the existence of God, holding instead that it is simply impossible for humans to possess knowledge of such matters.[1] It is to such beliefs—or the lack thereof—that Matthew Arnold refers when he writes in "Dover Beach" (1867) of the ebbing tide of the "Sea of Faith." Whereas in the twentieth century that ebbing tide was sometimes welcomed as representing a freeing of human potential, Victorians tended to hear it in the way that Arnold heard it, inextricably associated with an "eternal note of sadness."

The established church of England and Scotland—the Anglican denomination—remained a powerful entity throughout the Victorian era—with the reigning monarch heading the Church as the "Defender of the Faith," as had been the case since Henry VIII's break with Rome in the 1530s—but by century's end its power was more social than political. Though only Anglicans could be admitted to Parliament until the late 1820s, and non-Anglicans were barred from taking degrees at Oxford and Cambridge until 1871, the changes in both policies demonstrated that allegiance to Anglicanism was no longer a necessary criterion for admission to the bastions of power.

The Church was also profoundly influenced by the gradual severance of church-state relations, as well as the increasing popularity of Evangelicalism, a broad-based movement comprising numerous Protestant denominations including Methodism and Presbyterianism. These "Dissenting" or "nonconformist" faiths transformed religious practice in Britain, stressing the importance of

---

is more in man than the mere breath of his body." But, toward the end of his life, he wrote to a correspondent, "I am sorry to have to inform you that I do not believe in the Bible as a divine revelation, & therefore not in Jesus Christ as the Son of God."

1   Among Victorian authors George Eliot is perhaps the most prominent to have described herself as an agnostic.

an individual's personal relationship with God, of prudence and temperance, of conversion, of missionary work, and of humanitarian activism. In 1878, the Methodist minister William Booth founded the Salvation Army, which ministered to the poor in London's East End and became the center of social purity campaigns stressing chastity and public decency for both sexes. In general, Evangelical congregations were less hierarchical in organization than the traditional Anglican Church, were anti-Catholic in orientation, and attracted both middle- and working-class believers who felt that Anglicanism had lost its spiritual power and become a mere appendage of the state.

Evangelicalism—and the resistance to it—within the Church of England resulted in a split between Anglican Evangelicals (commonly referred to as Low Church), progressives (Broad Church, sometimes called Latitudianarians), and Anglo-Catholics (High Church). An important High Church reaction to Evangelicalism took place in the 1830s and 1840s through the Oxford Movement, also called Tractarianism, led by Oxford theologians and intellectuals, John Henry Newman, John Keble, and Edward Pusey chief among them. Celebrating the mystical and aesthetic elements of worship, they advocated an increased emphasis on religious ritual and a strict observance of clerical hierarchy within the Anglican communion. Newman's conversion to Roman Catholicism in 1845 spelled the end of the Oxford Movement, heralding a significant Catholic revival that saw many intellectuals rejecting Protestantism to embrace the Catholic faith and tradition. This was a significant religious as well as political development, since Catholics in England and especially in Ireland had for centuries been the objects of persecution. The Catholic Emancipation movement of the 1820s presaged the loosening of political and legal restrictions against members of the Catholic church, the majority of whom were barred from voting, holding office, running for Parliament, or attending the universities.

Henry Taunt, "Bible Stall at the St. Giles Fair, Oxford," 1880.

English Jews were also denied full rights of citizenship until a series of measures granted them access to Parliament, the military, the legal establishment,
and institutions of higher learning. Anti-Semitic stereotypes were legion in
Victorian novels such as *Oliver Twist*. In at least a few cases the writings of
non-Jewish novelists challenged the stereotypes—sometimes tentatively—in
ways that to some extent still participated in the culture of prejudice (as in
Anthony Trollope's wide-ranging novel of capitalism, marriage, and religion,
The Way We Live Now [1875]), sometimes more clearly and unequivocally (as
in George Eliot's *Daniel Deronda* [1876][1]). And a significant body of Anglo-
Jewish literature by writers such as Israel Zangwill and Amy Levy expressed a
range of Jewish responses to social prejudice on the part of England's Christian
majority.

Though the religious establishment suffered many challenges to its power, it
would be a mistake to assume that secularism, Utilitarianism, and Darwinian
theory stamped out religious faith or traditional religious practice: far from it.
The Victorian period can be fairly characterized as an age of religious doubt
that was also marked by intense religious feeling. As novels such as Anthony
Trollope's *Barsetshire Chronicles*—a series of six novels published from 1855 to
1867—vividly convey, religious affiliation (irrespective of the strength of one's
actual faith) shaped most people's sense of personal identity. And the quest for
spiritual meaning was itself the driving force behind some of the most moving
literary works of the age. One such work, Tennyson's *In Memoriam* (1849), an
elegy for his friend Arthur Henry Hallam, chronicles the spiritual crisis of one
man in the aftermath of his friend's death. By the end of the poem, the speaker
has reconciled his religious doubts and scientific skepticism to re-embrace a
Christian vision of the afterlife. In the closing lines of the poem the speaker

---

1   Eliot's novel has been cited by a number of early Zionist leaders—including Emma Laza-
     rus—as highly influential in their decision to embrace Zionism. The narrative's treat-
     ment of Jews—contrasting their spirituality and connection to their community to the
     materialism and corruption of English society—was met with some hostility, and many
     reviewers remarked that the parts of *Daniel Deronda* focusing on Jewish characters were
     its weakest.
         The critic Edward Said has suggested, in "Zionism from the Standpoint of Its Victims"
     (1979), that the novel was a propaganda tool, used to encourage patriation of British-
     controlled Palestine by Jews.

exalts "That God, which ever lives and loves, / One God, one law, one element, / And one far-off divine event, / To which the whole creation moves."[1]

Illustrations by George Cruikshank to Charles Dickens's Oliver Twist *(1838). The captions identify the figures in the above illustrations as "Fagin and the boys" and as "Monks [another character in the novel] and the Jew." As presented by Dickens and Cruikshank, the character of Fagin is a caricature of evil—and of Jewishness. In passages such as the following Dickens's descriptions of Fagin give expression to some of the most extreme anti-Semitic stereotypes: "It seemed just the night when it befitted such a being as the Jew to be abroad. As he glided stealthily along, creeping beneath the shelter of the walls and doorways, the hideous old man seemed like some loathsome reptile, engendered in the slime and darkness through which he moved: crawling forth by night, in search of some rich offal for a meal." By repeatedly naming him as "the Jew" Dickens crudely implied that the characteristics of Fagin were also those of Jews in general. Dickens received complaints from readers on this score, and over time he altered his views. Beginning with the edition of 1867 he made revisions to* Oliver Twist, *changing to "Fagin" the previous references to "the Jew." The last novel Dickens completed,* Our Mutual Friend *(1864–65), is notable not least of all for the inclusion of a Jewish character (Riah) who is portrayed by Dickens in a distinctly positive light.*

---

1   The importance of Tennyson's poem during the period is well illustrated by Queen Victoria's comment after the death of her husband Prince Albert in 1861 that "Next to the Bible, *In Memoriam* is my comfort."

Victorian Domesticity: Life and Death

The center of British religious, cultural, and emotional life in the nineteenth century was the family. As industrialization transformed the household from a workspace into its "opposite," the home came to be regarded as an almost sacred space, to be shielded from the aggressive competitiveness of the public world of work. The family, especially among the rising middle class, was increasingly nuclear in structure; the extended networks of friends and relations that had formed strong household connections in pre-industrial society became more and more tenuous. Increasingly, the social arrangement perceived as ideal among the better-off social classes consisted of a male breadwinner, employed outside the home, and his female helpmeet, who nurtured the children, managed the servants, and served as a paragon of domestic virtue. One of the key signs of a man's professional success was his wife's "idleness" within the home. The separation of work and family life was reflected in city planning with the construction of the first modern suburbs, supported by public transportation systems. Middle-class domestic architecture encouraged the display of wealth and the division of sexual labor amongst family members by dividing houses into "public" and "private" spaces. The middle-class family model became the ideal for the working class as well, although

Illustration, Wonders of a Toy-Shop, *c. 1852. Though it is sometimes claimed that children were treated as "little adults" in the nineteenth century, that was far less frequently the case than it had been a century or two earlier. In many respects, indeed, the nineteenth century marks the coming into prominence of "childhood" as a cultural entity. The changing attitudes toward children working in factories was one manifestation of change. Another was the evolution of "toy"—a word used before the nineteenth century to refer to a wide variety of trifles, but increasingly in the nineteenth century applied to playthings for children; toyshops specializing in such items became more and more widespread over the course of the Victorian period.*

economic necessity continued to force many working-class wives and children to contribute to household earnings through paid labor, both inside and outside the home.

The domestic ideal and the emphasis on the family circle was shaped and promoted within the most privileged sphere of society. Throughout her reign, Queen Victoria was a paragon of good manners, restraint, and moral uprightness. In this she stood in contrast both to the escapades and excess that had surrounded the monarchies of her predecessors, George IV and William IV, and to the moral hypocrisy that characterized the reign of her son, Edward VII. In 1840, three years after her coronation, she married her first cousin, Prince Albert of Saxe-Coburg-Gotha. Together, they had nine children, and Victoria became the nation's most revered icon of domestic femininity and maternal fecundity. She was a firm believer in separate spheres of influence and authority for men and women, voicing a then-conventional feminine distaste for power: "I am every day more convinced," she at one point declared, "that we women, if we are to be good women, feminine and amiable and domestic, are not fitted to reign." The royal family exemplified an ideal of Victorian domesticity, with Albert exercising much influence over his wife's decisions, and Victoria displaying unwavering devotion to the practical, manly Albert. Yet for all her outwardly conventional feminine attitudes, Victoria privately expressed ambivalence toward childbirth and marriage; she once complained in a letter to her daughter that giving birth made her feel like "a dog or a cow." In 1853, she agreed to undergo anesthesia during the birth of her son Leopold. This was a controversial new medical procedure, not least of all because it challenged the curse laid upon Eve (and therefore all women) in Genesis 1: "In sorrow shalt thou bring forth children."

When Albert died of typhoid in 1861, the entire nation went into a state of mourning. Victoria was overwhelmed with grief, and for 15 years after his death she was rarely seen in public, except at the unveiling of the many public monuments she arranged to have erected to his memory. Eventually many began to regard her seclusion as self-indulgent and excessive, and her popularity among her subjects suffered for several years. Yet Victoria's long widowhood was in many ways a sign of the times; it both reflected and influenced the Victorian vogue for elaborate mourning rituals and conventions governing the public observance of death.

Life expectancy during the Victorian period was almost certainly higher than it was in the late eighteenth century, and it did improve over the period, but for most of the century it was nevertheless extraordinarily low by the standards of the developed world today—probably no higher than 40 years in many areas of the country. The death of relatively young people was far more common than it is today—not only deaths of children but also of young adults—of diseases such as "consumption" (tuberculosis), for example, and of cholera, and very commonly, mothers dying in childbirth.

It is no exaggeration to say that death became a commercial industry in the nineteenth century; funer-

Advertisement from The Lady, *4 October 1900.*

als provided a public occasion to mourn the passing of a loved one as much as they offered an opportunity for rich and middle-income people to display wealth. Strict observance of funerary rituals in details of dress and deportment became a social necessity, and commemorative memorabilia, such as tea sets, photographs, and mourning jewelry—often made from the hair of the deceased—could be found in most homes. Many families were prepared to spend the bulk of their savings on the funerals of loved ones. For the poor, the story was of course much different. The indigent were buried with little or no ceremony in unmarked paupers' graves. Many working-class families contributed to burial clubs, an early form of insurance that guaranteed that at least a modest amount of money would be set aside for a respectable funeral for family members.

The obsession with death in the Victorian period is reflected in much of the literature of the period; in Gaskell's novel *Mary Barton*, no fewer than 13 deaths either take place or are recounted within the first ten chapters. Tennyson's

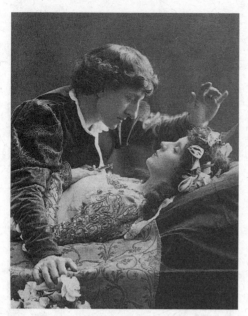

Romeo gazes at the dead Juliet: photograph of an 1895 production of Shakespeare's Romeo and Juliet, *with Mrs. Patrick Campbell as Juliet.*

famed elegy *In Memoriam* is as much a meditation on death as it is a lament for the loss of a loved one. Countless Victorian novels feature prolonged death scenes, with grieving or greedy family members keeping vigil by the bedside of the dying. One of Dickens's most beloved characters, Little Nell in *The Old Curiosity Shop* (1840–41), was modeled on his sister-in-law, Mary Hogarth, whose death had affected him deeply. Little Nell's death prompted an outpouring of grief from readers, many of whom wrote letters to Dickens in between installments of the novel imploring him to spare her.[1] The beautiful, often eroticized corpse was a favorite image in both visual art and poetry. In Christina Rossetti's "After Death" (1862), a female speaker observes her lover's attitude toward her corpse, and realizes, "He did not love me living; but once dead / He pitied me; and very sweet it is / To know he still is warm tho' I am cold."

Though mortality rates, especially among infants, remained high throughout the century, there were significant medical advances in disease control and sanitation. Prominent among these was the verification of the bacterial theory of disease. Until late in the century, most medical practitioners and lay people believed that disease was spread through miasma, or the spread of harmful odors through the atmosphere. Susceptibility was routinely blamed on moral and social factors such as poverty, overcrowding, and sexual behaviors. During the cholera epidemics of the 1840s, researchers began to make links between incidents of the disease and water sources. Joseph Lister's work in the 1850s and 1860s confirmed the existence of microorganisms, yet the miasma

---

1   Not all were so moved. Of the death of Dickens's beloved character, Oscar Wilde famously opined, "One would have to have a heart of stone to read the death of little Nell without dissolving into tears … of laughter."

theory of disease was so entrenched that it was not until late in the century that the bacterial theory was fully accepted. By 1890, the pathogens for several diseases, including tuberculosis, cholera, typhoid, rabies, and diphtheria, had been identified. Surgical practice was also transformed by Lister's work on antiseptic treatments and the adoption of anesthetics, particularly ether and chloroform.

Cultural Trends

When the Duke of Wellington died in 1852, a million and a half people lined the streets of London to pay their last respects to the military hero who had defeated Napoleon at Waterloo. The deaths of the eminent were marked by elaborate, theatrical state funerals that fed an increasing appetite for public

"View of the Grand Entrance to the Great Exhibition, 1851" *(from* The Official Illustrated and Descriptive Catalogue, *1852). The idea for what became the Great Exhibition grew out of a proliferation of smaller exhibitions of the products of craft and industry in the 1840s, and out of an awareness that Paris was contemplating its own large-scale international exhibition. Organized largely by Henry Cole, with the strong support of Prince Albert, the "Great Exhibition of the Works of Industry of All Nations" was held in Hyde Park in 1851. The Crystal Palace, centerpiece of the Exhibition, was later dismantled and re-assembled at Sydenham in south London as a home for permanent exhibitions, where it stood until it was destroyed by fire in 1936.*

spectacles, epitomized by the Great Exhibition of 1851. The culture of Victorian Britain was very much a visual one, with public amusements, popular shows, traveling exhibitions, circuses, sporting events, holiday resorts, and public gardens to cater to every stratum of a society that had a growing amount of both disposable income and leisure time. London's theaters drew thousands of spectators every night to witness ingenious visual effects created by London's theater impresarios; live animals, underwater sequences, mob scenes, flying machines, sumptuous interiors, and innovations in lighting stoked the public mania for stage realism.[1] Music halls aimed at lower middle- and working-class audiences featured a miscellany of comic songs, dance numbers, and magic shows by popular performers. Many public museums and galleries—which today draw thousands of visitors annually—were established in the Victorian period following the Great Exhibition, including the Victoria and Albert Museum, the National Portrait Gallery, and the Tate Gallery (founded by sugar magnate Henry Tate). Madame Tussaud's Wax Museum found a permanent home in London in 1835. From the 1870s and 1880s onwards, fashionable new shopping arcades and department stores filled with enticing consumer goods made shopping a respectable pastime for middle-class women.

Mass visual culture was inaugurated in the nineteenth century with the advent of a range of technologies, including the kaleidoscope, the daguerreotype, the photograph, and the cinema. As on the stage, visual technologies exploited light and movement in an effort to create the illusion of reality and transport viewers across time and space. Panoramas and dioramas[2] featured foreign cities, battlefields, landscapes, and natural disasters, and anticipated the "moving pictures" of the cinema. Innovations in print technology and the explosion of illustrated print material from the 1830s onwards signaled the public's increasing demand for the pictorial representation of daily events. The popular *Illustrated London News*, established in 1842, was the world's first illustrated weekly paper to hit newsstands; it used increasingly sophisticated technologies—from woodcuts to steel engravings to photographs—in its pictorial coverage of events

---

1   Perhaps not coincidentally, this era of special-effects theatricality is now generally said to have marked a nadir in the history of English drama as a literary genre.

2   In a diorama, spectators view a partially translucent painting in a specially designed building, with variations of light cast upon the image to simulate the movement of light in a daytime scene. The diorama was first exhibited in London in 1823.

at home and abroad. Serial novels published in periodicals were accompanied by wood-engraved illustrations intended to heighten the reader's appreciation of the narrative; popular engraver-illustrators such as George Cruikshank and Hablot K. Browne ("Phiz"), both of whom illustrated for Dickens, were initially as celebrated as the author himself.

Victorian painters benefitted both from the emergence of a wealthy middle class able to purchase art for their homes and from the public's fascination with visual representation of contemporary life and historical drama. Scenes of everyday life with a narrative dimension and a moral message were especially popular with the viewing public. Like Victorian novelists and poets, many Victorian visual artists came to document the hardships of an industrial culture and landscape, depicting agricultural laborers, factory workers, and the unemployed in a highly realistic, yet often sentimental mode that has come to be known as social realism. Childhood innocence and scenes of domestic harmony were also common themes for many Victorian artists; new and inexpensive methods of art reproduction meant that such pictures could be sold cheaply to a wide audience that was interested in seeing the values of home and family reflected on its walls. Panoramic views of Victorian life in all its colorful variety were also popular: William Powell Frith's *Derby Day* (1858) and *Railway Station* (1877) portrayed scenes of ordinary Victorians in such realistic detail that they caused a great sensation when they were first exhibited at the Royal Academy. Founded in the eighteenth century under George III, the Royal Academy of Arts was institutionalized as the most important mediator of public taste in art in the Victorian period. It offered a free training school to many of the century's most significant artists, and its annual exhibitions of what it deemed the best works of the year drew thousands of spectators and buyers—as well as accusations of bias and preferential treatment on the part of those whose work had been excluded from the exhibitions or poorly hung.

The most influential movement in Victorian painting was the Pre-Raphaelite Brotherhood, composed of the artists John Everett Millais, William Holman Hunt, Thomas Woolner, James Collinson, Frederick George Stephens, and the brothers of Christina Rossetti, artist and poet Dante Gabriel Rossetti, and critic William Michael Rossetti. At mid-century these artists began producing works that challenged the dominant taste for neoclassical style and subject matter by painting in the manner of medieval, pre-Renaissance artists. Close

William Powell Frith, The Railway Station *(detail), 1862.*
The painting depicts a scene at Paddington Station in London.

attention to natural detail, flattened perspective, vivid colors, an interest in
literary subject matter, and erotically charged images of spiritual and religious
devotion were some of the hallmarks of the group. Their paintings of female
figures as either ravishing "femmes fatales" or dreamy heroines in historical
dress are today instantly recognizable (and are much reproduced). These paintings conveyed both women's power and vulnerability in nineteenth-century
culture, and were sometimes twinned, in D.G. Rossetti's work especially, with
a companion poem or with a quotation from a literary work. ("The Blessed
Damozel" [1846] is one such example, in which the separation of two lovers
by death in the poem is conveyed with two separate panels in the painting.)

"Pre-Raphaelite," indeed, denotes a style of poetry as well as of painting; sensuous detail and a tendency to link earthly beauty to the divine are as characteristic of the poetry of Rossetti as they are of his paintings.

The Pre-Raphaelites should in part be considered alongside the Gothic Revival, a wave of interest in a medieval and Gothic aesthetic that had begun in the Romantic period and influenced Victorian painting, architecture, design, literature, and religious practice. The idealization of the Middle Ages is exemplified in the writing of Thomas Carlyle, John Ruskin, William Morris, and Alfred Tennyson. Ruskin, an art critic who championed the work of the Pre-Raphaelites, argued in *The Stones of Venice* (1851–53) for the moral superiority of the Gothic style, in part because it was the product of artisan-workers who were free to use their creativity in their work, and so express their individual and spiritual nature. Ruskin urged his readers to re-examine the

Arthur Hughes, The Long Engagement *(detail). Hughes (1832–1915) was one of the most prominent of the second wave of Pre-Raphaelite painters.*

"ugly goblins" and "stern statues" of Gothic cathedrals, for "they are the signs of the life and liberty of every workmen who struck the stone; a freedom of thought, and rank in scale of being, such as no laws, no charters, no charities can secure."

The Arts and Crafts movement of the last few decades of the century, led by William Morris and influenced by Ruskin's ideas, was dedicated to the production of hand-crafted furniture, glassware, books, and art objects. Design firms such as Morris and Co. and the Century Guild revived the medieval guild

William Morris and Edward Burne-Jones with their families (c. 1880).
Burne-Jones (1833–98) was, with Morris, a key figure in the Arts and
Crafts movement and the most significant of the second generation of
Pre-Raphaelite artists. Morris is standing in the back at the right of the
photograph, and Burne-Jones is seated in the center. Morris's wife Jane
(née Burden), the inspiration for and subject of many Pre-Raphaelite
works, is in front of Morris and Burne-Jones; Burne-Jones's father
stands at the rear left. Photograph by Frederick Hollyer.

system of production, rejecting the mass-produced manufactures of the assembly line in favor of the freedom and spontaneity of craft and its makers. In their critique of the ravages of industrial technology and the drudgery of mechanized labor, the practitioners of Gothic Revival imagined, and to some extent invented, the idea of the medieval past as a time of moral and religious stability, devotion to craft, and harmony with the rhythms of the natural world.

Technology

The technological invention that perhaps best exemplified the industrial age was the steam engine, a source and symbol of power both on land and at sea. Although the steam engine had been in use since the early eighteenth century, it was not until the nineteenth that steam technology helped transform an entire economy and a way of life. Steam engines were adapted for use in

The Palace of Westminster, home to both Houses of Parliament, was redesigned and rebuilt following the fire of 1834, in a vast project not completed until 1860. It is one of the most striking examples of the Gothic style applied to a secular construction.

the production of coal, textiles, heavy metals, and printing presses, thus becoming indispensable to Britain's industrial growth. Steamships powered the British Empire, with several major shipping lines established in the 1840s to serve routes to India, Africa, East Asia, and Australia. Railway steam locomotives epitomized the coming of the Victorian era, with the first local lines built in 1837 and 1838 as Victoria assumed the throne. In the "railway mania" of the 1840s, over 8,000 miles of new track were approved, and, by 1900, over nine hundred million passengers were using Britain's rail system annually. London's underground rail system opened its first line in 1863, though horse-drawn transportation continued to dominate the streetscape until the end of the century. The convenience and speed of rail travel caught on quickly with everyone from

Robert Howlett, "Isambard Kingdom Brunel and the Launching Chains of the Great Eastern," 1857. The ship (designed largely by Brunel) remained the largest in the world throughout its 31 years on the seas. Brunel, the leading engineer of the age, also played an important role in designing such Victorian landmarks as the Crystal Palace, the new Houses of Parliament, Paddington Station, and the Clifton Suspension Bridge at Bristol.

the Queen to the ordinary worker. Rail companies established excursions to special events, such as horse races or the seaside, inaugurating local and national tourism on a mass scale. So important was the advent of railway travel to the development of English daily life, railway stations even became essential to the book trade and the spread of leisure reading; from the 1850s onward, book stalls catering to thousands of daily commuters began to stock their shelves with newspapers, magazines, and cheap, popular fiction, which became known as "railway literature."

Cultural Identities

The adoption of new technologies, the reorganization of employment, and the shift in power from the monarchy to the institutions of the modern liberal state revolutionized people's experience of work, family life, civic duty, and leisure time in the Victorian era. Such developments are almost always accompanied by shifts in the way people understand themselves as individuals in relation to their society. In the nineteenth century, the conditions and practices of one's class, gender, race, and sexuality began to acquire new meanings, to take on new importance, and to attract a new kind of attention. Changes in living conditions developed in connection with prescribed gender roles, which began to seem "natural" and "innate," because they supported the logic of industrial capital and bourgeois family life. Though this process did not begin in the Victorian period, it was majorly extended and thoroughly revised during the time. Victorians tended to think about identity in terms of oppositions: male and female, rich and poor, black and white, and, later in the century, homosexual and heterosexual. Such oppositions had the effect of establishing seemingly stable types and suggesting that the differences were natural and unchangeable. For example, the ideology of separate spheres for men and women proposed that gender and sexual identity were fixed categories and that "true womanhood" was the inherent opposite of normative manliness. Still, in the literary works of the period, the line between "opposites" was constantly crossed and revealed as problematic and variable.

The "Angel in the House"[1] became a common label for the Victorian ideal of respectable middle-class femininity. Quiet beauty, purity, devotion and selflessness were some of the essential features of the domestic wife and mother, who was described and exalted in advice literature and popular domestic novels aimed at female readers. "She must be enduringly, incorruptibly good," advised John Ruskin, "instinctively, infallibly wise—wise, not for self-development, but for self-renunciation; wise, not that she may set herself above her husband, but that she may never fall from his side." The absolute other to this paragon of virtue was the "fallen woman," a label that encompassed

---

[1] The phrase originated in the title of Coventry Patmore's long narrative poem. Patmore's "The Angel in the House"—first published in 1854, but revised several times for subsequent publication—was written about the author's wife, Emily, who Patmore exalted as the perfect model of Victorian femininity and domesticity. The poem's opening lines— "Man must be pleased; but him to please / Is woman's pleasure"—rather neatly encapsulate the meaning and the message of the work. In "Professions for Women," a 1942 address given to the Women's Service League, Virginia Woolf argued that "part of the occupation ... of a woman writer" was to kill the "Angel in the House."

any form of female sexual experience deemed improper or immoral. Prostitutes, rape victims, unmarried mothers, adulteresses, homeless women, the insane, and any woman who displayed rebellious passions could be labeled "fallen." Yet the boundary between the domestic angel and the fallen woman was extraordinarily narrow; one false step and innocence became wickedness, followed by ostracism from society, poverty, and almost certain death for the transgressor, at least according to dominant narratives of fallenness.[1] On the other hand, some fallen women were portrayed as penitent victims who embodied the feminine ideal even more fully than their uncorrupted female counterparts. Writers such as Elizabeth Gaskell, Christina Rossetti, George Eliot, Mary Elizabeth Braddon, Augusta Webster, and Thomas Hardy explored the tropes of purity and fallenness, bringing "pure" and "impure" women into each other's (and the reader's) proximity in order to probe the limits of the feminine ideal.

The male counterpart to the domestic angel was the Victorian gentleman, an heir of the chivalric ideal updated for the industrial age. In *The Idea of a University* (a series of lectures published as one volume in 1873), John Henry Newman characterized the gentleman as tender, merciful, prudent, patient, forbearing, resigned, and disciplined. Yet despite Newman's apparent confidence in this description, gentlemanliness was difficult to define: was it based on a man's mode of income or on his behavior? Was it a hereditary, professional, or moral category, or some combination? While eminent men were celebrated with great gusto in biography and prose works such as Carlyle's *On Heroes and Hero Worship* (1841), men were also often regarded as morally inferior to women because of their greater contact with the competition and corruption of the public world. (On the other hand, women could just as easily be pressed into the role of evil temptress in accounting for a man's fall from grace.) Tennyson's dramatic monologue "Ulysses" (1842) wrestles with two competing versions of masculinity: the thwarted Romantic hero, who longs for adventure and freedom from domestic encumbrance, and the reliable, managerial male who faithfully adheres to professional duty.

---

1   In a famous moment in Dickens's *David Copperfield*, the narrator's recollection of a dangerous moment in the fallen Emily's early life leads him to wonder if it might not have been far better for her to have died rather to have survived only to later "fall."

The concepts of the Victorian lady and gentleman were also cl[a]
serving to both reinforce and blur distinctions between various soc
groups. The boarding schools for the sons and daughters of the [
middle classes promulgated notions of proper female and male conduct in
their curricula; increasingly, it was understood that one was not simply born
a lady or a gentleman, but must learn to become one through rigorous training and constant self-scrutiny. As the terms "lady" and "gentleman" gradually
lost their association with rank, socio-economic boundaries became increasingly difficult to distinguish, and novelists began to focus on the gendered and
class behaviors of individuals for their narrative content. In Charlotte Brontë's
Jane Eyre (1847), the moral awakening of the male hero, Edward Rochester,
is achieved via the superior moral guidance of the "servant" governess, Jane
Eyre, who avoids succumbing to becoming Rochester's mistress, thus teaching him the true nature of domestic love and Christian sacrifice; Jane finally
becomes Rochester's wife following his spiritual, moral rebirth. In Dickens's
novels, including *David Copperfield* (1850) and *Great Expectations* (1860), the
gentlemanly status of the male protagonists is achieved through diligence and
perseverance rather than by birthright.

The best-selling advice book for men, *Self Help* (1859) by Samuel Smiles,
stressed thrift, hard work, and optimism as essential qualities of the "self-made
man," who, no matter what his social status, could achieve respectability and
success, in part by following the example of heroic men whose accomplishments
Smiles recounted. More generally, advice books, novels, and poems about the
progress toward, or the fall from, "true" womanhood or manliness demonstrate
that gendered and classed identities were cultural constructs that seemed "natural." The lady, the gentleman, the fallen woman, the hero—these gendered
and class types, rationalized through the ideology of separate spheres—were
cultural myths through which individuals made sense of their relationship to
the social order.

As the century drew to a close, new styles of masculinity and femininity
emerged to compete with the prevailing gender models of the previous decades.
One of these emergent types was the "New Woman," a term that described a
figure of greater sexual, economic, and social independence than the "Angel in
the House." Although the term denoted a lifestyle and a literary category more
than a political perspective, the figure of the New Woman was in part a product

of the gains feminists had made by the 1880s and 1890s in the areas of higher education, employment, political and legal rights, and civic visibility. The New Woman quickly became a flashpoint for opinion makers on either side of the "Woman Question."[1] Smoking, swearing, riding a bicycle, debating in public, wearing men's clothes, and refusing marriage were some of the trademarks of the New Woman, who figured in novels, short stories, and popular journalism as someone either to emulate or to condemn. A number of male novelists, including George Gissing, George Moore, and Thomas Hardy, created memorable New Woman characters who grapple with the competing demands of personal autonomy and social expectation, while the works of female writers, like Sarah Grand's *The Heavenly Twins* (1893) and the semi-autobiographical *The Beth Book* (1897), presented New Woman characters who triumph over social convention and the sexual double standard.

Advertisement for Swift Cycles, c. 1895.

For Grand and other feminist writers, such as Mona Caird and Olive Schreiner, the portrayal of the New Woman hinged on a critique of the male sexual privilege that had already come under fire in the 1870s and 1880s during the social purity campaigns and the resistance to the Contagious Diseases Acts. This legislation, enacted in the 1860s, allowed for the forcible confinement and internal examination of prostitutes by doctors in order to prevent the spread of venereal disease, first among the military, and then within

---

1   The question was largely one of the nature—and consequently, the proper role—of women. The "Woman Question" came to encompass the debates about the rights and responsibilities, as well as the place, of women in Victorian society.

civilian communities. Underwriting these Acts was the assumption that because male sexual urges were "uncontrollable," prostitution was a necessary evil that should be regulated because it could not be eradicated. The Act of 1864 decreed that infected women could be held in locked hospitals for three months; the Act of 1869 extended the period of confinement to a year. In 1867, there were proposals to extend the Acts to the north of England and the civilian population. Though the laws were intended to combat the spread of disease by prostitutes, in practice, they essentially meant that any woman passing through a poor neighborhood was subject to compulsory medical examination and arrest. The campaign against the Acts, led by the charismatic Josephine Butler, condemned the sexual double standard and the humiliation of poor and vulnerable women by police and doctors, with Butler comparing the compulsory medical examinations to "instrumental rape." The Acts were struck down in 1886 after much public controversy; the movement to repeal them, led mostly by middle-class women, marked the first instance in which women publicly debated the subject of sex on a broad scale. It was also one of the most visible of the many social purity campaigns of the 1870s, 1880s, and 1890s, in which moral reformers engaged in the rescue and "reformation" of prostitutes and other "fallen women" and urged men to take a vow of chastity. The mandate of the National Vigilance Association, for example, was to "create a universal ethic of chastity, for all men and women alike." In calling for a single standard of behavior, many of the social purity groups espoused moral coerciveness and interventionist policies, which often ended up stigmatizing and further repressing the women and girls they were attempting to help.

The preoccupations of the purity campaigners were part of a renewed cultural and scientific interest in human sexuality among Victorians, dating from at least the early 1870s and the publication of Darwin's *The Descent of Man*. In that book, Darwin applied the theories from his *On the Origin of Species* to human evolution and behavior, positing that sexual selection among men and women accounted for their mental and physical differences. These "natural differences" were drawn straight from the catalogue of Victorian gender stereotypes, which held that men were inherently courageous, virile, and combative, and women intuitive, passive, and altruistic. The "complementarity" of these traits ensured the survival of the human "race," which evolutionists, anthropologists, and psychologists understood as a hierarchy: white European males at the top, followed by women, children, and the "primitive races." But, scientists wondered, how to explain the fact that some white men—seemingly nature's most civilized specimen—occasionally exhibited traits that resembled those of the women, children, primitives, and even the animals who were understood as biologically and mentally inferior? Such questions were compounded by fears that Britain's empire was crumbling because the purity of the "white race" was being diluted through crossbreeding and racial mingling among English imperialists and the "savages" they ruled in the benighted labyrinths of the Empire. Closer to home, the poverty, crime, and vice of England's urban districts was often racialized: "As there is a darkest Africa is there not also a darkest England?" asked William Booth, founder of the Salvation Army. "Civilisation, which can breed its own barbarians, does it not also breed its own pygmies? May we not find a parallel at our own doors, and discover within a stone's throw of our cathedrals and palaces similar horrors to those which Stanley[1] has found existing in the great Equatorial forest?"

Social Darwinist theories of atavism (the reappearance of "primitive" characteristics in "advanced" populations) and degeneration (retrograde evolution) were formulated in the second half of the century to account for the "tendencies" of criminals, alcoholics, the poor, the mentally and physically disabled, and homosexuals. It was not until the 1880s that the term "homosexual" entered the English language; before that time homosexual acts among men were illegal (sodomy was punishable by death until 1861), but there was no concept of "the homosexual"—either male or female—as a distinct identity or way of being. With the emergence of a gay male subculture in London in the 1870s and 1880s, homosexuals—also called "sexual inverts"—became subject to increased scientific and legal scrutiny. Although "the lesbian" also emerged as a distinct identity in the 1890s, women were not subject to the same kinds of persecution as gay men, in part because of the belief that women were unmotivated by sexual desire, and that their passionate female "friendships" were therefore innocent, merely temporary diversions from their true calling as wives and mothers.

The Criminal Law Amendment Act of 1885, which raised the age of sexual consent from 13 to 16 under pressure from the social purity campaigners,

---

1   Henry Morton Stanley (1841–1904) was a renowned journalist and explorer, best known for his travels in Africa and his successful search for David Livingstone (see above, p. 82).

"Two Seated Sicilian Youths," photograph from c. 1893 (Victoria and Albert Museum).

contained a clause—known as the Labouchère Amendment, after Member of Parliament Henry Labouchère, who had introduced it—that mandated imprisonment for any man found guilty of "gross indecency"—effectively, any sexual act—with another man, even if the "indecency" was conducted entirely in private.[1] The Labouchère Amendment served to demonize gay men as "degenerates" whose "unnatural" desires threatened the stability of marriage, the future of the race, and the strength of the Empire. Feminized male types—the dandy, the aesthete, the fop—surfaced in visual art and literature alongside the masculinized New Woman figure to characterize a climate of sexual and gender experimentation at the fin-de-siècle that was celebrated by a few and denounced by many. As the popular satirical magazine *Punch* joked, "A new fear my bosom vexes; / Tomorrow there may be no sexes!"

In 1895, celebrity playwright Oscar Wilde[2] was brought to trial under the terms of the Labouchère Amendment and sentenced to two years in prison for "gross indecency." The highly publicized Wilde trials brought the moral panic

---

1   Many sexual acts were already illegal; in particular, "buggery"—a British term for anal sex—whether between two men or between a man and a woman, had been illegal since the Buggery Act of 1553.

2   Wilde was a married father of two young children, but rumors about his dalliances with men—many of working-class backgrounds, known as "rent-boys"—had abounded as his popularity increased. It was Wilde's involvement with Lord Alfred "Bosie" Douglas, the son of the 9th Marquess of Queensberry, that resulted in the rumors becoming a legal matter. The eccentric Queensberry, who believed his son had been corrupted by the older Wilde, left a note for Wilde at his club, accusing the playwright of "posing as a somdomite [*sic*]." Encouraged by Bosie, who hated his father, Wilde sued for libel; the resulting trial revealed a number of graphic details about Wilde's sexual predilections, and he was subsequently himself tried for acts of gross indecency.

of the preceding two decades to a crisis point. Yet Wilde's trial testimony, his writing, and that of his contemporaries such as John Addington Symonds, Algernon Charles Swinburne, "Michael Field," Sarah Grand, Mona Caird, Vernon Lee, and Edward Carpenter signaled a new level of consciousness about sexual and gender identity. With remarkable candor the sexologist Havelock Ellis wrote that while "we may not know exactly what sex is ... we do know that it is mutable, with the possibility of one sex being changed into the other sex, that its frontiers are often mutable, and that there are many stages between a complete male and a complete female." Ellis broke new ground with his multi-volume *The Psychology of Sex* (1897–1910), an early volume of which, *Sexual Inversion* (1897), was particularly noteworthy for treating homosexuality in a purely descriptive fashion, rather than as a pathology. (In other volumes Ellis took a similar approach to many other topics, including "autoerotism," or masturbation, and sado-masochism.) Sexuality and sexual practice had become topics of public conversation in a way that belies twentieth-century stereotypes of Victorian culture as sexually conservative or naïve. The apparent "repression" of sexual behaviors deemed improper or immoral only seemed to prohibit what was in fact an intense interest in the passions, proclivities, and practices of the "other" Victorians.[1]

Realism

"Art is the nearest thing to life," wrote George Eliot in "The Natural History of German Life" (1856). "It is a mode of amplifying experience and extending our contact with our fellow-men beyond the bounds of our personal lot. All the more sacred is the task of the artist when he undertakes to paint the life of the People." Eliot's essay anticipated the masterpieces of realist fiction she would begin writing in just a few years—*Adam Bede* (1859), *The Mill on the Floss* (1860), and *Middlemarch* (1874) among them. For Eliot, as for many of her contemporaries, the true, even "sacred," purpose of art was to present an objective representation of real life that reflected the habits, desires, and aspira-

---

1   Steven Marcus's seminal exploration of Victorian expressions and repressions of sexuality, *The Other Victorians: A Study of Sexuality and Pornography in Mid-Nineteenth Century England* (1966) helped complicate the sometimes overly simplified early and mid-twentieth-century view of the Victorians as simply repressed and "asexual."

tions of readers. For many novelists, realism seemed to be the form best suited to this purpose.

Victorian poetry too, especially at mid-century, was influenced by the predominance of realist fiction; long narrative poems, such as Tennyson's *Idylls of the King* (1856–85) and Robert Browning's *The Ring and the Book* (1868–69), appropriated novelistic forms of storytelling, combining trenchant social critique with formal experimentation. In Elizabeth Barrett Browning's "verse novel" and female Bildungsroman,[1] *Aurora Leigh* (1856), the speaker, Aurora Leigh herself, defines and defends her poetic practice of social engagement with the contemporary world, sounding very much like Eliot:

> Nay, if there's room for poets in this world
> A little overgrown (I think there is),
> Their sole work is to represent the age,
> Their age, not Charlemagne's …
> …
> … this is living art,
> Which thus presents and thus records true life.

Much realist fiction of the Victorian period tended to center on the everyday experiences, moral progress, and inner struggles of an ordinary individual, while giving a sense of the connections between that individual and his or her broader social networks. Many realist novels, including those by Anthony Trollope, William Thackeray, Dickens, and Eliot contained multiple plot lines and a range of characters across socio-economic strata, representing both the cohesiveness and the disintegration of various social communities in an industrialized, commercializing society. Detailed descriptions of landscapes, city streets, and domestic interiors and close attention to the emotionally complex motivations of characters—these too are characteristic of the realism of the Victorian novel. However, such broad vision is typically viewed from a single narrative perspective, whether that of the novel's protagonist or of an omniscient narrator.

Why did realism hold such appeal for Victorian novelists and their audiences? One explanation is that the revolutions of the nineteenth century created a climate in which people longed for a sense of verisimilitude in their literature

---

1   "Novel of Education" (German).

in order to guide them through the changes and upheavals, both private and public, which they themselves faced. Many Victorian readers sought moral and ethical guidance from their authors, who assumed—or were thrust into—the role of "secular clerics" with varying degrees of confidence and authority. Realist fiction, along with other forms of writing such as biography, criticism, poetry, and history, was accepted as having a pedagogical function; such texts not only taught readers how to navigate the changes they were experiencing, but also how to imagine sympathetically the authenticity of others' experience. "We want to be taught to feel," wrote Eliot, "not for the heroic artisan or the sentimental peasant, but for the peasant in all his coarse apathy, and the artisan in all his suspicious selfishness."

In rejecting the heroic and the sentimental, Eliot positioned the realist novel in opposition to the heightened, "falsifying" sensibilities of the romantic mode, as did many others. In 1785, distinguishing between the romance and the newly emergent genre of the novel, Clara Reeve had observed that "the Novel is a picture of real life and manners, and of the times in which it was written. The Romance in lofty and elevated language, describes what never happened nor is likely to happen"; Reeve's description of the novel could be applied to most Victorian fiction. Nonetheless, many of the best-known Victorian novels contain elements of the fantastic, the supernatural, or the mysterious: while Dickens's *Oliver Twist*—as is true, indeed, of most of his novels—sets out to realistically document the ravages of industrial poverty, but the novel's plot depends on outrageous coincidence, its story peopled with broadly drawn character types befitting the romantic mode.[1] The novels of Charlotte and Emily Brontë memorably combine psychological realism with Gothic elements such as female imprisonment and suggestions of ghostly presences. The persistence of romantic elements in Victorian realist novels not only unsettles the confidence of our formal definitions, but also prompts us to consider just whose versions of "the real" were recognized as the most truthful.

Inevitably, realism's dominance in literature and in visual art came under attack. As early as the 1850s, but more widely in the 1880s and 1890s, visual

---

1   *Oliver Twist* is one of many orphans in Dickens's novels. Dickens's orphans inevitably confront the urban nightmares of Victorian life with well-nigh angelic purity—and, in Oliver's case, perfectly grammatical English.

artists, writers, and critics began to question the moral imperatives of realist art in a series of movements that have come to be referred to under the umbrella term "Aestheticism." In poetry, drama, criticism, and fiction, Aestheticism stressed experimentation in form and composition, independence of imagination and expression, and freedom of content, however perverse, morbid, or tawdry. In rebelling against the harsh brutalities of British industrial culture, the Aesthetes sought a "pure" art and formal beauty dissociated from the concerns and surroundings of the everyday. The Aesthetes were not interested in instructing or edifying a mass readership; rather, they advocated aesthetic withdrawal in order to pursue the essential forms of art. "Art for art's sake,"[1] translated from the French by art critic Walter Pater, became the rallying cry of the Aesthetes. "Art never expresses anything but itself," declares one of Oscar Wilde's speakers. "It has an independent life, just as Thought has, and develops purely on its own lines. It is not necessarily realistic in an age of realism, nor spiritual in an age of faith. So far from being a creation of its own time, it is usually in direct opposition to it." Similarly, Wilde concludes his preface to *The Picture of Dorian Gray* (1891) with the assertion that "All art is quite useless," having earlier stated that "There is no such thing as a moral or an immoral book."

By the 1890s, the aesthetic movement had been charged with elitism, hedonism, self-absorption, and homosexuality.[2] Aestheticism by that time had shifted into Decadence, a term of either censure or praise, depending on who wielded it. The Decadents extended the precepts of Aestheticism in their affirmation of the perversity, artificiality, and overindulgence of a culture and a century that was nearing its end, and their works were often taken as evidence of social degeneration; in *Degeneration* (1892), the German critic Max Nordau attacked degenerate, Decadent artists—including Wilde—and argued that social decay is both reflected in and driven by art.

---

1 The French writer Théophile Gautier (1811–72) is generally credited with coining the phrase "l'art pour l'art" in the preface to his novel, *Mademoiselle de Maupin* (1836). A number of critics have contended that the idea—if not the precise phrase—dates back to ancient Rome.

2 Wilde's *The Picture of Dorian Gray*, which first appeared in Lippincott's *Monthly* Magazine in 1890, was immediately accused of having homoerotic overtones and deemed "unclean," "effeminate," and "contaminating." Wilde made a number of changes to the novel before its publication as one volume in 1891, but these were not enough to keep the book from counting against him during Wilde's trial for acts of "gross indecency."

Advertisements.

COMIC HISTORY OF ENGLAND.

On the First of July, 1846, will be published, price One Shilling,

THE FIRST PART

OF THE

COMIC HISTORY OF ENGLAND.

BY GILBERT ABBOTT à BECKETT.

WITH NUMEROUS ILLUSTRATIONS BY JOHN LEECH.

IN announcing a Comic History of England it may be necessary to observe that the levity implied in the title will relate to the manner, but by no means to the matter of the work, which will be collected with the gravest regard to the truth and accuracy that the subject requires. The aim of the writer will be to present a faithful narrative, for which the best authorities will be most carefully consulted, and to serve it up to the reader in a more palatable form than has hitherto been thought compatible with the dignity of history. There is not the smallest intention to sacrifice fidelity to fun in the forthcoming production, which is designed to show that the *utile et dulce*—are not inseparable. The advantages of blending amusement with instruction are universally allowed ; and there is an end to the once favourite fallacy that food for the mind requires the uninviting flavour of physic.

It will appear in Monthly Parts, price ONE SHILLING each, handsomely printed in octavo, and copiously illustrated by JOHN LEECH, with

ONE LARGE ETCHING,

AND

FROM SIX TO TWELVE WOOD ENGRAVINGS.

THE COMIC HISTORY OF ENGLAND will comprise from Twelve to Twenty Parts, and will appear regularly with the monthly Magazines until its completion .

PUBLISHED AT THE "PUNCH" OFFICE, 85, FLEET STREET.

AN INFALLIBLE HAIR DYE.

ROWLAND'S
MELACOMIA,

The most successful LIQUID PREPARATION ever known in this or any other Country, for Dyeing the HAIR OF THE HEAD, WHISKERS, MUSTACHIOS, and EYEBROWS a *natural* and *permanent* BROWN or BLACK, so exactly resembling the natural colour of the hair as to defy detection. It is perfectly innocent in its nature, is free from any unpleasant smell, and can be used by any Lady or Gentleman with the greatest ease and secrecy. Its effect is so permanent that neither water nor perspiration will influence it ; and it is entirely free from those properties (usual in Hair Dyes) which give an unnatural *red* or *purple* tint to the Hair. Price 5s.

Prepared by A. ROWLAND & SON, 20, Hatton Garden, London.

ROWLAND'S ODONTO,
OR PEARL DENTIFRICE,

A WHITE POWDER FOR THE TEETH, composed of the Choicest and most *Recherché Ingredients of the Oriental Herbal* ; the leading requisites of *cleanliness* and efficacy being present in the highest possible degree. It extirpates all *tartarous adhesions* to the Teeth, and insures a PEARL-LIKE WHITENESS to the *enamelled surface*. Its ANTI-SEPTIC and ANTI-SCORBUTIC PROPERTIES exercise a highly beneficial and salutary influence; they arrest the further progress of decay of the Teeth, induce a healthy action of the GUMS, and cause them to assume the brightness and colour indicative of perfect soundness ; while, by confirming their adhesion to the TEETH, they give unlimited enjoyment and fresh zest to appetite, by perpetuating effective and complete mastication. The BREATH also, from the salubrious and disinfecting qualities of the ODONTO, attains a sweetness and fragrance truly grateful to its possessor.

The Proprietors of this Dentifrice pledge themselves, that its efficacy in preserving and embellishing the Teeth far surpasses anything of the kind ever offered to the Public.

As the most efficient and fragrant aromatic purifier of the BREATH, TEETH, and GUMS ever known, ROWLAND'S ODONTO has for a long series of years occupied a distinguished Place at the TOILETS of the SOVEREIGNS and the NOBILITY throughout Europe; while the general demand for it at once announces the favour in which it is universally held.

Price 2s. 9d. per Box.

CAUTION.—To protect the Public from Fraud, the *Hon. Commissioners of Stamps* have directed the Proprietors' Name and Address, thus—A. ROWLAND & SON, 20, Hatton Garden, to be engraved on the Government Stamp, and which is affixed on each Box.

*** All others are FRAUDULENT IMITATIONS.

The Genuine Preparations are sold by the Proprietors, as above, and by Chemists and Perfumers.

Page of advertisements from the eighth number of the 1846 serial publication in ten numbers of Dickens's Oliver Twist. *(Pages of advertisements appeared at the front and back of each number.)*

The Victorian Novel

The dominant Victorian literary form was the novel. Although the genre novel emerged well in advance of the Victorian period, the literary legitimacy and cultural authority the novel wields today were solidified in the nineteenth century. The novel was a dynamic form, shifting according to popular taste and critical assessments of its potential value to readers, who were offered an ever-expanding list of authors and subgenres from which to choose. The early and mid-Victorian novels of Dickens, Thackeray, and Trollope were wildly successful, both with the critical establishment and the reading public. Female novelists, including the Brontës, Eliot, Braddon, Gaskell, Charlotte Yonge, and Ellen Price Wood were some of the most respected and prolific novelists of the century, and paved the way for legions of other women to enter the field of fiction writing. Although the profession of "novelist" achieved new respectability in the period for both men and women alike, the novel continued in some circles to be maligned as lightweight and "pernicious," associated with frivolous lady scribblers and their female readers. As George Henry Lewes, George Eliot's partner, observed in "The Lady Novelists" (1852), "Of all departments of literature, Fiction is the one to which, by nature and by circumstance, women are best adapted.... The very nature of fiction calls for that predominance of Sentiment which we have already attributed to the feminine mind."

The taste for particular subjects and approaches shifted regularly: the "silver fork" novels of the 1820s and 1830s centered on the extravagances and corruptions of the rich and fashionable, while the "social problem" novels of the 1840s depicted the minute details of life at the very opposite end of the social scale. Domestic novels by both the famous and the obscure focused on the quotidian; George Eliot's *Middlemarch*, rich in psychological complexity and moral analysis, is one of the most outstanding examples of domestic fiction of the Victorian period. A heightened form of this domestic-centered fiction was the "sensation" novel, which flourished in the 1860s and 1870s. Strong on dramatic incident and scandalous subject matter, such as bigamy, murder, madness, and crime, sensation novels exposed the hidden corruptions and dirty secrets of the outwardly respectable middle class; Wilkie Collins, Braddon, and Wood were some of the leading practitioners of this wildly popular and much maligned subgenre. The immense popular appeal of sensation novels helped inaugurate the concept of a "mass readership," much to the chagrin of the critical elite, who bemoaned the "degradation" of literature as the century drew to a close. In the latter decades of the century, mystery novels, detective fiction, horror, and adventure stories soared in popularity, partly on the strength of an expanding audience of lower-income readers, rising literacy rates, and cheaper methods of book production. The counterpart to these often lurid and shocking tales were the naturalistic novels of Thomas Hardy, George Gissing, and George Moore, whose late-century fiction offers bleak, social Darwinist portraits of urban class struggle, slum life, rural poverty, and sexual frustration.

Cover, Famous Crimes, *Police Budget Edition, c. 1890. Sensationalized stories of crime and horror, priced at one penny each and known as "penny dreadfuls," became hugely popular in the late nineteenth century.*

If the vogue for particular kinds of subject matter in novels shifted regularly, so too did their modes of publication, distribution, and consumption. One significant mode of publication was the three-volume edition, known as the "triple-decker." Readers who could not afford to buy the volumes themselves borrowed one volume at a time from lending libraries for a fee, generating huge profits for the most successful of these, Mudie's Select Library and W.H. Smith and Son. The triple-decker format was eventually supplanted by cheap single-volume editions that were sold in national book chains and at rail stations. Another mode of publication, one that made the novel a household word, was the monthly or weekly serial. Monthly installments of a few chapters, often accompanied by illustrations and advertisements, were initially published and purchased in separate parts with paper wrappers, generally appearing over a period of 19 months. By the 1860s, these serializations were more often appearing in monthly or weekly literary magazines. Dickens's enormously successful *Pickwick Papers* appeared in installments in 1836–37, launching the serial format as the most important publishing medium for Victorian fiction.[1] Serialization allowed readers with modest incomes to purchase new works when bound volumes were beyond their financial reach, and the regular continuation of a novel over a period of months or years meant that novels and novel reading became woven into the fabric of daily life, mingling with news, opinion, and readers' personal experience. The serialized format also had an influence on the novelistic genre, establishing a particular pace and necessitating "cliff-hangers," ensuring the return of the audience week after week.

Poetry

The novel's predominance and popularity have often meant that the significance of Victorian poetry is overlooked. Victorian poets throughout the century were greatly influenced by poets of the Romantic period, but key departures in form, content, and purpose set the Victorians apart from their predecessors. One of the most important of Victorian innovations was the development of the dramatic monologue, a lyric poem in the voice of a speaker who is not the poet and who occasionally addresses a silent auditor. Although the Victorians did not invent the dramatic monologue, Robert Browning and Alfred Tennyson are typically credited with developing it into a form expressive of psychological complexity. Victorian psychologists were interested in exploring the boundary between sanity and madness, and the possibility of a lucid yet mentally unbalanced narrating persona appealed to Browning and Tennyson, who used the dramatic monologue to expose not only the unstable character of their speakers' passions, but also the social and cultural contexts that either produced or reflected their instability. Browning, in particular, chose a range of unstable, deluded, or even mentally deranged speakers whose self-perception is ironically distanced from the reader's, thus participating in pre-Freudian ideas about the divided self; perhaps the most famous of these is "My Last Duchess" (1842), which slowly reveals the fate of the speaker's wife. The dramatic monologue was also notably employed by Elizabeth Barrett Browning, D.G. Rossetti, Augusta Webster, Thomas Hardy, Rudyard Kipling, and by many twentieth-century poets.

---

1   Long poems and works of non-fiction prose were also sometimes published serially; important examples include Robert Browning's *The Ring and the Book* and Matthew Arnold's *Culture and Anarchy* (serialized in *Cornhill Magazine* in 1867–68).

Many other poetic forms also flourished in the period. Perhaps surprisingly in an "age of realism," epic poems were a feature of the Victorian literary landscape, from Tennyson's *Idylls of the King* to George Eliot's *The Spanish Gypsy* (1868) and William Morris's *The Earthly Paradise* (1868-70). Sonnet sequences too were a popular form, particularly among female poets; notable examples include George Eliot's *Brother and Sister Sonnets* (1869), Christina Rossetti's *Monna Innominata* (1881), Augusta Webster's *Mother and Daughter Sonnets* (1895), and—most popular of all—Elizabeth Barrett Browning's *Sonnets from the Portuguese* (1850), a collection of 44 sonnets chronicling Barret Browning's courtship with Robert Browning. Through the work of these writers and a host of others—from Felicia Hemans and Letitia Landon at the beginning of the period to Charlotte Mew and Mathilde Blind at its end—the "poetess" became an accepted part of the literary landscape

The lyric introspection and self-exploration that is the hallmark of much Romantic verse was augmented in both form and content by a Victorian poetry of social engagement that strove to contextualize a speaker's moral and spiritual questions within the vicissitudes of contemporary life. In Tennyson's monologue *Maud* (1855), the tormented speaker's mental deterioration and reawakening are represented as continuous with the effects of industrialization and England's entry into the Crimean War. In Augusta Webster's dramatic monologue *A Castaway* (1870), a high-class prostitute's self-scrutiny illustrates the relationship between political economy and the commodification of female identity, with "coin" as a central metaphor for the connection between the two.

Not all poets accepted the view that poetry should speak to the issues and concerns of the present. In 1853, Matthew Arnold wrote that poets should respond to their world by mining "those elementary feelings which subsist permanently in the race, and are independent of time." In some of his later poetry, Arnold turned to classical rather than contemporary subjects as a way of rejecting what he saw as the crass materialism and spiritual futility of modern life. Yet for all his melancholia, Arnold did not advocate artistic isolation; whereas many poets of the second half of the century called for the independence of art from the imperative to offer moral instruction, Arnold continued to insist that the aesthetic endeavor necessarily involved ethical responsibility.

In contrast, Swinburne's poetry of sensual experience, his carnal subject matter and verbal pyrotechnics revel in the corporeality of poetry, so much so that he was accused in one famous review of "fleshliness" to the exclusion of "meditation" and "thought."[1] Swinburne's verse was important to the development of Aestheticism, influencing later poets such as Wilde and Symonds, whose poetry tended to emphasize formal beauty, sonic effects, and the momentary over the timeless. Like the Spasmodic poets of the 1840s and 1850s, like Arthur Hugh Clough in the late 1850s and early 1860s, and, at the century's end, like Gerard Manley Hopkins, Swinburne also engaged in many challenging experiments with poetic form and meter, thereby anticipating some of the innovations and deliberate difficulties of modernist writing.

Drama

The Victorian period is not remembered for great stage dramas or for penetrating comedies, at least until the last decades of the century. Although Victorian audiences were avid theatergoers, they tended to prefer light-hearted entertainment to more serious fare. Comedies, pantomimes, farces, and musicals attracted audiences from across the social spectrum, but it was melodrama that became the most popular dramatic genre. For most literary critics, melodrama has little or no literary value and is thus easy to dismiss as an aesthetically vacant genre. Yet popular texts can reveal much about a culture because they are so intimately connected with everyday assumptions and values. The melodrama of the Victorian period opens a window onto the nature of power relations within modern market culture and the patriarchal family; sometimes it seems to support, and at other times to contest, these relations. With its sensational plots, stock characters, unadorned language, and a moral economy that unambiguously separates good from evil, melodrama exploited an audience's emotions, and invariably ended on a happy note. (We need look no further than the mass appeal of Hollywood films to begin to understand why stage melodrama was so popular.) Early in the century, melodramas often featured Gothic plots, settings, and characters, but the vogue for such subject matter gave way in the Victorian period to storylines centered on workaday conflicts

---

1   The charge was made in Robert Buchanan's "The Fleshly School of Poetry," a review essay that first appeared in Volume 18 of *The Contemporary Review* in 1871. The review focused on D.G. Rossetti's *Poems*, citing Swinburne and Morris as other key figures in what Buchanan derisively termed "the Fleshly School," a mode he took to task for its "morbid deviation from the healthy forms of life."

in familiar settings, such as factories, cottages, and manor houses.

The most prolific and successful writer and adapter of melodramas was Dion Boucicault; his 1852 play *The Corsican Brothers* was such a hit with Queen Victoria that she saw it five times. Tom Taylor's popular *The Ticket-of-Leave Man* (1863) was set in recognizable London locations and featured a sleuth named Jack Hawksure who became a prototype for later stage detectives. Many popular novels, including works by Dickens, Collins, and Braddon, were adapted or pirated for the stage soon after they had been published. Ellen Price Wood's *East Lynne* (1861), a novel with a fallen woman theme, was adapted into several stage versions on the basis of its enormous success as one of the earliest sensation novels.

In 1881, theater impresario Richard D'Oyly Carte opened the Savoy Theatre in London for the express purpose of staging the comic operettas of W. S. Gilbert and Arthur Sullivan, whose collaboration had begun in 1875. Their most popular plays, such as *H.M.S. Pinafore* (1878), *The*

"A Gaiety Girl," music hall poster, 1893.

Mikado (1885), and *Patience* (1881), are still regularly staged today. Gilbert's storylines and lyrics combined frivolous romance with witty and genial mockery of certain contemporary values,[1] as well as of the formulaic nature of most

---

1   *Patience*, for example, satirized Aestheticism, prominently featuring a character known as Bunthorne, an aesthete poet. Though some critics have identified Oscar Wilde as the model for Bunthorne, Wilde's relative obscurity at the time of the operetta's composition suggests that the character is more likely a representation of then-better-known poets such as Swinburne and D.G. Rossetti.

London stage fare; Sullivan's alternately lilting and bouncy melodies proved irresistible, and "Gilbert and Sullivan" rapidly became a popular phenomenon. The Savoy Operas, as they came to be known, anticipated the new directions in British theater of the 1890s, epitomized in the comic plays of Oscar Wilde and the "problem plays" of George Bernard Shaw; both Wilde and Shaw offered serious critiques of their society while dazzling their audiences with their audacious wit, brilliant dialogue, and shocking candor.

Prose Non-Fiction and Print Culture

Victorian writers of essays, criticism, history, and biography fully embraced the role of the public intellectual, whose particular mission was to instruct and edify readers about the day's key issues. Virtually no subject remained untouched: writers of non-fiction prose, also known as "sages," probed everything, from the latest scientific developments to religious controversies, from political and economic questions to gender issues, from aesthetic developments to social values and mores. In an age of growing religious skepticism, readers looked to their "sages" as latter-day prophets and interpreters who were uniquely qualified to offer an almost divinely inspired wisdom. This role of the secular cleric emerged along with the rise of the professional writer, or "man of letters," who could earn a comfortable living by the pen and maintain a level of gentlemanly respectability. Carlyle, Arnold, Ruskin, Mill, Newman, Pater, and Wilde produced some of the most influential cultural criticism of the age, using a variety of rhetorical techniques, verbal styles, and literary forms.

For female writers, the decision to offer social and cultural critique often came at a price, since women were discouraged from involvement in—and even knowledge of—political issues. Writers such as Frances Power Cobbe, Florence Nightingale, Harriet Martineau, Caroline Norton, George Eliot, and Harriet Taylor Mill exploited a variety of "voices"—some gendered "male"—in their critiques of the role of women in Victorian society, as well as in their writing on a variety of other topics, from political commentary to literary criticism. What united most of these writers, male and female, was their simultaneous position as societal outsiders and insiders: in a range of rhetorical styles, from prophetic to disinterested, prose writers typically argued from a marginal position under the assumption that their particular viewpoint had been abandoned or would be resisted by their readers. Yet it was precisely this outsider perspective that guaranteed the sage's unique authority within a society hungry for moral guidance by a voice from "beyond."

For every writer or sage celebrated by his or her reading public as a visionary, there were countless, often nameless "hack" writers who also contributed non-fiction prose, or, more properly, journalism, to newspapers and periodicals. Indeed, the periodical and newspaper press afforded both the sages and the hacks, novelists, and poets a space to disseminate their work and reach ever-expanding audiences. In Wilkie Collins's words, it was "the age of periodicals." Early in the century, prominent literary journals such as the *Edinburgh Review*, *Blackwood's Magazine*, the *Quarterly Review*, *Fraser's Magazine* and the *Athenaeum* attracted the most eminent writers. In the early Victorian era, writers in these journals generally published anonymously or under a pseudonym, no matter how distinguished they might be; not until the latter half of the century did signatures gradually begin to replace anonymity in many of the periodicals. Throughout the period, the number of periodicals steadily increased, until there was a magazine for every taste, every income level, every hobby group, every political and religious organization. Domestic magazines aimed at female readers, children's magazines, satirical or humor magazines, and monthly and quarterly miscellanies publishing fiction, poetry, criticism, and news all competed with each other for readers' interest, loyalty, and purchasing power in an increasingly diverse literary marketplace. Nearly all of the best-known literary writers across the genres saw their work published in magazines and newspapers: Barrett Browning's "The Cry of the Children" (1843) in *Blackwood's*, Dickens's *Oliver Twist* in *Bentley's Miscellany*, Arnold's *Culture and Anarchy* in the *Cornhill Magazine*, Yonge's *The Clever Woman of the Family* (1865) in the *Churchman's Family Magazine*.

The periodical press was also instrumental in the development of modern literary criticism. Book reviews in influential periodicals, such as the *Athenaeum*, could make or break a writer's reputation; prominent literary reviewers—some of whom, such as Henry James, were also celebrated authors in their own right—both forged a professional identity for themselves as literary critics and formulated principles of literary analysis that are today's tools of the trade.

Victorians were, in general, fascinated with characterizing their "age": Carlyle's "Signs of the Times," Mill's "Spirit of the Age," and Eliza Lynn Linton's

"Girl of the Period" became popular catchphrases that signaled a self-conscious awareness of a society in transition. It was the "age of steam," the "age of doubt," and, perhaps most notably for students of literature, the "age of reading." Reading, like many other social institutions and cultural practices, gradually became democratized during Victoria's reign. The 1870 Education Act instituted compulsory elementary education in England and Wales for the first time;

The opening of the Manchester Free Library, 1852. In 1845, local governments were given the authority to raise tax revenues to support the establishment of public libraries and museums. Free public libraries were distinguished from fee-charging circulating libraries such as Mudie's and W.H. Smith's.

adult literacy was nearly universal by century's end. Readers were everywhere: in pubs, on trains, around the family hearth, at gentlemen's clubs, and in reading rooms.[1] The single reader—particularly the female reader—was a common subject for Victorian painters. Reading aloud was also a popular pastime; it was common for middle-class fathers to gather together their dependents, including the servants, at the end of the day or week to read edifying family literature, such as sermons, tracts, and didactic fiction. Drawing on his background in the London theater, Dickens delivered public readings of his novels that attracted huge crowds and increased sales of his books. His performance of Little Nell's death scene famously left audiences weeping.

The explosion of reading and reading cultures in Victorian England went hand in hand with new print technologies, the removal of prohibitive taxes on reading material, the ease of distribution made possible through the rail system, the rise of cheap, mass-produced print, and political, economic, and social reforms that affected people at all levels of their existence. At the beginning

1   Private libraries where readers could pay an annual fee for access to current newspapers and the latest books and periodicals.

of the century, mass literacy was regarded as a recipe for political revolution. From at least the middle of the century onwards, some worried that reading was becoming too popular, that it was a kind of "mania" or "disease" that "consumed" people. Critics such as Matthew Arnold argued that the newly literate but untutored masses lacked the necessary skills to distinguish between the timeless and the trashy, signaling the demise of English culture. Yet there were also those who argued that literacy was a human right, and it was ultimately this viewpoint that prevailed. In 1840, Carlyle wrote, "Books are written by martyr-men, not for rich men alone but for all men. If we consider it, every human being has, by the nature of the case, a *right* to hear what other wise human beings have spoken to him. It is one of the Rights of Men; a very cruel injustice if you deny it to a man." The history of reading—the history of what and how different people read, the expectations that existed about what women and men should read, both in their leisure time and professionally—is ultimately inseparable from the history of the Victorian period.

The English Language in the Victorian Era

The English vocabulary continued to expand throughout the period. New words entered the language to name aspects of the changing world of work (*trade-union* is recorded as first having entered the language in 1831, for example; *margin*, used with reference to profit to mean "amount of money available once certain costs are covered," in the 1850s). New words were also needed to name aspects of human nature that were being seen in new ways or acknowledged for the first time (*personality*, used in the modern sense of "distinctive personal identity," in 1835; *sadism* in 1888; *homosexual* in 1892). New words were coined to name new religious movements (such as *evangelicanism*, *disestablishmentarianism*, and its famously long opposite *antidisestablishmentarianism*) and to name new developments in the culture of sports (*caddie* is first recorded in 1857). Less innocuously, new ways kept springing up to express old prejudices; *jew* is first recorded as being used derogatively as a transitive verb in 1845.

The coining of new words from Latin and Greek roots—especially new scientific terms—continued at a quickened pace, from *lithograph* and *locomotive*, to *photograph* and *phonograph*, to *telegraph*, *telephone*, and *dictaphone*. Far fewer new words were entering English from French, however; the flow of new words

The Western Electric multiple telephone switchboard, the Royal Exchange, Manchester, 1888. The spread of English as the leading language of communication world-wide was aided by the invention of the telegraph in 1837, and of the telephone later in the century.

from French into English,[1] which had continued in the second half of the eighteenth century and the early years of the nineteenth at about the same pace as it had been a century earlier, slowed to a trickle in the Victorian era; it was far more characteristic of the eighteenth-century English to turn to the French for *etiquette* (1750) than it was for Victorians to turn to the French for *élan* (1880).

The expansion of English in the nineteenth century was not restricted to new noun coinages. A lively feature of the growth of the language during this period was an expansion in the use of verb-adverb combinations (e.g., *bring up, hold up, let up, pass up, shut up*—to name only a few of those involving *up*). With the spread of such coinages (as well as of an ever-growing number of slang expressions) into the written language came a gradual reduction in the level of formality of standard English.

A reduction in dialect differences and in range of variation in English pronunciation had begun centuries earlier, with the imposition of English authority over Wales, Scotland, and Ireland; no doubt it was influenced, too, by the inherently stabilizing effects of print culture following the introduction of the printing press to England in the late fifteenth century. This trend toward greater standardization of vocabulary and of pronunciation continued through the nineteenth century. The spread of standardized pronunciation in particular was assisted by the growing influence of the elite boarding schools (known as "public schools") as the preferred sites of education for the privileged classes and for those who aspired to join them. Increasingly, in the late-Victorian period, girls as well as boys were sent to such schools; boarding

---

1   The importation of French words into English, often thought of as beginning with the Norman conquest in 1066, in fact did not occur with any great frequency until roughly a century later; the flow reached its peak in the late fourteenth century.

schools such as St. Andrews (1877) and Roedean (1885) were the first institutions for girls that paralleled centuries' old boys' schools such as Eton, Har-
row, and Rugby.

Perhaps the greatest development relating to the history of the English language in the Victorian period was the initiation of a dictionary "on historical
principles"—one that would record not only the various different meanings
of words, but also how they had changed over time, and precisely when each
meaning was first recorded in surviving written English. *The Oxford English
Dictionary*, which was to be among the most ambitious of projects in an age
of famously ambitious projects, had its origins in the work of the Philological
Society, founded in 1842. In 1858, following the lead of a similar project initiated in Germany[1] and following years of discussion, the society issued a formal
"Proposal for the Publication of a New Dictionary by the Philological Society."
The society would invite volunteers to assist in sending in records they found
of early or significant uses of words; eventually some six million slips with
quotations written on them were submitted. By 1879, the Philological Society
concluded that the project was so vast that it would not be able to complete it
on its own, entering into an agreement with the Oxford University Press. Even
with this assistance, it was not until 1884 that it proved possible to publish a
volume covering one part of the letter *A*. By 1900, only four and one-half volumes had been published, and it was not until 1928 that a complete version of
the full dictionary was available. (By then, of course, much of the early work
was outdated; a second edition was published in 1989, and the *OED* is now
continually being updated online.)

A less successful Victorian initiative was a multifaceted campaign to rationalize spelling—a campaign that extended in one form or another through almost
the entire period; the prevalence of spellings that bear no relation to phonetic
principles increasingly came to be criticized as antiquated and illogical.[2] In the

---

1   The *Deutsches Wöterbuch* was begun by the classicist Franz Passow and the philologists
     (and compilers of fairy tales) Jacob and Wilhelm Grimm.

2   As a late-Victorian spelling reformer pointed out, the ways in which English words are
     spelled often bear so little connection to pronunciation that it would be possible to spell
     fish as *ghoti*, with the *gh* pronounced as we do the *gh* in *cough*; the *o* pronounced as we do
     the *o* in *women*; and the *ti* pronounced as we do the *ti* in *nation*. This now-famous example
     is thought to have been first given common currency by Bernard Shaw (who later became
     a crusader for spelling reform).

early years of the Victorian era, interest in such matters was spurred by the introduction of Isaac Pitman's system of shorthand, with Pitman himself acting as a leading advocate for reform. By the 1850s, the Bible and a number of works were available in phonetic spelling versions, and by the end of the following decade, the Philological Society was taking an active role in airing all sides of the debate. Its American counterpart adopted a less impartial stance, calling in particular for the adoption of simplified phonetic spellings of words such as *tho*, *altho*, and *thruout*. Of their list only two—*program* and *catalog*—became generally adopted in the United States. In Britain resistance to such Americanisms carried the day—and in both countries, the campaign to rationalize spelling faltered by century's end in the face of a growing recognition of the degree to which English had become a written as well as a spoken language, with words comprehended very largely through the appearance on paper of the entire written word.

Resistance to Americanisms generally was felt not only in Britain herself, but also—indeed, perhaps even more strongly—in English Canada, in its unique position as staunchly British by history and by disposition but unavoidably "American" in the geographical sense. Complaints, such as those of a contributor to the *Canadian Journal* in 1857 against words and expressions "imported by travellers, daily circulated by American newspapers, and eagerly incorporated into the language of our colour Provincial press," were far from uncommon. Words such as *travellers* (in its British spelling; *travelers* according to common practice in the United States) themselves became points of contention. As the American spellings of such words—introduced by Noah Webster in his dictionary in 1825—became entrenched in the United States, Canadians began to develop a hybrid somewhere in between British and American spellings.

Conventions for marking direct speech and quoted material finally stabilized in the Victorian period in something close to their current form, though with what are now established differences between American and British conventions of punctuation still unsettled. Quotation marks themselves are a relatively recent invention; they became widely used only in the eighteenth century. Even in the late eighteenth century a number of different indicators for quoted material were still being used, the most of common of which was to include quotation marks not only at the beginning of the quoted passage, but also at the beginning of each subsequent line for as long as the quotation extended.

In the early Victorian period, it had become conventional to mark quotations with only an open quotation mark at the beginning of a passage and a closed quotation mark at the end—though it remained acceptable to use either single or double quotation marks.

The period also saw significant changes in the evolution of the paragraph as a primary means of signaling the shape of ideas in prose. The paragraph was originally simply a short horizontal marker added beneath a line in which a break in meaning occurred; in the sixteenth century, it became conventional to mark such shifts by setting off blocks of text through indentation at the beginning of each block. Until the late eighteenth century, however, paragraphs of English prose were often extremely long by modern standards, and one paragraph of expository or argumentative prose might hold a large number of only loosely related ideas. Even in the Romantic era, a paragraph might often run to a page or more. Through the nineteenth century, however, paragraphs gradually but steadily became shorter, and the principle of restricting each paragraph to a set of closely related ideas became much more widely followed.

Introduction to
the Early Twentieth Century:
From 1900 to Mid-Century

The first half of the twentieth century saw a fracturing of almost every aspect of British life. At the beginning of the century, Queen Victoria, monarch for 63 years, still reigned over a nation that had become the world's greatest economic and political power. Over the course of the nineteenth century, the Industrial Revolution had transformed the economy, and Great Britain had become "factory to the world." Despite a high level of religious anxiety among the educated classes of the late-Victorian period, the established church retained its authority over a God-fearing society. The working class was not always contented with its lot—and with reason—but the class hierarchy remained extraordinarily stable. So, too, did gender roles; a small minority of women was pressing to be given the vote, but they were regarded as extremists by the vast majority of the population. Expressions of sexuality were tightly circumscribed, and the possibility of having an orientation other than heterosexual was unmentioned (except for occasional veiled references to difficulties or scandals "of the Oscar Wilde sort"). And the British Empire had reached its zenith. The vast dominions of Canada and Australia had become semi-autonomous (in 1867 and 1901 respectively), but overwhelmingly their people were proud to call themselves British subjects. Despite a lively debate in the latter half of the nineteenth century as to whether Britain's imperial ambitions were truly benefitting either the colonizers or the colonized, the majority of British citizens were not "little Englanders" looking to reduce Britain's overseas commitments; they were pleased that British rule extended over all of India, a very large part of Africa, and a considerable amount of the rest of the world. England was seen by the English, in the words of the popular poet W.E. Henley, as the "Chosen daughter of the Lord." Still, Britain had certainly not been immune to change in the second half the nineteenth century; indeed, many of the lines along which twentieth-century society would fracture were in place in the late-Victorian era. Political and ideological strains that would shake class structure were already forming; categories of gender and sexuality were already becoming far less stable than they had been a decade or two earlier; and the "Aesthetes" had begun in the 1890s to break free of characteristically Victorian patterns of anxiety over the religious, the moral, and the aesthetic. Nonetheless, for most British people the world in 1900 seemed recognizably the same world as that of 1850, and Britain held a central place within it.

By 1950 that world had been distinctly altered. The four years of World War I had resulted in the deaths of millions and had had a catastrophic effect on the nation's spirit; the great economic depression of the 1930s had bred poverty and despair; the seven years of World War II had threatened Britain's survival and left the nation exhausted, even in victory; and immediately in its wake, with Britain still physically and emotionally devastated, a new war—a "Cold War" against the Soviet Union—had begun. Exhausted by these struggles, Britain in 1950 had lost its place as the world's leading power to the United States. Daily life had been radically altered by the radio, the telephone, and the automobile.

The streets of London decorated for the coronation of Edward VII, 1902.

Wyndham Lewis, Workshop, *c. 1915. The Canadian-born writer and artist Wyndham Lewis (1882–1957) lived largely in England from 1908 onwards. In the period 1912–15 he was a leader among those painters variously described as Futurist, Cubist, and "Vorticist"— the last of these a term that Lewis himself coined. Though his writing—like that of Pound and others in their circle—is tainted by anti-Semitism, misogyny, and, in Lewis's case, venomous portrayals of homosexuals, Lewis is unquestionably a figure central to British Modernism.* Workshop *is one of the works that extend furthest his vision of harsh lines and fragmented shapes conveying a sense of the modern city, and of modernity itself.*

World War I recruiting poster used in Ireland, c. 1915.

"Dig for Victory" poster, distributed in Britain's West African colonies, 1940.

A bombed street in London, 1940. The photographer is unknown.

(Above) Sirkka-Liisa Konttinen,
Kendal Street, 1969. *A member of*
the Amber collective, between 1969
and 1983 Finnish-born Konttinen
documented the life and eventual
demolition of Byker, a terraced com-
munity in Newcastle upon Tyne in
northern England. In 2003 she and
Amber returned to document the
Byker Wall Estate that replaced it.

(Left) Bill Brandt, The Lambeth Walk,
1936. This photo, originally published
in the illustrated weekly magazine
Picture Post, *was taken in the Bethnal*
Green area of London. The girl per-
forms a dance popular at the time.

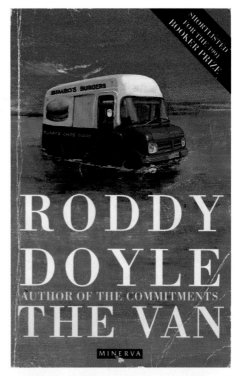

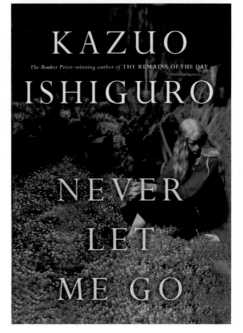

A sampling of book covers: Graham Greene's
Journey Without Maps (1936; Pan paperback
edition, 1948), Roddy Doyle's The Van (1991;
Minerva paperback edition, 1992), and
Kazuo Ishiguro's Never Let Me Go (2005). The
image on the Ishiguro cover is "Christina,"
from a famous 1912–13 series of photographs
by Lieutenant-Colonel Mervyn O'Gorman of
his daughters, whom he photographed both
in autochrome color and in black and white,
sometimes on a beach near their Dorset home,
sometimes (as here) in a garden setting.

THE BEATLES.. LONDON PALLADIUM
.. ROYAL COMMAND PERFORMANCE. 1963

Poster, The Beatles London Palladium Royal Command Performance, 1963. The Royal Variety Performance (also known as the Royal Command Performance) is a gala variety show held every year, the proceeds of which go to charity. When The Beatles performed at the show on 4 November 1963, the audience included the Queen Mother, Princess Margaret, and Lord Snowdon, but not the Queen. As the group was about to play their hit song "Twist and Shout," John Lennon made a request: "Will the people in the cheaper seats clap their hands? And the rest of you, if you'll just rattle your jewelry."

David Hockney, My Mother, Bolton Abbey, Yorkshire, *1982. Painter and photographer David Hockney (b. 1937) has long maintained his reputation as one of Britain's leading visual artists. Hockney initially created controversy with his open homosexuality, and in recent years he has incited debate with his views on art history, arguing strenuously that the old Masters employed camera-like techniques in order to achieve realistic effects. A native of Bradford, Hockney has lived largely in California since the 1970s.*

Peel Square, Bradford, c. 1995. From the 1950s onwards many immigrants from Asia have settled in Bradford.

Notting Hill Carnival, Notting Hill, London, 1979. The Carnival was started in 1964 to celebrate Caribbean culture within Britain.

Church-going was in decline, and the nation was well on its way to becoming a secular society. Though Britain remained more class-conscious than North America or Australia, the class structure itself had seen great change; only the wealthy had servants, and all social classes partook of the same culture to an unprecedented extent. The Labour Party government of Clement Attlee, elected in 1945 in a clean break from Winston Churchill and the glorious but conservative path that he represented, had for five years been building a welfare state; this was Britain's first avowedly socialist government. "Votes for women"—to most minds a far-fetched notion in 1900—had in 1950 been a reality for over 30 years; women had done

King Edward VII.

Members of a slum-dwelling family in London, c. 1913. Though Britain was the world's wealthiest nation, the poor often lived in appalling conditions of hardship.

A sternwheel steamer and trading canoes at Okopedi on the Eyong River, Nigeria, 1909. Nigeria was among the last British possession to be governed through a trading company; in 1900, control was transferred from the Royal Niger Company to the government, and the territory became the Protectorate of Southern Nigeria. The Niger Company continued as the leading trading entity in the region.

"men's work" during two long world wars, and were starting to wonder if winning the vote might represent the beginning rather than the end of the struggle for gender equality. Much of Britain was as repressed sexually as it had been in 1900—but more and more people were starting to see the awkwardness that surrounded sexual matters as an obstacle to be overcome rather than as the expression of a necessary and appropriate sense of modesty. And the sun was rapidly setting on the British Empire. The dominions were now fully independent and beginning to drift away from the mother country culturally; India had been partitioned in 1947 into two independent nations; and, in Britain's African and Caribbean possessions, the stirrings of unrest that would lead to independence had already begun. In terms of literature, Britain had, in the years between 1900 and 1950, undergone the modernist revolution.[1] The sometimes fractured, sometimes free-flowing approaches to form that the poetry of T.S. Eliot, the plays of Samuel Beckett, and the prose fiction of James Joyce and Virginia Woolf represented had not been taken up by the majority

---

1   "Modernist" and "Modernism" are commonly used as umbrella terms to describe a wide range of interconnected intellectual and aesthetic developments of the first half of the twentieth century that occurred in France, Italy, the United States, and other areas, as well as in Britain. A connecting thread is that expressions of Modernism tend to shun the linear, the decorative, and the sentimental. They tend too toward the presentation of reality fractured into its component pieces—and conversely, toward a rejection of aesthetic traditions by which reality is represented through the construction of conventionally unified wholes, through a single point of view, or through a single, unbroken narrative. Modernism is discussed more fully later in this introduction.

of writers. Yet many serious writers in 1950 were aware of the expanded possibilities of literary form that Modernism had revealed—and many wrote with
a sense that the world was not the ordered and coherent whole that it had been
widely assumed to be at the dawn of the twentieth century.

The Edwardian Period

If it is true that the first half of the twentieth century may be characterized
as a period in which the old Britain and the old world broke apart, it is also
true that much of that fracturing did not begin to be readily visible until the
years after 1910. 1910 was marked by the death of Edward VII, but more significantly this was the time of the first explosions of Modernism—Cubism in
painting, Imagism in poetry, in music such ground-breaking works as Stravin-
sky's *The Rite of Spring* (1913). With these began the fracturing of form that
would become a dominant theme in the cultural history of much of the rest
of the century. With 1914 came the outbreak of World War I, and with 1915
and 1916—the years of the gruesomely drawn-out battles of Ypres and of the
Somme—came a more visceral sense of fracturing as the full horror of the war's
unprecedented carnage began to sink home.

The deaths of Victoria in 1901 and of her son Edward nine years later have
often been seen as defining moments in the change from the Victorian to the
modern world. Edwardian Britain liked to see itself as highly distinct from its
Victorian predecessor. And certainly there were some changes; architectural
style became rather less ornate, for example, and social style rather less formal.
But at its core the Edwardian era was as much a continuation from the Victorian one as a break with it. Established religion, a hierarchy of social class, a
largely inflexible set of attitudes toward gender roles, a complacent confidence
in Britain's dominant position in the world—all these remained largely un-
changed. In the literary world Victorian traditions were being carried forward
by novelists such as George Moore and Arnold Bennett, dramatists such as
Arthur Wing Pinero, and poets such as Robert Bridges and W.E. Henley, the
immensely popular author of "Invictus" (1888) and "Pro Rege Nostro," also
known as "England, My England" (1892). And even much of the literature
that we now think of as recognizably modern may as readily be seen as connecting with that of the late-Victorian era as anticipating the later literature of
the century. The prose fiction of Joseph Conrad, for example, with its laying

bare of the dark corners of the human soul (and of the dark realities of colonialism), touches the nerves of the reader in ways that we think of as distinctively modern. Indeed, the cry "that was no more than a breath" of the dying ivory agent Kurtz in Conrad's *Heart of Darkness* (1899, 1902)—"The horror! The horror!"—is often regarded as a defining expression of the anguish that came to be felt as characteristic of the twentieth century. And some of Conrad's narrative techniques break ground that would become heavily tilled in the twentieth century; through layering of viewpoints (stories within stories, multiple narrators) Conrad found ways to create a narrative density that at once intensifies and destabilizes the reader's experience of the events being recounted. But Conrad was an extraordinary innovator, not a revolutionary; however original, the threads of most of his fiction are still woven through a storytelling art that draws on the conventions of fiction writing that held sway through the nineteenth century—conventions of realism through which implausible coincidences or exotic adventures could be made believable to the reader. As a *New York Times* reviewer put it in 1903, "the adventures he describes are little short of miraculous and are laid among scenes wholly alien to commonplace life, [but] they are wrought into a tissue of truth so firm and so tough as to resist the keenest scepticism.... Not even his Kurtz, the man of impenetrable darkness of soul, is either a bloodless or an incredible figure."

In some respects a "Victorian" sense of empire carried on into the 1920s and 1930s. Here Queen Mary (wife of George V) is shown visiting the Burma pavilion at the British Empire Exhibition, London, 1924. Though some complained that the Exhibition's strongly patriotic flavor was excessively self-congratulatory, it was highly popular with most Londoners.

The novelist E.M. Forster is recognizably an author of the twentieth century in his treatment not only of the sexual (see below for a discussion of his novel *Maurice*) but also of the spiritual; his approach to the spiritual realities that transcend everyday life connects to the work of later twentieth-century writers such as Elizabeth Bowen, Graham Greene, and Kazuo Ishiguro. And in some stylistic respects (particularly the shifting, ironic narrative voice of *A Passage to India* [1924]), his fiction has affinities with modernism. But the texture of his work—most notably of the novels *A Room with a View* (1908) and *Howard's End* (1910)—is woven of nuances of social interaction and of subtle modulations of feeling, and relates at least as strongly to the conventions of Victorian realism as it does to those of Modernism. Forster is above all a social novelist, whose work recognizably connects with the traditions of his nineteenth-century predecessors.

Much of H.G. Wells's fiction was forward-looking in a more precise sense. Beginning in 1895, with the publication of *The Time Machine*, and continuing with *The Island of Dr. Moreau* (1896), *The Invisible Man* (1897), and *The War of the Worlds* (1898), Wells had founded the genre of science fiction as we still know it today. He continued in this vein in the new century with such works as *The First Men in the Moon* (1901) and *The War in the Air* (1908). But, in

David Lloyd George, 1906. Lloyd George was a leading advocate of the interests of the working class in the early years of the century. As Chancellor of the Exchequer, he introduced the "Peoples' Budget" of 1909, calling for new taxes on the better-off to pay for measures to improve the lot of the poor, including an old age pension. The Old Age Pensions Act was resisted so strongly by the House of Lords that the Liberal government acted to reduce the power of the House; both that Act and the Parliament Act, which established the supremacy of the House of Commons, became law in 1911. Lloyd George was also responsible for the National Insurance Act (1911), which provided some protection for workers who lost earnings through illness or unemployment.

the style of his fiction, Wells, too, was a traditional storyteller. And, though he is remembered today primarily for his science fiction, he wrote in a vein of social comedy with at least as much frequency, and with even greater success in his own lifetime. *Love and Mr. Lewisham* (1900), *Kipps: The Story of a Simple Soul* (1905), and *The History of Mr. Polly* (1910) are comic novels that draw on Wells's own struggles in painting an entertaining but strongly critical picture of the English social class system.

Like many writers of the time—playwright Bernard Shaw perhaps most prominent among them—Wells became a committed socialist in the early years of the twentieth century. The chief vehicle of socialist response in Britain at the time was the Fabian Society, founded in 1884 to promote *evolutionary* socialism (thus disavowing violent class struggle). The Fabian Society, led by Shaw, Sidney Webb, and Beatrice Potter Webb, was instrumental in forming the Labour Representation Committee in 1900; that committee, with substantial input as well from the Trades Union Congress, transformed itself into a political party in 1906, and over the course of the next generation the Labour Party managed to displace the Liberal Party as the main political alternative to Britain's Conservative Party. *Mrs Warren's Profession* (1893) is among the earliest of a long series of plays that give dramatic life to Shaw's progressive views; among its most memorable successors are *Major Barbara* (1905) and *Pygmalion* (1913). Shaw continued to write for the stage well into the 1920s (and lived until 1950), but he too expressed a powerful sense of change more in the content of his work than in its form. And other writers of the Edwardian era— including novelists and dramatists of thoroughly modern views such

Workers share a paper to read the news during the General Strike of 1926. The condition of the working class had improved somewhat by the 1920s, but in some sectors—notably coal mining—efforts were being made to roll back improvements in wages and working conditions. The 1926 General Strike in support of the coal miners lasted nine days.

as Sarah Grand, Ella Hepworth Dixon, and Cicely Hamilton (all of whom expressed their strong feminist views through their work), for the most part structured their texts in traditional ways.

The World Wars

As Lord Earl Grey, the British Foreign Secretary, watched the streetlights being lit from his office window one evening just before the outbreak of war in August 1914, he is famously reported to have remarked to a friend, "The lamps are going out all over Europe; we shall not see them lit again in our lifetime." At the time, such thinking went against the grain; at the outset of the "Great War," many in England firmly expected their soldiers to be home before Christmas. But over the next 30 years many came to believe that the moment at which World War I broke out had heralded nothing less than the collapse of civilization as it had long been known. At the outset of World War II in 1940, George Orwell adopted this vein of apocalyptic pessimism in his long essay "Inside the Whale":

> The war of 1914–1918 was only a heightened moment in an almost continuous crisis. At this date it hardly needs a war to bring home to us the disintegration of our society and the increasingly helplessness of all decent people....While I have been writing this book another European war has broken out. It will either last several years and tear western civilization to pieces, or it will end inconclusively and prepare the way for yet another war that will do the job once and for all.

Western civilization has proved to be rather more resilient than Orwell had feared, but his view of the period beginning in 1914 as "an almost continuous crisis" is now widely shared by historians; increasingly the two world

The Western Front in World War I, 1915.

wars of the twentieth century are being seen as part of a continuum. From more than one angle this makes sense. In both wars, Britain and her Empire/Commonwealth allies, joined belatedly by the United States, were fighting against a militaristic and expansionist Germany. In both wars, much of the rest of the world was drawn into the conflict, though there was no parallel in World War I to the crucial importance of the Pacific theater and the struggle between the Allies and Japan in World War II.

The two wars are also linked through a chain of causation. Though all authorities agree that both wars had multiple causes, it is also universally agreed that one vitally important cause of World War II was the decision by the Allies after World War I to demand reparations—a decision that had the effect of crippling Germany economically in the short term and that had the even more pernicious longer-term effect of so embittering the German people as to make a majority highly receptive to Hitler's appeals to nationalism, expansionism, anti-Semitism, and hate. The British economist John Maynard Keynes had been among those prescient enough to foresee the problem early on. In his chapter on "Europe after the Treaty" in *The Economic Consequences of the Peace* (1919), he summarized the matter with blunt eloquence:

> This chapter must be one of pessimism. The treaty includes no provisions for the economic rehabilitation of Europe—nothing to make the defeated ... into good neighbours, nothing to stabilise the new states of Europe; ... Nor does it promote in any way a compact of economic solidarity amongst the Allies themselves.... It is an extraordinary fact that the fundamental economic problem of a Europe starving and disintegrating before their eyes, was the one question in which it was impossible to arouse the interest of the Four [powers that imposed the peace treaty].

Hitler's eventual rise to power, then, was partly fueled by the hardships imposed on the Germans by the Allies at the conclusion of World War I.

If there are similarities and connections between the two world wars, there are also important differences. There are differences in the way the wars were fought, to start with—the trench warfare, stagnation, and machine gun carnage of World War I contrasts with the tanks, submarines, airplanes, and bombs of World War II. There is usually also agreed to be a substantial difference in the moral context in which the two wars were fought. Many have suggested that ethically there was little to differentiate the two sides in World War I—that the essential nature of the conflict was simply a power struggle between Britain and Germany as co-aggressors. And it has often (and rightly) been suggested that the tangle of Old World alliances that existed prior to World War I did much to facilitate the sort of stumbling into war that occurred in the wake of the assassination of Archduke Franz Ferdinand of Austria on 28 June 1914. In fact there probably was to some degree a legitimate moral case to be made on the side of Britain at the outset of World War I—much as the jingoism of the time on all sides may now strike us as repulsive. There is no question, though, that the moral imperative that lay behind the Allies' decision to go to war with Germany in 1939 was far stronger than it was at any time during World War I. Nazi atrocities against the Jews had in 1939 not yet reached their full extent, but already Hitler had shown that he was a dictator willing to persecute minorities ruthlessly and to invade neighboring countries on the flimsiest of pretexts. World War II, then, was driven far more persuasively than was the first by a moral imperative, and there was thus much less of a disconnect than there had been in World War I between idealistic calls for sacrifice and the reality as it was sensed by the ordinary soldier; few looked at Nazi Germany in the autumn of 1939 with the detached tone

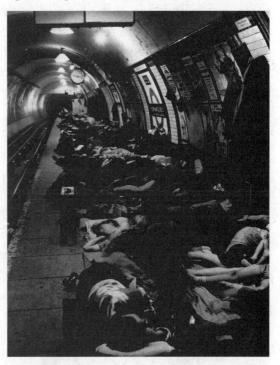

Londoners sleeping in the Elephant and Castle underground station during the bombing raids of 1940. These raids, popularly referred to as "the Blitz," were intended by the Nazis to "soften up" the English in preparation for a German invasion. Though much of London (and of other cities) was destroyed, the efforts of the British Air Force against superior numbers in what came to be known as the "Battle of Britain" were highly successful, and Hitler eventually decided against attempting an invasion of the British Isles; only the two Channel Islands fell to the Nazi forces. The Battle of Britain during the Blitz subsequently became a defining event in the British national consciousness.

that the poet W.H. Auden famously adopted in "September 1, 1939" in seeking to explain the phenomenon of Hitler, the "psychopathic god": "Those to whom evil is done / Do evil in return." To most it seemed clear that both in the case of Hitler as an individual and in the case of the people of Nazi Germany as a whole, the evil that was being done was far disproportionate to whatever evil had been committed against them. (Even today, many who admire Auden's poem as an affirmation of the humane in the face of the more basely human and in the face of war as a general proposition find the feelings the poem expresses odd or inappropriate in the moral context of World War II.)

A crucial difference between the experience of World War I and II was that in World War II the horrors of war had less shock value. Paul Fussell, whose *The Great War and Modern Memory* (1975) is a landmark study of the connections between wartime experience and literature, was a soldier himself in World War II; by the time of World War II, as he put it, "we didn't need to be told by people like Remarqué [author of *All Quiet on the Western Front* (1928)] and Siegfried Sassoon how nasty war was. We knew that already, and we just had to pursue it in a sort of controlled despair. It didn't have the ironic shock value of the Great War." It should perhaps not surprise us, then, that the body of serious literature that arose *directly* from the experience of World War II turned out to be slighter than the body of such literature that emerged during and after World War I. Certainly works such as Robert Graves's *Goodbye to All That* (1929), Siegfried Sassoon's *Memoirs of an Infantry Officer* (1930), David Jones's *In*

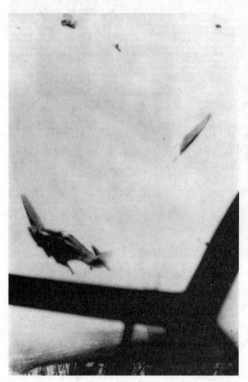

This image of the 1940 Battle of Britain was taken from the cockpit of a German fighter plane. It shows a British Hurricane fighter with its left wing torn off; the wing is visible in the top right of the photo, and the pilot, parachuting to safety, is seen in the top left.

Parenthesis (1937), and the poetry of Wilfred Owen, Isaac Rosenberg, and others all seem to have secured a place in the canon of British literature, whereas few if any works emerging directly out of the combat experience of World War II have staked such a claim. Indeed, Auden's "September 1, 1939" and Virginia Woolf's *Between the Acts* (1941) are among the few works still widely read from that time on themes that relate to the experience of the war even tangentially.[1]

Two aspects of the 1939–45 conflict have come to be seen as defining elements of twentieth-century experience. The first of these was the planned extermination of an entire people—the event that resulted in the murder of approximately six million Jews (as well as significant numbers of other groups deemed "undesirables" by the Nazis, notably homosexuals and Roma, or Gypsies), and that has come to be known as "The Holocaust." The second is the use of the atomic bomb against Japan by the United States in 1945—and the consequent dawning among the world's population of an awareness that humans now had the capacity to destroy the entire human race. From those most horrific aspects of World War II has emerged a literature that will surely be lasting (including the works of Primo Levi, the diaries of Anne Frank, John Hersey's *Hiroshima*)—but few if any of its most important works are by British writers.

As in World War I, however, there was a rich body of literary work produced in Britain during World War II that was not directly *about* the war.

THIS IS A WARTIME BOOK

THIS POCKET BOOK INCLUDES EVERY WORD CONTAINED IN THE ORIGINAL, HIGHER-PRICED EDITION. IT IS PRINTED FROM BRAND-NEW PLATES MADE FROM COMPLETELY RESET, LARGE, CLEAR, EASY-TO-READ TYPE, AND IS PRODUCED IN FULL COMPLIANCE WITH THE GOVERNMENT'S REGULATIONS FOR CONSERVING PAPER AND OTHER ESSENTIAL MATERIALS.

F-I

Printed in Canada

Notice from copyright page of a 1945 printing of the paperback edition of Mazo de la Roche's Jalna, *one volume of the family saga that has remained extraordinarily popular from its publication in 1927.*

---

1   Perhaps another major difference among the works of World Wars I and II is that the famous texts of World War I were written by combat veterans, who recorded their experiences, whether in memoirs or autobiographical novels, while literary works about World War II tend to offer the impressions of civilians.

Brighton Rock *(1938), Graham Greene's "entertainment" about the lives of young British gangsters, was first issued in a Penguin paperback in 1943. The price of 2 shillings is equivalent to a little over £3 in 2006 UK currency.*

Works of this sort in the years 1914–18 include T.S. Eliot's *Prufrock and Other Observations* (1917) and James Joyce's *Portrait of an Artist as a Young Man* (1916).[1] In the years 1939–45, the list of such works is both long and remarkably diverse. It includes the exuberant verse of Dylan Thomas's *The Map of Love* (1939); Eliot's *Four Quartets* (1935-43), which he regarded as his finest work; many of Auden's finest lyrics, including "Lay Your Sleeping Head, My Love," "Musée des Beaux Arts," and "Song (As I Walked Out One Evening)" (all first published in 1940); the bubbling hilarity of Noel Coward's play about the afterlife, *Blithe Spirit* (1942); the memorably self-deprecating and socially observant light comedy of Monica Dickens's memoir *One Pair of Hands* (1939); now-classic memoirs by Vera Brittain (*Testament of Friendship*, 1940) and Flora Thompson (*Lark Rise to Candleford*, 1940); Joyce Cary's novel of the memorable artist and outsider Gulley Jimson, *The Horse's Mouth* (1944); Graham Greene's tragic novel of a disillusioned "whisky priest" in revolutionary Mexico, *The Power and the Glory* (1940); and two very different but equally devastating fictional treatments of the horrors of totalitarian communism, Arthur Koestler's grim novel of the suffering endured by a "deviationist," *Darkness at Noon* (1940), and Orwell's fable of a collectivist society that comes to be based on the principle that "all animals are equal, but some are more equal than others," *Animal Farm* (1945). In writing the following comments in 1940 about the literature of World War I, Orwell clearly also had World War II in mind:

> In 1917 there was nothing a thinking and sensitive person could do, except remain human, if possible.... By simply staying aloof and keeping in touch

---

1   See below under "Modernism" for a discussion of these authors.

with pre-war emotions, Eliot [in publishing *Prufrock* in 1917] was carrying on the human heritage…. So different from bayonet drill! After the bombs and the food queues and the recruiting posters, a human voice! What a relief!

Marx, Einstein, Freud, and Modernism

Several towering figures in the intellectual and cultural life of the twentieth century played a key part in shaping the world view according to which human life was subject to forces over which, individually, humans could have little control, and of which they would often be entirely unaware. The first of these figures—Karl Marx—died 17 years before the end of the nineteenth century. But his vision of economic forces and class struggles saturated with historical inevitability continued to shape political and social attitudes (as well as a good many literary ones) throughout the twentieth century. An intellectual underpinning derived from Marx is, to a large extent, what differentiates the attitudes of social realist writers such as Shaw, Wells, and George Gissing from those of predecessors such as Charles Dickens and Elizabeth Gaskell. Much as Dickens and Gaskell had deplored the conditions of inequality that beset Victorian Britain, they believed that the actions and the goodwill of individual human beings could ameliorate social problems. The approach of 1890s and early twentieth-century socially progressive writers, in contrast, derived largely from the Marxist view that individuals are typically caught in a web of large social and economic forces over which they have no control; that class oppression is a systemic matter; and that mass struggle and political action (rather than appeals to the higher natures of the ruling classes) are the appropriate means of bringing about a better world. Thus for Shaw, for example, the "fundamental condition of the existence" of prostitution was that "a large class of women are more highly paid and better treated as prostitutes than they would be as respectable women." The activist writer and publisher Nancy Cunard was equally alert to the interactions of class, gender, money—and race. Author of some of a number of important essays on colonialism (and publisher of such key modernist works as Samuel Beckett's *Whoroscope* [1938] and Pound's *Cantos* [1922–62]), Cunard spoke of the British Empire in unvarnished terms of class and race as few had before: when writing in *Negro* (1934), an anthology of African literature and art she edited, about the system of British rule in Jamaica, for example, she understood it clearly as having been purposefully structured as "white at the top, mulatto in the centre and black at the bottom of the economic and social scale" so as to rule by dividing "the peoples of African and semi-African descent."[1]

If the socially progressive literature of the early twentieth century had intellectual underpinnings derived largely from Marx, the intellectual underpinnings of twentieth-century modernist literature are intimately connected with the ideas of physicist Albert Einstein, of philosophers of language such as Bertrand Russell, and of the psychoanalyst Sigmund Freud. Einstein's paper, "The Electrodynamics of Moving Bodies" (1905), later to become known as his Special Theory of Relativity, posited that both time and motion are not absolute but rather relative to the observer. In the same year he completed his thesis on "A New Determination of Molecular Dimension" (1905), a major step forward in the development of quantum theory in which he postulated (among other things) that light was both waves and tiny particles of light quanta, or photons. Much as they may have been imperfectly understood, the broad outlines of Einstein's theories became widely disseminated in subsequent years and clearly contributed to a growing sense of a world that was being discovered to be in a far less stable form than it had been thought.

New language-based trends in analytic philosophy were also undermining certainties. The ideas developed by Gottleib Frege, Bertrand Russell, and Ludwig Wittgenstein in the late nineteenth and early twentieth centuries had the effect of destabilizing what had been thought of as largely fixed relationships between words and meanings. The focus of these philosophers was on analyzing the content of what we mean when we make statements, whether they be statements referring to objects in the "real" world or statements involving claims of a more abstract sort. They endeavored to design symbolic systems that could convey meaning more reliably than words, for their work suggested that relationships between a word and a presumed referent were exceedingly complex and inherently unstable; Wittgenstein's work, in particular, suggested

---

1   Cunard was greatly assisted in these endeavors by George Padmore (1902–59), a Trinidadian-born writer and activist who later lived in the United States and in Britain and who played an important role in various progressive causes in the 1930s. A strong panAfricanist, Padmore eventually became personal advisor to Kwame Nkrumah, Ghana's first President.

that it was in the nature of language for words to float largely free of fixed referents in any world of "objective truth." Indeed, Wittgenstein suggested in his groundbreaking 1921 work *Tractatus Logico-Philosophicus* that "Language disguises thought. So much so, that from the outward form of the clothing it is impossible to infer the form of the thought beneath it, because the outward form of the clothing is not designed to reveal the form of the body, but for entirely different purposes."

The perceived unreliability and instability of language and of meaning affected the realm of ethics as much as it did those of metaphysics and epistemology, and, from about 1910 onwards, moral relativism was a subject of lively debate. (G.E. Moore's *Ethics*, an influential attempt to hold such relativism at bay, was published in 1912; T.S. Eliot read a paper on "The Relativity of the Moral Judgement" in the Cambridge rooms of his friend Bertrand Russell in 1915.) Russell became famous as a result of his pacifism (for which he was jailed in 1918), his efforts to undermine the authority of Christianity over Western society, and his challenge to societal constrictions on sexual behavior. But the changes that he helped to bring about to the foundations of analytic philosophy[1] may have been even more revolutionary—and more influential in the literary realm—than his shocking views on social issues.

Just as important as the work of Marx, Einstein, or the philosophers of language to the intellectual shape of the twentieth century was that of several explorers of the human psyche. Of these, pride of place is traditionally accorded to Sigmund Freud, an Austrian psychiatrist who advanced groundbreaking notions of the importance and complexity of sexuality in the human psyche, and of the significance of the unconscious in human thought and behavior. Both notions had an enormous effect on twentieth-century intellectual life in general and on imaginative literature in particular, as writers sought ways to represent sexuality as a much more central element of human experience than

---

[1]   The major tenets of analytic philosophy, as espoused by Russell, include the positivist view that there are no specifically philosophical truths (in contrast to foundationalism, which claims for philosophy a special status as a system of thought); an insistence on the logical clarification of thought; and a rejection of grand systems of thought in favor of detailed attention to common sense and everyday language.

had been the habit of the Victorians and sought ways in which to represent the richness of the human unconscious.[1]

Another key pioneer in the study of the human mind was the American William James (brother of novelist Henry James). Among James's most important contributions was his conceptualization of the fluidity of consciousness. James entitled a chapter in his *Principles of Psychology* (1892) "The Stream of Consciousness," beginning by observing that "within each personal consciousness states are always changing" and that "each personal consciousness is sensibly continuous." The connections between the ideas of James and twentieth-century literary developments are not difficult to discern. Most obviously, the "stream of consciousness" technique of prose fiction that features so prominently in core modernist texts such as Dorothy Richardson's *Pilgrimage* (1915–67), Virginia Woolf's *Mrs. Dalloway* (1925), and James Joyce's *Ulysses* (1922) represents a new form of realism that is psychological rather than social in character. These writers aim at an increased awareness of the ways in which the mind associates freely, in which "irrelevant" thoughts may connect with repressed impulses or emotions that are central to the psyche, and in which unpredictable but meaningful details are constantly jostling together with the quotidian.

A similar apparent disconnectedness is also an obvious feature of modernist poetry—most obviously in the disjunctions that characterize many of the poems of Ezra Pound and T.S. Eliot. To be sure, many have argued persuasively that a unity both of thought and of feeling emerges from the extended allusive density of poems such as *The Waste Land* (1922). But it is abundantly clear that any such unity is very different in character from the unity that emerges, say, from a defining long poem of the Victorian period such as Tennyson's *In Memoriam* (1849), just as whatever unity emerges from Joyce's *Ulysses* (serialized

---

1   Though Freud's important work began in the 1890s, he began to become well known in the English-speaking world only after 1910, with the publication of a series of lectures he had given at Clark University in the United States on *The Origin and Development of Psychoanalysis*. Of his most important works, *The Interpretation of Dreams* (1900) was translated in 1913, *The Psychopathology of Everyday Life* (1901) in 1914; soon after his work came to the attention of the Bloomsbury Group in England, and both Leonard Woolf and Lytton Strachey wrote reviews of or commentaries on Freud's work. (In the 1920s, the Woolfs' Hogarth Press became for a time the leading publisher of English translations of Freud's work.)

1918–20 and published as a single volume in 1922) is very different in character from that of the classic realism of Victorian novels such as George Eliot's *Middlemarch* (serialized 1871–72 and published as a single volume in 1874) or Anthony Trollope's *The Way We Live Now* (1875).

Less frequently discussed is the modernity of Eliot's later poetry—most notably, *Four Quartets*, an extended poetic expression of the search for meaning and truth in a context of instability. As much as the poem is infused with the Anglo-Catholicism to which Eliot had converted in 1927, it is also deeply colored by the sorts of destabilizing awareness that were so central to the habits of thought that came to the fore in the first half of the twentieth century. The poet continually struggles to conceptualize the movements of time, but finds that

> Words strain,
> Crack, and sometimes break, under the burden,
> Under the tension, slip, slide, perish,
> Decay with imprecision, will not stay in place,
> Will not stay still.

Samuel Beckett, one of the first to appreciate that most disconnected of all Joyce's works, *Finnegan's Wake* (1939), became the last great figure of modernist literature. It was Beckett, above all, who pioneered the expression in action of the psychological insights of Modernism and the despair that so often accompanied them. It is perhaps the case that "action" should here be put in quotation marks, however, for Beckett's plays—perhaps most notably *Waiting for Godot* (1952), *Krapp's Last Tape* (1958), and *Endgame* (1957)—are informed by an unprecedented awareness of the degree to which a *lack* of action may be as expressive as action, just as silences may be as expressive as words. Beckett extended the modernist project in his prose fiction as well as in his plays—and in French as well as in English through to the 1970s; it is perhaps due more to his influence than that of any of the other great figures of Modernism that ripples from the modernist tradition have continued to radiate in British literature even into the twenty-first century.

A common tendency is to assume that what is aesthetically revolutionary will substantially overlap with what is politically revolutionary (or at least with what is progressive). In fact there is no necessary connection between the two—and, indeed, a striking feature of twentieth-century Modernism is that many of its key figures were politically conservative or even reaction-ary.[1] During his lifetime, T.S. Eliot was probably almost as influential for his political, religious, and cultural conservatism as he was for his revolutionary aesthetic. Writer and artist Wyndham Lewis, whose concept of Vorticism[2] was for a time central to the intellectual currents of Modernism, embraced political views that could fairly be characterized as reactionary rather than conservative. Ezra Pound, for his part, who was even more revolutionary than Eliot in his modernist aesthetic, ended even further to the right politi-cally—notoriously lending his support to the fascist cause, and calling for the extermination of Jews during World War II.[3] Eliot and Pound were also far from progressive in their attitudes on gender and sex; many have sug-gested that a dark sense of sexuality is a fundamental aspect of Eliot's world view—and almost as many have suggested that a disturbing element of mi-sogyny lurks not far below the surface of much of his writing, his early writ-ing in particular.

Leading modernist women writers, by contrast, more often combined the freedom of modernist forms with progressive, unconventional, or even revolu-tionary political and social views. The futurist poet Mina Loy, for example, was a strong feminist and decidedly left of center politically; Nancy Cunard was a pioneer of left-of-center class analysis as well as of modernist publishing; and Virginia Woolf, though she rarely shared the unqualified sense of political con-viction that came to motivate her husband Leonard (who ran for Parliament as a Labour Party candidate in 1920), was herself not only a powerful voice for feminism but also a Labour Party member and a supporter of a variety of socialist and progressive causes. It was Woolf who famously assigned a specific

1   The roots of this conservatism are in part in various nineteenth-century political and ideological developments—especially a strain of ultra-conservatism in France that devel-oped in the second half of the century and that connects both with Pound and the Sym-bolists and with twentieth-century fascism. A number of scholars have also remarked on the impulse toward totality that marks much of the modernist project and fascist ideology.

2   The short lived but highly influential movement was named by Ezra Pound for its empha-sis on dynamic movement, drawing the viewer's eye to a painting's center.

3   Pound was indicted for treason by the American government in 1943. He was found incompetent to stand trial and spent 12 years in St. Elizabeth's Hospital in Washington, DC.

point in time to the great change that Modernism represented: "on or about December 1910," she commented in her 1924 essay "Character in Fiction," "human character changed." She was, of course, exaggerating for effect; few in her era were more acutely aware of how erratically change may occur, and of the ways in which the characteristics of one era may extend into the next. In that connection, it is worth reminding ourselves that, much as the Modernism of Eliot, Joyce, and Woolf has come to take on the character of the defining spirit of British literature in the 1910s and 1920s, its centrality was far from obvious at the time. For every admirer of the Cubist paintings of Picasso and Braque, there were many who reacted with contempt or ridicule. For every gallery-goer who was stirred by the modernist sculptures of Jacob Epstein (such as the young colonial P.K. Page, as recounted in her poem "Ecce Homo" [1946]), there were many chuckling over the way in which such sculpture was lampooned in the pages of the satirical magazine *Punch*. And for every dedicated reader of *The Waste Land* or *To the Lighthouse* (1927), there were dozens of readers of the ballads of Robert Service, and of the traditionally structured novels of Arnold Bennett and John Galsworthy. Not until 1948 and 1969 respectively were T.S. Eliot and Samuel Beckett awarded the Nobel Prize for Literature; the only British writers to receive the award before 1940 were Rudyard Kipling (1907), W.B. Yeats (1923), Bernard Shaw (1925), and Galsworthy (1932).

Illustration by Ernest H. Shepard from the chapter "The Further Adventures of Toad" in Kenneth Grahame's The Wind in the Willows *(1908). The early decades of the twentieth century are remembered for the dawn of Modernism, but they were also something of a golden age for children's literature; in addition to Grahame's work, Sir J.M. Barrie's* Peter Pan *(1906), Lucy Maud Montgomery's* Anne of Green Gables *(1908), and A.A. Milne's* Winnie the Pooh *(1926) and* The House at Pooh Corner *(1928) all remain popular classics.*

The Place of Women

As well as being a central figure of Modernism in the British literary tradition, Woolf is central to what is arguably the most important historical development of the twentieth century, the attempt to free women from the dense network of social, economic, and legal restrictions that had always ensured male dominance and control. If *To the Lighthouse* and *Mrs. Dalloway* (1925), with their psychological realism, are key documents of Modernism, *A Room of One's Own* (1929) is a key document of the struggle by women in the twentieth century for full equality. Woolf's call for change, as well as her evocation of personal experience in a male-dominated social and literary milieu, continues to resonate with readers in the present century.

Illustration accompanying the article "Presentation Day at London University," by "A Lady Graduate" in The Girl's Own Paper, *July 1898. The University of London had begun to admit women as full degree students at the undergraduate level in 1878, but it was not until the 1920s that Oxford and Cambridge followed suit, even at the undergraduate level.*

As the twentieth century opened, women were still second-class citizens in almost every respect—unable to vote, subject to a variety of employment limitations, restricted for the most part from higher education, and restricted too in myriad intangible ways by social nuance and convention. Oppression in the workplace in the context of the Industrial Revolution has long been widely acknowledged; at least as pervasive in the late nineteenth and early twentieth centuries was the exploitation of retail workers, as the Report of the Royal Commission on Labour detailed:

The maximum salary in addition to board and lodging ever paid to women in the shop working 70 3/4 hours was stated at 35 to 40 shillings

The arrest of Emmeline Pankhurst during a suffragette demonstration near Buckingham Palace, 1914.

Sylvia Pankhurst (daughter of suffragette leader Emmeline Pankhurst) painting the slogan "Votes for Women" on the front of the Women's Social Defence League offices in London, 1912.

[equivalent to roughly £200 in 2006]; in the other shops 30 shillings was stated as the maximum salary ever given. The girls declared that they had nothing to complain of, except the long hours of work and the short time allowed for meals, which had seriously affected their health. No one closed earlier than 11:00 p.m. on Saturdays, 9:30 on Fridays, and 9:00 on Mondays, Tuesdays, and Wednesdays, beginning in each case at 8:30 a.m.

Women's contingent to the 1930 "Hunger March,"
a demonstration in London's Hyde Park.

For decades, those in the suffrage movement and other women's groups struggled to bring change. In 1903, Emmeline Pankhurst, together with others frustrated with the pace of change and with the "ladylike" tone of the protests by other women's groups, formed The Women's Social and Political Union, taking as their motto "Deeds Not Words." As Pankhurst recalled in 1914,

From the very first, in those early London days, when ... we were few in numbers and very poor in purse, we made the public aware of the woman suffrage movement as it had never been before. We adopted Salvation Army methods and went out into the highways and byways after converts.

Real change finally began to take effect just before the end of the war in 1918, with the Representation of the People Act granting the vote to all men over the age of 21 and to women over the age of 30 who also met one or more of several restrictive criteria regarding marital status and property.[1] The London *Times* provided a (doubtless oversimplified) summary of the effect of the war on the suffrage movement in an article on the occasion of the 1930 commemoration by Prime Minister Stanley Baldwin of a statue of Pankhurst:

> The World War came. In the twinkling of an eye ... the militant suffragettes laid aside their banners. They put on their overalls and went into the factory and into the field; they were nursing, they made munitions, and they endured sacrifices with the men, and the effective opposition to the movement melted in the furnace of the War.

The success of the suffrage movement and the change in the role women played in the workplace were the most dramatic gender-related changes during this period, but there were many other important developments; the era was also characterized by changing notions regarding gender and education, contraception and reproductive technology, and the nature of masculinity.

Avant-Garde and Mass Culture

The concept of the avant-garde, of a tiny minority far in advance of the popular taste in culture (or of the majority view politically) came into its own in the twentieth century. No doubt it may have resonated with particular force simply because of the degree to which cultural activity was being extended to "the masses"; with primary education having been made compulsory in Britain through the Education Act of 1870, the twentieth century was the first in which the vast majority of British people were fully literate. The expansion of libraries had helped to spread the habit of reading through the nineteenth century, and with the publishing industry's shift in the 1890s away from "triple-deckers" intended for purchase by libraries and toward one-volume novels of modest length aimed at individual buyers, the habit of book-buying began to spread at a comparable rate. In the early years of the century, publishers introduced series of relatively affordable hardcover editions of literary

---

1   Not until 1928 were all such restrictions lifted and all women over 21 granted the franchise.

classics, aimed at a broad popular market (chief among them the Everyman's Library series from Dent and the World's Classics series from Oxford University Press).

An even more revolutionary step came in 1936, with the introduction of Penguin Books' series of affordable paperback editions. "The Penguin books are splendid value for sixpence," wrote George Orwell in reviewing Penguin's third batch of ten titles, "so splendid that if the other publishers had any sense they could combine against them and suppress them. [If instead] the other publishers follow suit, the result may be a flood of cheap reprints which will cripple the lending libraries ... and check the output of new novels." Within a few years, the paperback novel had indeed become ubiquitous in British society, but with none of the disastrous effects Orwell had feared; the size of the market for books had been expanded sufficiently by the arrival of the paperback to more than compensate authors and publishers for the lower revenue per copy sold.

Along with the spread of a mass literary culture—and the spread as well of the cinema and of radio—came huge social and cultural changes. If Modernism was a cultural movement concentrated in a small elite, modernity swept through every corner of society in the 1920s and 1930s. The social and cultural attitudes of the late-Victorian age may have persisted through to the end of the

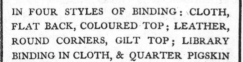

THE PUBLISHERS OF *EVERYMAN'S LIBRARY* WILL BE PLEASED TO SEND FREELY TO ALL APPLICANTS A LIST OF THE PUBLISHED AND PROJECTED VOLUMES TO BE COMPRISED UNDER THE FOLLOWING THIRTEEN HEADINGS:

TRAVEL ❧ SCIENCE ❧ FICTION
THEOLOGY & PHILOSOPHY
HISTORY ❧ CLASSICAL
FOR YOUNG PEOPLE
ESSAYS ❧ ORATORY
POETRY & DRAMA
BIOGRAPHY
REFERENCE
ROMANCE

IN FOUR STYLES OF BINDING: CLOTH, FLAT BACK, COLOURED TOP; LEATHER, ROUND CORNERS, GILT TOP; LIBRARY BINDING IN CLOTH, & QUARTER PIGSKIN

LONDON: J. M. DENT & SONS, LTD.
NEW YORK: E. P. DUTTON & CO.

Preliminary advertising page from Captain Cook's Voyages of Discovery, one of the Everyman's Library volumes published in 1906, the year the series was founded. Eventually its list grew to include over 1,000 titles.

Edwardian era, but within ten years "Victorian" had become a synonym for "stuffy and old fashioned." The book that set the tone more than any other was Lytton Strachey's *Eminent Victorians* (1918), a series of biographical essays on four leading members of Victorian society (Henry Edward Cardinal Manning, Florence Nightingale, Matthew Arnold, and General Charles George Gordon). Strachey's work is often characterized as "satirical," but "irreverent" is perhaps a better adjective. He writes in a breezy, brilliant, style, but he is interested in the depths of human emotion as well as the surfaces. He pokes fun at his subjects, to be sure, but he is more interested in exploring the workings of what he sees as pretension, hypocrisy, ambition, and self-deception than he is in ridiculing them. Here is how Strachey begins his essay on Florence Nightingale:

> Everyone knows the popular conception of Florence Nightingale. The saintly, self-sacrificing woman, the delicate maiden of high degree who threw aside the pleasures of a life of ease to succour the afflicted, the Lady with the Lamp, gliding through the horrors of the hospital at Scutari, and consecrating with the radiance of her goodness the dying soldier's couch—the vision is familiar to all. But the truth was different. The Miss Nightingale of fact was not as facile fancy painted her. She worked in another fashion, and towards another end; she moved under the stress of an impetus which finds no place in the popular imagination. A Demon possessed her. Now demons, whatever else they may be, are full of interest. And so it happens that in the real Miss Nightingale there was more that was interesting than in the legendary one; there was also less that was agreeable.

The deft touch of Strachey's satire became simplified and coarsened in the ridicule popularly directed at Victorian styles—and, in particular, at Victorian attitudes toward sexuality—as

The British film industry was competitive with that of the United States in the 1920s and early 1930s. In this 1920s photograph a scene from the (now lost) film The Thrill *is being shot on a beach near Brighton.*

World War I and the years that followed brought huge changes in women's fashion, with shorter skirts and dresses and more freedom of movement. This photograph, from the 1920s, shows two London models.

an emerging mass society sought to define itself against the backdrop of supposed Victorian narrowness and prudery. The reaction may have been overdone, and certainly the characterization of the Victorians was simplistic, but there could be no doubt that the short skirts, jazz music, and sexual attitudes of the 1920s and 1930s were as far removed from those of only 15 or 20 years before as those of 1905 or 1910 had been from the attitudes and styles of a full century earlier. Virginia Woolf's recollections of a Bloomsbury scene from the 1920s in which Woolf, her sister Vanessa Bell, and her husband Clive Bell are together in the drawing room at 46 Gordon Square give something of the flavor of the time:

Suddenly the door opened and the long and sinister figure of Mr. Lytton Strachey stood on the threshold. He pointed a finger at a stain on Vanessa's white dress.

"Semen?" he said.

Can one really say it? I thought and we burst out laughing. With that one word all barriers of reticence and reserve went down…. So there was now nothing that one could not say, nothing that one could not do, at 46 Gordon Square.

Indeed, few places in Britain in the 1920s and 1930s had left Victorian conventions of respectability so firmly behind as had 46 Gordon Square; few others had traveled so far in the same direction, or so fast, as had the "bohemians" of the Bloomsbury Group.

Indeed, the literary portrayal even of heterosexual love (let alone of homosexuality) remained largely off-limits through to the 1960s. A litmus test was

D.H. Lawrence's *Lady Chatterley's Lover*, which was published in 1928, but with certain passages, which were considered objectionable on account of their sexual content, removed. Not until 1960, after a high-profile court case, was the unexpurgated text of the novel (by today's standards still far from explicit in its portrayal of sexuality) finally published. Despite such strictures, however, change was occurring throughout society, and "Victorian" attitudes seemed to many to be part of the distant past.

Sexual Orientation

The number of leading writers in the first half of the twentieth century who acknowledged a same-sex sexual orientation, at least among their circle of friends, was probably greater than it had been in any previous era of British history—certainly greater than at any time since the early years of the seventeenth century. The list of writers and intellectuals who are now known to have been gay, lesbian, or bisexual includes not only W.H. Auden and Christopher Isherwood, but also A.E. Housman, Nancy Cunard, E.M. Forster, Radclyffe Hall, John Maynard Keynes, Lytton Strachey, Sylvia Townsend-Warner, and a number of others.

It should be emphasized here that sexual identities are far from being stable, trans-historical categories. Notions of and attitudes

Two women (above), outside a London bookshop, holding copies of the newly published paperback edition of Lady Chatterley's Lover *(1960), while a London commuter (right) chooses* Lady Chatterley's Lover *over* The Times.

toward same-sex orientation were in flux throughout the late nineteenth and early twentieth centuries. Until well into the second half of the twentieth century, however (interestingly, at about the time that the word *gay* began to be used to identify those with a same-sex sexual orientation), there was little or no tolerance of same-sex sexuality in most sectors of society. As Auden and his friend and sometime literary collaborator Isherwood tacitly recognized when they moved to the United States, Britain in the 1920s and 1930s was even less ready than was America to openly acknowledge the legitimacy of same-sex relationships. Famously, the novelist and playwright Oscar Wilde had been tried and imprisoned in 1895 for "acts of gross indecency," and homosexuality continued to be widely regarded (in a somewhat contradictory fashion) both as a sin and as a disease throughout the first half of the century. E.M. Forster's novel on the theme of homosexual love, *Maurice*, which was not published until after his death in 1971, but which he had completed in 1914, gives a strong sense of the reality. When Maurice, having realized that "he loved men and had always loved them," confesses to his doctor that he is "an unspeakable of the Oscar Wilde sort," he is met with disgust and denial:

> "Rubbish, rubbish!... Now listen to me, Maurice, never let that evil hallucination, that temptation from the devil, occur to you again."
>
> The voice impressed him; was not science speaking?
>
> "Who put that lie into your head? You whom I see and know to be a decent fellow! We'll never mention it again. No—I'll not discuss. I'll not discuss. The worst thing I could do for you is to discuss it."

Maurice eventually does accept his sexual identity, but not before a further consultation, this one with a Mr. Lasker-Jones, who claims a 50 per cent rate of "cure" by means of hypnotism for what he terms "congenital homosexuality."

If male homosexuality remained "unspeakable" through much of this period, female homosexuality remained for many unimaginable. In 1921, the British Parliament debated adding "acts of gross indecency between women" to the list of acts prohibited in the criminal statutes, but elected not to do so for fear of advertising homosexuality to "innocent" women. A few years later Hall's novel *The Well of Loneliness* (1928) was the occasion for the greatest literary storm of the era, over its alleged "obscenity." The novel recounts the story of a young woman named Stephen (whose parents had hoped for and expected a boy, and gone forward with the planned name regardless when the baby turned out to be a girl), and the romantic relationships she forms with other women. That the book could have been deemed obscene is astonishing to many readers today. In many ways the book is striking for the sense of normalcy it evokes as to the quotidian aspects of love:

> And now for the first time the old house was home. Mary went quickly from room to room humming a little tune as she did so, feeling that she saw with a new understanding the intimate objects that filled those rooms— were they not Stephen's? Every now and again she must pause to touch them because they were Stephen's.

Radclyffe Hall, c. 1920.

Even when the novel's prose becomes effusive over the physical and spiritual aspects of the union, the most specific suggestions of the expression of sexual love between two women are passages such as the following: "Stephen bent down and kissed Mary's hands very humbly, for now she could find no words any more … and that night they were not divided."

Such effusive attestations of the rapturous purity of unions at once physical and spiritual as one finds in *Maurice* and *The Well of Loneliness* may seem unexceptionable today, and even at the time many people were supportive; *The Well of Loneleiness* was published to a generally favorable reception in the press. In the view of *The Sunday Times*, Hall's novel was written "with distinction, with a lively sense of characterization, and with a feeling for the background of her subject which makes her work delightful reading. And, first and last, she has courage and honesty." *The Daily Herald* asserted that there was "nothing pornographic" in the book:

> The evil minded will seek in vain in these pages for any stimulant to sexual excitement. The lustful [figures] of popular fiction may continue their sadistic course unchecked in those pornographic novels which are sold by the million,

but Miss Radclyffe Hall has entirely ignored these crude and violent figures of sexual melodrama. She has given to English literature a profound and moving study of a profound and moving problem.

The Daily Express was the lone dissenter; a 19 August 1928 article headed "A Book That Must Be Suppressed" accused the novel of "devastating young souls" with its story of "sexual inversion and perversion." It seems probable that the *Express* represented popular feeling at the time more accurately than did the *Sunday Times* or the *Daily Herald*; soon after the *Express* article appeared, the Home Office advised the publishers to discontinue publication, and the police then charged the publishers under the 1857 Obscene Publications Act. Despite the support of dozens of high-profile authors and intellectuals, the magistrate Sir Charles Biron ruled against *The Well of Loneliness*:

> Unfortunately these women exist, and the book asks that their existence and vices should be recognised and tolerated, and not treated with condemnation, as they are at present by all decent people. This being the tenor of the book I have no hesitation in saying it is an … offence against public decency, and an obscene libel, and I shall order it to be destroyed.

The inevitable focus of history on landmark cases such as those of Oscar Wilde and *The Well of Loneliness* has to a considerable degree sensationalized and darkened our sense of late nineteenth- and early twentieth-century life outside the heterosexual mainstream. That it could be a dark and depressing existence there can be no doubt—the pessimism that Forster expressed even as late as 1960 ("police prosecutions will continue …") is surely understandable. But, as documents such as the letters exchanged between Strachey and Keynes attest, it could also be one of self-assured candor, zestful comedy, and a whole-hearted enjoyment of life. "Our time will come," declared Strachey, speaking confidently in an 8 April 1906 letter to Keynes of the situation of homosexuals in Britain, "about a hundred years hence." A hundred years later it is beginning to seem that Strachey's optimism may have been at least as well-founded as Forster's more pessimistic view.

Ireland

If a remarkable amount of memorable literature emerged in Britain from the years of turmoil between the two World Wars in the first half of the twentieth century, the same statement could be made of Ireland, as the Irish endured the state of turmoil that remained a constant throughout the first half of the century. The fiction of James Joyce and the plays of Samuel Beckett have already been mentioned as central to the evolution of modernist literature. The other important Irish literary work of the period includes J.M. Synge's vivid portrayals of the elemental life of the Aran Islanders on the coast of western Ireland in plays such as *Riders of the Sea* (1904) and *The Playboy of the Western World* (1907); the plays of Lady Augusta Gregory; the sweeping expressiveness of Sean O'Casey's great dramas *Juno and the Paycock* (1924) and *The Plough and the Stars* (1926); and the extraordinary range of the poetry of William Butler Yeats from the 1890s through the 1930s—lyrical, Romantic, Symbolist, mystical, political, Existential, and perhaps above all, passionate.

To this list should be added the plays of Bernard Shaw, who was born in Dublin and lived there for the first 20 years of his life. Shaw has often been called the most important dramatist in English after Shakespeare; he was a socially committed writer who understood, as he puts it in the "Preface" to his 1905 play *Major Barbara*, that "it is difficult to make people realise that an evil is an evil." Shaw *was* able to make people realize such things, not only through effective polemic but also (and more memorably) through the sparkling wit of his plays. Shaw's important work extends from brilliantly biting works of the 1890s and early 1900s such as *Mrs. Warren's Profession*, *Arms and the Man* (1894), and *Major Barbara* (on the topics of prostitution, militaristic attitudes, and religion and social reform, respectively); to *Pygmalion*, a satire of attitudes toward social class and its expression through language, on

Cover, Major Barbara: A Screen Version, *Penguin, 1945. This early "film tie-in" publication (number 500 in the Penguin series) was still in the standard early Penguin format; not until the 1960s did it become common for book publishers to employ a different cover design in such situations.*

which the 1950s musical *My Fair Lady* was based; to the epic historical drama *Saint Joan* (1923).

If the Irish Shaw is arguably the greatest "British" dramatist of the twentieth century, one of the greatest "British" writers of the 1890s, Oscar Wilde, had also been born and raised in Ireland before moving to London. Indeed, many have judged the literary outpouring from Irish writers during the period 1890–1960 to amount to a more important body of work than the entire literature of Britain over the same period—despite the fact that the combined population of England, Scotland, and Wales, at almost 50 million, was more than ten times that of Ireland.

But how are Britain and Ireland to be defined? Here matters become tangled, for during this period Ireland, for centuries a predominantly Catholic (and mostly unwilling) component of the United Kingdom, finally achieved the status of an independent republic. In the process, however, it became geographically split, with several largely Protestant counties of Northern Ireland remaining a political unit of the United Kingdom.

The Irish had been treated as second-class citizens throughout the centuries of English rule over Ireland. But the hardships they endured in the nineteenth century were particularly severe; the potato famine of 1845–51 alone is estimated to have killed almost a million Irish—almost 10 per cent of the population. By the 1880s and 1890s, political pressure in Ireland for radical change had become extremely powerful. And there was pressure for cultural change too; the Celtic Revival (also known as the Irish Literary revival), begun in 1896 by Irishmen and women such as Yeats and Lady Augusta Gregory, was remarkably successful both in increasing appreciation for the traditions of Irish culture and in encouraging the creation of new works in those traditions.

In the late nineteenth century, too, many in England became more sympathetic to Irish aspirations. In an effort to end the long history of oppression and resistance in British-controlled Ireland, Liberal governments twice introduced bills providing for one form or another of "Home Rule" (the term used to refer to limited Irish self-government) in the British House of Commons. The second of these was passed by the House of Commons but defeated in the Conservative-dominated House of Lords. In 1912, another Home Rule Bill was passed, and again the House of Lords rejected it. But now the rules had been changed; as a result of the previous year's Parliament Act, a veto by the House of Lords retained force for only three years. As the date in 1914 approached when the veto was due to expire and Home Rule would thus come into effect, tension rose to such a pitch that many felt civil war to be a real possibility. Substantial areas of the north of Ireland that had been forcibly settled by the English in earlier eras were now staunchly Protestant and vowed resistance to any government order to allow an Ireland dominated by "Papists" to become independent of Britain. And since Protestants from Ulster, in the north of Ireland, were heavily represented in the British army's contingent of troops stationed in Ireland, the military could not be relied on to carry out orders. With the onset of World War I, however, the implementation of the Home Rule Bill was postponed until after the war—and in a fateful move, Prime Minister Herbert Asquith promised that the British government would never force Ulster Protestants to accept Home Rule involuntarily.

Given the long history of vetoes and postponements—and given that the promised self-government in any case was to bring only a limited independence from Britain—it is unsurprising that Irish nationalists were impatient. On Easter Monday, 1916, rebels stormed public buildings in Dublin and proclaimed a republic. In the struggle, as Yeats famously wrote in "Easter, 1916," the Irish were "transformed utterly" and "a terrible beauty" was born. The uprising was brutally suppressed, but the nationalist Sinn Fein continued to wage a guerrilla opposition to British rule. Yet another Home Rule Bill was passed in 1920, providing for six counties of Ulster to be partitioned at independence, and the remainder of the island to remain a part of the British Empire but to be granted Dominion status (parallel to that of Canada, Australia, New Zealand, and South Africa) as the Irish Free State. That limited form of independence came

A young boy sings nationalist songs to a crowd outside Mountjoy Prison, Dublin, where an Irish Republican Army prisoner is about to be executed (1921).

into effect in 1922, but many Irish Republicans refused to accept any form of subservience to the British Crown, and the Irish Republican Army continued a clandestine struggle. In 1937, a new constitution changed the status of the country to that of a sovereign state within the British Commonwealth—a status sufficiently independent of Britain that Ireland was able to remain neutral in World War II—and in 1949 an Irish Republic was finally proclaimed, with the nation withdrawing from the Commonwealth. But the long struggle was still not fully over; tensions within Northern Ireland would continue to haunt Britain into the twenty-first century.

An understanding of the politics and religion of Ireland is essential background for an understanding of Irish history—and Irish literary history—during this period. But it gives little sense of the daily reality of Catholics and Protestants who lived largely in isolation from each other, Catholics overwhelmingly the majority in Ireland, Protestants forming the majority in Northern Ireland. The novelist Elizabeth Bowen, who was raised mainly in Dublin in an Irish Protestant family (she "was taught to say 'Church of Ireland,' not 'Protestant'") later described her experiences in *Seven Winters: Memories of a Dublin Childhood* (1943):

> It was not until the end of those seven winters that I understood that we Protestants were a minority, and that the unquestioned rules of our being came, in fact, from the closeness of a minority world.... I took the existence of Roman Catholics for granted but met few and was not interested in them. They were, simply, "the others," whose world lay alongside ours but never touched. As to the difference between the two religions, I was too discreet to ask questions—if I wanted to know. This appeared to share a delicate, awkward aura with those two other differences—of sex, of class. So quickly in a child's mind does prudery seed itself and make growth that I remember, even, an almost sexual shyness on the subject of Roman Catholics. I walked with hurried steps and averted cheek past porticos of churches that were "not ours," uncomfortably registering in my nostrils the pungent, unlikely smell [of incense] that came round curtains, through swinging doors.

Ideology and Economics in the 1930s and 1940s

How do ideologies differ from ideas? In part they are simply sets of ideas, but the question goes beyond that: an ideology is a systematic set of beliefs that is

shared widely, and that prescribes a program of political action in
with those beliefs. In the twentieth century, such ideologies as c
socialism, fascism, and liberalism all exerted enormous power. The central concepts of liberal democracy took shape in the nineteenth century, and by the
end of the twentieth century had spread to much of the world. But for much
of the twentieth century they were powerfully challenged by those of other
ideologies: socialism (and its relative, communism) and fascism.

Fascism is identified as an ideology of the far right and it has indeed often
co-existed with capitalist economic structures. But the strength of its appeal
is—like that of communism—collectivist in nature. As the official name of
the Nazi party in Germany (the National Socialist Party) suggests, fascism is
"socialist" in its appeal to the egalitarian instincts of the populace. But whereas
socialism and communism are (in theory at least) internationalist, appealing
to the fellow-feeling of humans *as humans*, fascism appeals strongly to nationalist feeling—to the instinct of the population to pull together *as a nation*.
More broadly, the egalitarian ideals of fascist societies are never inclusive; the
nation defines itself not only against other nations, but typically also against
a backdrop of a perceived "other" within its midst. Whether the "other" be
immigrants, those of a different skin color, those of a different religion, or a

group such as the Jews that is defined
by race, culture, and religion, the oth-
erness is typically used as a focal point
for defining the nation's identity, and
for lending intensity to the ideological allegiance of the fascist core.

If fascism weirdly approaches socialism from one direction, communism departs from socialist ideals in
another. Socialist ideals are above all
those of fairness and equality in a society in which government is prepared
to intervene consistently on behalf of
the greater good—to control capitalism, in socialism's weaker version (social democracy), or to replace it with

*Nazi authorities affix a poster to a shop as
part of their campaign of persecution, 1935.
The sign reads "Buy nothing from Jews!"*

a system of government ownership of the means of production on behalf of the entire population, in the full-fledged socialist model. Such ideals are built on foundations very similar to those of communist ideology, but the differences turn out in practice to be crucial. Perhaps the most important difference is that communist ideology—especially as it attained full force in the twentieth century—embodied the paradoxical notion that an elite could act as the "vanguard" for the masses, and that a "dictatorship of the proletariat" could reasonably act on behalf of all the people, without the people in practice having a direct say in who was to govern, or how. With the benefit of hindsight, it seems obvious that such an ideology was likely to result in almost as much oppression and cruelty as was the ideology of fascism. But in a Russia that had been laboring under the inequalities of a semi-feudal system, or indeed in Depression-era North America or Great Britain, when the engines of capitalism seemed to be merciless and unrestrained by government, to many communism seemed the only realistic path toward a society that would be both more free and more fair for all citizens.

The greatest ideological struggles of the first half of the century were unquestionably those that unfolded in Russia in 1917 and in Germany and Italy in the 1930s, but an ideologically charged climate was a worldwide reality. In some ways, the twentieth-century ideological tapestry may be seen in sharpest focus in the context of the Spanish Civil War (1936–39). Under the banner of those fighting for the Republican cause were liberals, socialists, communists, and anarchists—all ranged against the fascist forces of Generalissimo Francisco Franco. As George Orwell details in his account of the ideological and physical battles of the war, *Homage to Catalonia* (1938), the Spanish Civil War became a battleground not only between democracy and fascism, but also between the various factions on the Republican side, with idealism all too often being trumped by self-interest or by the dictates of outside governments lending support. In the end, the Communist government of the Soviet Union was as reluctant as were the capitalist governments of Britain or the United States to stand in the way of the anticipated "stable" government that the fascist General Franco represented.

The Spanish Civil War is often regarded as central to 1930s' intellectual currents, and certainly the degree to which intellectuals from Britain (and indeed, from throughout the Western world) rallied to the Republican side was remarkable. Sylvia Townsend Warner was among the leading British writers in Spain during the war; as she reported in a 1937 magazine article, the conflict was extraordinary not least of all for the bond that grew up between intellectuals and common citizens: "It is unusual for writers to hear words such as 'Here come the Intellectuals' spoken by working-class people and common soldiers in tones of kindliness and enthusiasm." Others spoke out not only against fascism but against all forms of militarism—and against war itself. Notably, Virginia Woolf's polemic *Three Guineas* (1938) inquired into the role that women could play in the prevention of war, concluding that war is not merely a public issue—that, rather, "the public and the private worlds are inseparably connected; that the tyrannies and servilities of the one are the tyrannies and servilities of the other."

Even before the Spanish Civil War became a focal point for literature and politics, literature in the 1930s had become more highly political than that of the 1920s. Writers such as Auden (in his early work), Christopher Isherwood, C. Day Lewis, Louis MacNeice, Stephen Spender, and Edward Upward were all, in the view of MacNeice in his *Modern Poetry* (1932), "unlike Yeats and Eliot ... emotionally partisan":

> Yeats [in the 1930s] proposed to turn his back on desire and hatred; Eliot sat back and watched other people's emotions with ennui and ironical self-pity.... The whole poetry, on the other hand, of Auden, Spender, and Day Lewis implies that they have desires and hatreds of their own and, further, that they think some things *ought* to be desired and others hated.

A young woman takes aim during target practice, Spain, 1936.

Like Orwell's 1984, *Aldous Huxley's* Brave New World *(1932) is a dystopia in which the State effectively controls the minds of its citizens, who are convinced that they are expressing human potential to its fullest.*

Many of these writers joined or were sympathetic to the Communist Party through much of the 1930s. In the later twentieth century, it would have been unimaginable for most of the important writers of a generation to be sympathetic to "the Party," as it came to be called, but, in the early 1930s, the brutality of Soviet communism under Stalin was not yet public knowledge—and the mainstream parties in Britain (Labour as well as the Conservatives) were dealing timorously and ineffectively with an economic downturn of unprecedented severity.

The Great Depression that began late in 1929 and lasted until the outbreak of war ten years later was a worldwide phenomenon—and one exacerbated in Britain (as in North America) by the determination of governments not to go into debt in order to provide support for the unemployed and otherwise impoverished, or to invest in getting the economy moving. Individuals, too, reacted with fear, and strove to increase their savings, thereby contributing to what British economist John Maynard Keynes termed "the paradox of thrift": when people saved rather than spending what little they had, they further reduced the demand for goods, which in turn led to further reductions in production, more unemployment, lower wages for those still working—and so the cycle continued. By the end of 1930, some 20 per cent of the British workforce was unemployed, and by the mid-1930s it was estimated that a quarter of the population had been reduced to a subsistence diet.

Keynes—an important figure in the Bloomsbury Group, and something of a cultural icon as well as one of the most important twentieth-century economists—broke new ground with his arguments for government intervention in the economy—recommending both that governments intervene to control inflation and that they act to "even out" the imbalances of the economic cycle by spending more during downturns. Conservatives argued that such imbalances would right themselves in the long run in any case, and should not be tampered with; Keynes's response was that "the long run is a misleading guide to current affairs. In the long run we are all dead." It was not until after World War II, though, that governments in Britain and elsewhere adopted Keynes's prescriptions for smoothing out the business cycle; although economic conditions improved somewhat in the south of Britain in the late 1930s, it was not until the war that economic growth resumed throughout the country.

A turn toward the political left is to be expected during any severe and prolonged economic downturn; given that the Great Depression was more severe and prolonged a downturn than any in the twentieth century, it is unsurprising that writers and intellectuals moved further to the left politically during the 1930s than at any other time during the century. But why did they embrace, in such large numbers, the relatively rigid doctrines of the Communist Party? As Orwell looked back in 1940, he took the view that the ideological coloring of the intellectual life of the 1930s had been as broadly connected to cultural as it had been to economic trends:

> By 1930 … the debunking of western civilization had reached its climax…. How many of the values by which our grandfathers lived could now be taken seriously? Patriotism, religion, the Empire, the family, the sanctity of marriage, the Old School Tie, birth, breeding, honour, discipline—anyone of ordinary education could turn the whole lot of them inside out in three minutes. But what do you achieve, after all, by getting rid of such primal things as patriotism and religion? You have not necessarily gotten rid of the need for something to believe in…. It is significant that [those intellectuals who did embrace religion in these years] went almost invariably to the Roman Church…. They went, that is, to the church with a world-wide organization, the one with a rigid discipline, the one with power and prestige behind it…. I do not think one need look farther than this for the reason the young writers of the thirties flocked into or towards the Communist Party. It was simply something to believe in. Here was a church, an army, an orthodoxy, a discipline.

With World War II, however, another form of discipline inevitably took hold; even though Britain and the United States became allies, the ties between the

British and American intellectual communities and the Soviet Communist Party steadily loosened. With the beginning of the "Cold War" between the West and the USSR immediately following the end of World War II (and a new sense of purpose in the Labour Party under Clement Attlee), the link between British intellectuals and the Communist Party had for the most part come to an end.

The Literature of the 1930s and 1940s

George Orwell may be seen as one of the writers who most fully expresses the ideological conflicts over socialism, communism, fascism, and liberal democracy that were at the heart of so much of twentieth-century life. His earlier works detail the appalling toll that capitalism was exacting on the working class. In *Down and Out in Paris and London* (1933), he recounts from personal experience the reality of the life of a vagrant, and of the life of the lowest of workers in the Paris hotel and restaurant industry. In *The Road to Wigan Pier* (1937), Orwell details the hardships of miners in the north of England, and of the working-class population throughout the country. Orwell was an avowed socialist; ironically enough, however, the two works for which he remains best known have often been portrayed as attacks on socialism; they are both novels in which he attacks the corruption of socialist ideals under Soviet-style communism. *Animal Farm* is a fable that shows the ways in which power may readily be seized by the most powerful and unprincipled in a "collectivist" system; *1984* (1949) is a futurist view of a society in which "Big Brother" controls people's minds as much as their actions.

Another writer of central importance to twentieth-century literature who was initially defined against a backdrop of ideology is the poet W.H. Auden. Auden first became famous as a political poet, particularly with his memorable call to arms against fascism in "Spain, 1937": "But today the struggle." Auden quickly became disenchanted with political polemic, however, not least of all his own. He became disillusioned with the Republican side in the Spanish Civil War after witnessing the persecution of Catholic priests by members of the Republican army, and after traveling through China in the wake of the 1937–38 Nanking Massacre he became convinced that violence is a disease that lurks within every human heart. "The act of taking sides," he became convinced, "spelled out the death of free culture and the triumph ... of its enemies." Auden's poetic response to the outbreak of World War II, "September 1, 1939," was famously equivocal, the emphasis being placed on the expiration of the 1930s—dubbed by Auden "a low, dishonest decade"—rather than on the imminence of the fascist threat to freedom.

"Spain, 1937" and "September 1, 1939" were among those poems that Auden refused to allow to be printed in later volumes of his poetry. Even in the 1930s, his work was extraordinarily diverse, and more and more as the years went by his name became paired with that of T.S. Eliot; after the death of Yeats in 1939, Eliot and Auden were almost universally regarded as the leading poets of the day. But the two may in more than one respect be seen as polar opposites. Whereas Eliot had moved permanently from the United States to England as a young man, Auden moved permanently from Britain to New York in 1939. Eliot's first marriage had failed in the face of the mental illness of his wife, Vivienne; she was eventually confined in a mental institution, and Eliot embraced the stiff collar traditions of Church and of respectable society with ever-greater conviction. Auden's marriage to novelist Thomas Mann's daughter Erica also ended, but it could hardly have been said to have "failed," since it had been entered into only to protect Erica from persecution at the hands of the Nazis. Auden made no secret of his same-sex sexual orientation (at a time when it took considerable courage to do so), and felt stifled by the society of which Eliot was a pillar; he moved in 1939 to New York, where he soon entered into a lifelong relationship with the poet Chester Kallman, and where his rumpled figure became a quiet fixture on the literary scene. If Eliot was a central figure of Modernism, Auden's connections to the forms of Modernism were more tenuous. His skill with poetic forms was extraordinarily wide-ranging, but unlike Eliot he kept returning to accentual-syllabic meters, and to the use of rhyme.

The explosive sexuality of D.H. Lawrence's fiction has been touched on above. If sexual love was one of the great themes of his work, the other was surely the corrosive effect that the British class system exerted on human relationships. In the 1930s that became a theme more and more widely taken up by novelists, in works such as Henry Green's *Living* (1929), Walter Greenwood's *Love on the Dole* (1933), and J.B. Priestley's *Angel Pavement* (1930). With the notable exception of the novels and stories of Edward Upward, however, expressions of outrage against the capitalist order of things tended to be

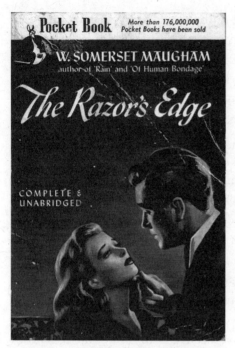

Somerset Maugham's The Razor's Edge *(1944), a novel of romance and spirituality, became one of the twentieth century's bestselling novels both in Britain and in North America. It was issued in paperback editions on both sides of the Atlantic in 1946. Pocket Books, which had followed Penguin's lead and introduced mass market paperbacks into the United States in 1941, published the American paperback edition (shown here).*

fewer in number and milder in tone in the prose fiction of the time than they were in its poetry.

At least as numerous and at least as popular in Britain during this era were fiction writers of a more conservative political stripe, including Somerset Maugham, with his tightly crafted novels and short stories; Evelyn Waugh, with his bitingly satirical novels; and P.G. Wodehouse, with his more light-hearted brand of satirical fiction. Many have seen an inherent conservatism, too, in what was then a new genre of popular fiction, the detective novel. The genre saw few if any worthy successors to Sir Arthur Conan Doyle's nineteenth-century creation, Sherlock Holmes, until Agatha Christie introduced her detective Hercule Poirot and the equally astute Jane Marple to readers in the late 1920s and 1930s. Together with the Father Brown novels of the Catholic conservative G.K. Chesterton, Christie's works founded an enduring tradition of English mystery novels.

The revolutionary experiments of Modernism that are so central to the literary history of the 1910s and 1920s were for the most part not extended in the following decades. To this generalization, David Jones's *In Parenthesis* is a notable exception; written partly in prose, partly in free verse, Jones's epic of World War I bears the unmistakable stamp of Modernism. And some other authors continued to experiment with literary form. Henry Green's *Living* (1929), for example, is written with an economy of expression that mirrors the economies of the working-class life it depicts, with articles and nouns frequently omitted from the normal syntactical flow. But most fiction writers of the period adopted a traditional approach to narrative, and even T.S. Eliot seemed to be backing away from Modernism with his ritualized play *Murder in the Cathedral* (1935)—and, following World War II, with a series of drawing-room comedies.

From the late 1930s well into the 1970s, one of the leading figures of British literature was unquestionably Graham Greene. Greene exploded onto the literary scene in 1938 with the publication of *Brighton Rock*, a tautly written exploration of the seediness and cruelty that lurked not far below the surface of much of British life. In subsequent novels, perhaps most notable among them *The Power and the Glory* (1940) and *The Heart of the Matter* (1948), Greene went on to explore the same qualities in human life generally. The setting of Greene's novels might be colonial Africa, rural Mexico, or war-torn London, but it is always recognizably "Greeneland"; always in the background is a sense of anguished Catholicism tinged with a bleak sense of despair.

Literature and Empire

No matter how widely Greene's geographical imagination ranged, the human souls he was interested in exploring were mostly those of white males from the Western world. Other British writers of the time, however, were beginning to reach for an understanding of the world that would take fuller account of the lives and the souls of those who lived under British rule in Africa, India, and much of the rest of the world. The essays of Nancy Cunard, along with those of Orwell, expressed a wide-ranging understanding of the mechanisms of imperial rule, and of the reality of life for many who suffered under it. In fiction, the novelist Joyce Cary broke new ground with his *Mr. Johnson* (1939), a comic novel with a Nigerian clerk as its protagonist. The novel represents the Nigerian in ways that are bound to make today's reader wince. Yet it also gives expression to a specifically Nigerian sense of humor, and conveys a genuinely sympathetic understanding of the situation both of Johnson and of Nigerians generally under British rule. *Mr. Johnson* is a long way from the literature of the closing decades of the twentieth century in its approach to colonial and multicultural realities (let alone the debates of the late twentieth century over "appropriation of voice"). Yet in a very real sense it marks a step forward for British literature in the possibilities it demonstrates for the British imagination of connecting with the rest of the world. In a very direct sense there is also a connection between

Mr. Johnson and the explosion of African literature later in the century (in the first half of the century exceedingly few African writers were published). As Chinua Achebe, author of *Things Fall Apart* (1958), perhaps the most widely read work of African literature, later recalled, reading the Cary novel was one of the things that led him to become a writer; "in spite of [Cary's] ability, in spite of his sympathy and understanding, he could not get under the skin of his African. They just did not communicate. And I felt if a good [English white] writer could make this mess perhaps we ought to try our hand."

The twentieth century had begun for Britain with a war in South Africa that had ended with a Pyrrhic victory. In a struggle against white colonists of Dutch background (Afrikaaners, or "Boers") that came to involve the Zulus and other native populations, the superior firepower of the British prevailed—but not without the adoption of a variety of brutally oppressive measures as the British struggled to control a guerrilla campaign by the Afrikaaners. At the time, the war seemed an extension of the British struggle against the Afrikaaners that had been continuing on and off for more than 50 years—and, as with previous conflicts, this one resulted in an expansion of the size of the British Empire. The war aroused objections to the imperial project to an unprecedented degree, however; more than a century later, it is difficult not to see in it a foreshadowing of the loss of the Empire. The brutalities in which the British allowed themselves to engage as they struggled to assert control seem a foretaste of the struggles against the Independence Movement in India in the 1930s and 1940s that would end with the independence of India in 1947, and of the struggles in Kenya and elsewhere in Africa in the 1950s that could be resolved only through the independence of those colonies. In one of his most famous speeches during the dark days of the Battle of Britain in 1940, Prime Minister Winston Churchill alluded to the possibility of the British Empire lasting for "a thousand years." Even then its foundations had crumbled, and within another 20 years the edifice of Empire would be almost entirely dismantled.

The English Language in the Early Twentieth Century

Many trends in the development of the English language that had begun in the nineteenth century or earlier continued through the first half of the twentieth. Punctuation became simpler: whereas, for example, it remained common in Britain through to the end of the nineteenth century and into the twentieth to precede a dash with a comma, by mid-century the norm was always to use one or the other, never both. Long periodic sentences had been on the decline through most of the nineteenth century, and this trend continued into the twentieth; on both sides of the Atlantic, sentences became shorter. Paragraphs also became shorter. To these generalizations, however, there were significant exceptions. With the growth of universities and the expansion of business, government, and political bureaucracies came an increase in academic, administrative, and political jargon of the sort of which Orwell complained in his famous essay "Politics and the English Language" (1946). While the majority of people (including most writers of fiction) were using shorter sentences, in other quarters writers were, in Orwell's words, "gumming together long strips of words which have already been set in order by someone else, and making the results presentable by sheer humbug."

In the twentieth century, spelling was largely stable on both sides of the Atlantic; though shortened forms of some of the more archaic spellings in standard English became common in down-market forms of advertising, particularly in the United States (*thru*, *donut*), even there few of these came close to displacing the longer traditional forms. Conventions for marking direct speech also stabilized on both sides of the Atlantic, with the British using single quotation marks and the Canadians adopting the American convention of using double quotation marks.

Vocabulary, of course, continued to expand, with many new coinages entering the language as the result of new developments in science and technology. Interestingly, Britain and the United States developed largely separate terminologies regarding that most influential of twentieth-century developments in technology, the automobile; in Britain cars run on *petrol*, the engine is under the *bonnet*, the luggage goes in the *boot*, and you drive on the *motorway*—without much noise unless there is a hole in your *silencer*. In numerous other areas in which new coinages were necessary, British usage developed as quite distinct from that in the United States—from television *presenters* (hosts); to *breeze block* construction (concrete block), to battery-powered *torches* (flashlights), to *Wellingtons* (rubber boots), to *hire purchase plans* (installment plans), British English remained distinct from American English. (Former British possessions such as Canada and Australia partook of both in forming their own national patterns.)

Perhaps the greatest structural shift in English in the first half of the twentieth century was the simplification or elimination of forms marking the subjunctive mood. In constructions such as "If I were to travel through time I would...," for example, the old subjunctive form came to be largely replaced by the simple past form of the verb ("If I traveled through time I would ...").

Throughout the nineteenth century, the spread of literacy and of mass transportation led to a steady decrease in the distinctiveness of the various dialects of English spoken in Britain, and in the distinctiveness of regional accents. That movement toward standardization continued in the twentieth century, with radio and television as its new vehicles. In 1922, the government set up the BBC (at first the initials stood for British Broadcasting Company, but the name was soon changed to British Broadcasting Corporation), and it remained the dominant force in British radio—and, from the 1950s on, British television—for most of the century. In 1926, John Reith, the BBC's managing director, created an Advisory Committee on Spoken English, chaired by Robert Bridges, then the Poet Laureate, with the task of making recommendations to facilitate a standard of pronunciation over the air. Reith specifically asked that the committee seek a "style or quality of English that would not be laughed at in any part of the country." In practice, the standardized pronunciations recommended by the committee—which remained largely mandatory for announcers until 1989—were broadly similar to the pronunciations taught in the nation's elite "public" schools in southern England. Indeed, the three terms "public school pronunciation," "BBC pronunciation," and "Received Standard Pronunciation" (a term introduced by Henry Cecil Wyld in the early twentieth century to denote "the form which ... is heard with practically no variation among speakers of the better class all over the country") are all roughly synonymous. Despite the ongoing trend toward standardization of speech in the twentieth century, however, the varieties of British English remained extraordinarily diverse throughout the century—so much so that someone from London could at century's end still have great difficulty understanding the accent of a Glaswegian or a "Geordie" (a native of the Newcastle area).

INTRODUCTION TO THE LATE TWENTIETH CENTURY AND BEYOND: 1945 TO THE TWENTY-FIRST CENTURY

The End of the War and the Coming of the Welfare State

Winston Churchill had inspired the nation—many said saved the nation—in the dark days of 1940, and remained over the following five years, by all accounts, one of the greatest war leaders in British history. Yet in 1945, the electorate unceremoniously dumped him and the Conservative Party from office, and installed the Labour Party under Clement Attlee in its place. Much as people were grateful to Churchill for his leadership in the war effort, he was seen very much as a war leader and a figure of the past at a time at which people felt strongly that they had fought not so much to preserve the world of the past as for their right to make a better world.[1] All too clearly, voters had seen that Churchill's fondest wish at the end of the war was to return to the peacetime Britain of earlier days—a Britain with a vast empire abroad and a rigid class system at home. Unlike the Prime Minister, at war's end the British people were increasingly seeing imperial possessions as a drain on the nation's scarce resources, and the class system as an impediment to prosperity and an affront to notions of equality. With remarkably little fanfare, the old British world of masters and servants had already largely disappeared, but its husk still gave shape to many social attitudes; it remained almost impossibly difficult to "get ahead" if one came from a working-class background and had

---

1   Churchill might still have been elected had it not been for his veer to the extreme ideological right during the course of the campaign. Apparently strongly influenced by having read F.A. Hayek's polemic against socialism, in his speech on 4 June 1945 Churchill likened Britain's Labour Party to Hitler's secret police, suggesting that no Labour government "could afford to allow free expression of public discontent.... They would have to fall back on some sort of Gestapo."

the "wrong accent," one could never be fully accepted in many social milieus if one's background was "in trade," and so on. It may be argued that a degree of class-consciousness persists into the twenty-first century.

Quite aside from the issue of increasingly anachronistic social attitudes, the working class and the lower middle class continued to face great obstacles simply in their daily physical existence. For many, conditions at the end of World War II were little better than they had been at the end of World War I; with

Wartime rationing in Montreal, 1942. Unlike in Britain, hardships on the home front ended soon after the war in countries such as Canada and Australia.

its calls to redistribute wealth and to engage the forces of government throughout the economy on behalf of general good, Labour represented a real change. And unquestionably, the various measures enacted by the Attlee government (many of them following on the recommendations of the 1942 and 1944 Reports to Parliament of William Beveridge) made Britain a much fairer society than she had been at any time previously in her history. The new initiatives included the establishment of the National Health Service (1946) and the National Insurance Act (1946),[1] which provided a measure of protection against poverty resulting from unemployment—or indeed from any other source.

If British life became more egalitarian during the Atlee years, however, much of what was being shared was still hardship. In a fifty-years-on retrospective, Doug Saunders memorably summarized the situation in postwar Britain:

> Food rationing during the war was bad. After the war it was terrible. Posters were put up reading "Eat Less Bread: Eat Potatoes Instead." Then, in the spring

---

1   The National Insurance Act was initially passed in 1911, but it was significantly expanded by the Attlee government.

of 1946, those posters went down: there was no bread at all.... Coal supplies were cut back to almost nil, so that in the winter of 1947, the coldest in British history, people were ordered not to heat their homes.... If the economies and buildings and cities were fractured, even worse damage was done to families. About four million children had been shipped away from their parents to unknown locations and with almost no contact, for years. Children and parents alike returned from the war to find things utterly different.... Susan Goodman, who was ten years old at the end of the war, had lived in the countryside, with her mother in London and her father in the armed forces. She recalls the moment when "this man got off the train—he was very tall and very yellow. He came up and said, 'Hello Sue, I'm Daddy,' and I put out my hand and said 'How do you do.' It was not auspicious."

Even into the 1950s, food and fuel shortages persisted—and as the hardships continued, people grew as tired of Attlee and Labour as they had been of Churchill and the Conservatives in 1945. With the 1950 election, Churchill was returned to office, and he presided over a period of relative calm from 1950 to 1955. In terms of the ideological direction of the nation, however, it was the election of 1945 that had represented the great turning point. From the late 1940s through to the late 1970s, periods of Labour rule (first under Attlee, later under Prime Ministers Harold Wilson and James Callaghan) alternated with periods of Conservative rule (first under Churchill again, later under Prime Ministers Harold Macmillan and Edward Heath). Under Labour, the growth of what came to be known as the "welfare state" was fostered, while under the Conservatives, the social activism of Labour was eschewed—but even while the Conservatives were in power, little attempt was made to dismantle the structures through which Labour was attempting to reshape British society;

The "London fog" for which the city became famous in the nineteenth and twentieth centuries was primarily created by air pollution. From December 1953 to March 1954, conditions became worse than ever, and there were more than 12,000 smog-related deaths. Since the 1950s air (and water) quality in London has improved dramatically as a result of anti-pollution measures.

for 30 years the domestic agenda for Britain remained one of building a more egalitarian society.

If the political shape of the 1950s, 1960s, and 1970s in Britain has something of a unity to it, the same cannot be said for the shape of its economic and cultural life over that period. Britain recovered far more slowly economically after World War II than did North America and many other parts of the world. The 1950s in North America are thought of as years of contentment in the midst of robust economic growth. Not so in Britain; for many, through much of that decade British life remained dreary and unsatisfying. The major literary movement of the era—the writings of the so-called angry young men—represented a reaction against the dreariness and lack of opportunity that characterized so much of British life. John Osborne's play *Look Back in Anger* (1956), which depicted the struggles of the rebellious Jimmy Porter, became the touchstone in discussions of the movement, but works of prose fiction such as John Braine's *Room at the Top* (1957) and Alan Sillitoe's *Saturday Night and Sunday Morning* (1958) and *The Loneliness of the Long Distance Runner* (1959), which also dealt with the conflicts and resentments of young working-class or lower middle-class males struggling to get on in society, had almost as great an impact.

Two other writers—Kingsley Amis and Philip Larkin—were initially often mentioned in the same breath as Osborne and Sillitoe, but even in the 1950s these two were on quite different literary paths, and, in the 1960s and 1970s, their work diverged even further both from that of angry young men and from each other's (though the two remained lifelong friends). With *Lucky Jim* (1954), a social satire about class distinctions, romantic bungling, and university life, Amis achieved literary celebrity at an early age. His subsequent novels were written in a similar vein—social satire bordering on farce—but as the years went on, the humor was tinged more with bitterness than with insight and discolored by misogyny. Larkin, too, tried his hand early on in his career with social satire—*A Girl in Winter* (1947) being the more notable of his two novels—but with Larkin, the satire was more gentle and did not sit entirely at ease with his evident aim of achieving a high degree of psychological realism. It was as a poet that Larkin made a lasting mark; poetry turned out to be the perfect medium for his unique variety of psychological understanding, his sometimes wry biting wit, and his bleak honesty about old age and death. Like

Amis, Larkin had his share of bitter and misogynist feelings (as his posthumously published letters revealed), but these are far less obtrusive in his work than they are in that of Amis, and where Amis's work became more coarse and superficial over the years, Larkin's became more varied, more resonant, and more memorable. In its subject matter but also in its form, Larkin's poetry was quite out of step with the vast majority of British poetry published in the second half of the twentieth century; almost all his poems are built on a foundation of accentual-syllabic meter, and most have a regular rhyme scheme. Yet they found a remarkably large audience; his final book, *High Windows*, made some British best-seller lists in 1974. Increasingly, critics and literary historians are coming to regard Larkin as the most important British poet of the second half of the twentieth century.

Another quite different group of writers might with equal appropriateness be described as "angry young men": those who emigrated to Britain from her overseas possessions. Particularly prominent were immigrants from the Caribbean; large numbers were recruited from Jamaica, Trinidad, and other Caribbean islands in the decade following World War II to help rebuild Britain's bombed-out cities. Though they made a real contribution to that re-building, they were often treated as second-class citizens, discriminated against in virtually every public sphere; the reaction was a series of race riots, beginning in the late 1950s.

The Caribbean-led wave of immigration in the postwar years was the beginning of a movement that would transform Britain demographically and culturally. Amongst their number were many of the founding voices of what would become known as post-colonial literature, including Samuel Selvon, George Lamming, and Derek Walcott. From the beginning, they wrote largely in opposition to (rather than within) British literary traditions; this was the beginning of the literary movement that Salman Rushdie memorably characterized a few years later with the phrase, "The Empire writes back."

The important women writers from this period were far less angry in their work than their male counterparts—though doubtless they had at least as much cause to be. The novels of Iris Murdoch, of Muriel Spark, and of Doris Lessing work with vastly different settings and story materials, ranging from the story of the life of a school mistress at a girls' boarding school in Spark's *The Prime of Miss Jean Brodie* (1961) to a philosophically tinged exploration of faith and moral imagination in Iris Murdoch's *The Bell* (1958) to an evocation of the gritty edges of colonial existence in Southern Rhodesia in Lessing's *The Grass Is Singing* (1950). Almost all are written in the vein of social or psychological realism—and most have something of an ethos of stoicism in the face of adversity. As a character in Murdoch's *Under the Net* (1954) puts it, "one must just blunder on. Truth lies in blundering on."

The End of Empire

If, in the generation following World War II, the Conservatives came to accept many of the egalitarian social principles in which Labour believed, they also came to accept that the old approach to empire was no longer workable. Britain's stature as a world power suffered serious damage during the Suez crisis of 1956, when it attempted unsuccessfully to block the nationalization by Egypt of the Suez Canal, and it suffered as well in the face of increasing resistance to imperial rule in British colonies. (Perhaps most notably, the Mau Mau rebellion in East Africa of 1952–56 showed to what extent a relatively small uprising could destabilize colonial rule, inspiring brutal reprisals and widespread fear). By the early 1960s the die was cast; Harold Macmillan's 1960 "Wind of Change" speech signaled Britain's intention to grant independence to virtually all of its remaining colonies, in Asia and the Caribbean as well as in Africa.[1] Independence in a significant number of these nations also meant majority rule by blacks, which was anathema to many white settlers. In some new nations, independence was followed by an exodus of whites, while in Rhodesia, the government of Ian Smith unilaterally declared independence from Britain in order to maintain the white minority's privileged position and prevent majority rule. Most nations joined Britain in refusing to recognize Smith's regime and imposing sanctions against it, but it was not until 1980, after a ten-year guerrilla war, that the people of Rhodesia—renamed Zimbabwe—established a state based on the principles of majority rule. By 1980, then, all of Britain's former colonial possessions in Africa were independent, as were most in Asia and the Caribbean; the only remnants of the British Empire were a scattering of small territories such as Hong Kong, Gibraltar, the Falkland Islands off the coast of Argentina, and several Caribbean islands.

---

1   Macmillan, the Conservative Prime Minister, delivered the speech to the South African Parliament during a tour of African Commonwealth states.

Doris Lessing was one of many post-war writers to focus in their fiction on the failings of colonialism. A few years before her novels and stories of southern Africa began to appear, Alan Paton's *Cry the Beloved Country* (1948), a simple and emotionally powerful tale of the hardships suffered by black South Africans under white rule, had achieved enormous success. At first such hardships were recounted for a wide audience only in novels by white writers. In the 1960s and 1970s, however, a new generation of writers of color emerged, and were rapidly accorded a place in the first rank of writing in English. Among the most important of these are V.S. Naipaul, whose major works include novels set in India (*A House for Mr. Biswas* [1962]), in Africa (*A Bend in the River* [1979]), and in his native Trinidad (*Miguel Street* [1959]); the Nigerian playwright Wole Soyinka, awarded the Nobel Prize for Literature in 1986; the Nigerian novelist Chinua Achebe, whose novels of struggle, corruption and loss in the post-colonial era (*Things Fall Apart* [1958] most notable among them) have taken on iconic status; the Trinidadian poet Derek Walcott; and the Kenyan novelist Ngũgĩ Wa Thiongo.

The HMS Antelope *under attack during the Falklands War, 1982. One case in which the British forcibly resisted efforts to wrest a colonial possession from their control was that of the Falkland Islands off the coast of Argentina, to which Argentina also laid claim. When the Argentinian Armed Forces invaded in April 1982, Margaret Thatcher's government declared war. By early June, the British had retaken the Islands, and on June 14, Argentina surrendered. Before the war Thatcher had been deeply unpopular; in its wake her popularity soared, and in 1983 she was re-elected in a landslide.*

All of these authors deal pointedly with issues of colonialism and post-colonialism in their work. It is Ngũgĩ, however, who has raised most pointedly the issue of the ways in which politics and literature connect also with language. Ngũgĩ's early novels—including *A River Between* (1965), a novel about young people grappling with the conventions of tribal life in a world in which almost no one speaks English—were written in English, and Ngũgĩ established a worldwide reputation as an English novelist. In midlife, he decided both for personal and political reasons to write instead in his first language, Kikuyu; he argues persuasively in *Decolonizing the Mind* (1986) that English is inherently tainted by the culture of the colonizer: "language has a dual character; it is both a means of communication and a carrier of culture." The debate over this issue involved many of the leading writers in Britain's former colonies; Achebe and Soyinka were among those who decided to write some works in English, others in their first language. Even those who chose to write in English, however, no longer felt obliged to adopt the "correct" English of the English themselves; whether through the use of idioms, of non-standard syntax, or of local dialects and rhythms of speech, they have extended the linguistic range of literature in English.

While the 1960s and 1970s saw an explosion of literature in English in nations newly independent from Britain, these decades also ushered in a new vibrancy and maturity in the literatures of Canada and Australia, which had long been formally independent from Britain but had retained into the 1950s a pervasive sense of Great

Stories from Black Orpheus

One of the most important vehicles with which African writing was brought to the attention of the rest of the world was the African Writers Series, launched by the UK publisher Heinemann in 1962 at the instigation of Alan Hill and initially under the general editorship of Chinua Achebe. By the end of 1969, the year that Political Spider: Stories from Black Orpheus *was published, the series had grown to 82 titles, including Achebe's* Things Fall Apart *and* Arrow of God; Weep Not, Child *and* A Grain of Wheat *by "James Ngũgĩ" (Ngũgĩ wa Thiong'o); and Wole Soyinka's* The Interpreters.

Britain as "the mother country." By the 1960s and 1970s both nations were beginning to define themselves as much in terms with their relationship with the United States (and, in the case of Australia, with Asian countries) as they did in connection with their old relationship toward Britain. Here and there, the work of important Canadian and Australian authors such as Margaret Atwood, P.K. Page, and Judith Wright illuminated the old connections with Britain, but just as often the work of these writers—like that of other major Australian and Canadian authors such as Patrick White (winner of the Nobel Prize in 1973), Les Murray, Peter Carey, Alice Munro, Carol Shields, and Michael Ondaatje—bears few traces of a British connection. Increasingly, indeed, literature in English had started to become more broadly international. Ondaatje, for example, has shown himself to be as comfortable writing about Italy and North Africa in World War II (in his Booker Prize-winning novel *The English Patient* [1992]) as he has writing about his native Sri Lanka and Canada. Rohinton Mistry has lived in Canada since he was 23, but he continues to set his major work—most notably his novel *A Fine Balance* (1996)—in his native India.

From the 1960s to Century's End

Within Britain, the 1960s and 1970s were also a time of cultural explosion—though here literature may be said to have shared the stage with other forms of cultural expression, most notably popular music. The music of The Beatles and The Rolling Stones played a central part in defining "the swinging '60s," but these groups were part of a much broader movement as a large generation of young people sought—through long hair, the lively clothing styles of Carnaby Street, and a newfound sexual freedom—to reject the values of their parents' generation.

Ironically, the most lasting literary reflections of this memorable cultural moment may not be in any literary expression of exuberance from the 1960s, but in detached and faintly critical after-the-fact poems on the subject by Larkin, such as "Annus Mirabilis" (1967):

> Sexual intercourse began
> In nineteen sixty-three
> (which was rather late for me)—
> Between the end of the *Chatterley* ban
> And the Beatles' first LP.

Lord of the Flies *has sold exception-*
ally well ever since its publication in
1954—including to high schools. This
still from Peter Brook's 1963 film ver-
sion of Lord of the Flies *was also used*
as a cover image for the "educational
edition" of the book the same year.

The comic novels of Amis and of David Lodge (notably *Changing Places,* 1975) also give some sense of the cultural moment. But several of the most important figures of British literature of these years maintained a considerable distance between their own work and the cultural ferment of the times. Lawrence Durrell completed the last of his series of evocative novels of the Anglo-Egyptian world, *The Alexandria Quartet,* in 1960; Anthony Powell continued to publish novels in his unique sequence *A Dance to the Music of Time;*[1] and William Golding, who had burst onto the literary scene in 1954 with *Lord of the Flies,* a horrific depiction of young boys forced to create a society for themselves, continued to publish novelistic explorations of the psyche and of ethical questions.

One of the most important poetic voices to emerge in Britain in the 1960s and 1970s also maintained a certain distance from the cultural mainstream; the focus of Ted Hughes's work remained largely on the natural world, and on the ways in which humans might connect to that world on a primal level. Doris Lessing, however, with the publication of her novel *The Golden Notebook* (1962), most certainly did connect with the mainstream of social and cultural change. Along with the nonfiction work *The Female Eunuch* (1970) by the Australian Germaine Greer, *The Golden Notebook* became a touchstone for women as they realized the extent to which they had been suppressed by the patriarchal structures and attitudes of society.

Committed as politicians had been to egalitarianism from the 1940s through to the 1970s, they had been largely unable to loosen the control that the British

---

1   This 12-volume work was published between 1951 and 1975 to much critical acclaim.

upper class and upper middle class continued to exert over key elements of British society. Perhaps the most egregious expression of this control was the connection that continued to exist between the best jobs and the old established universities. In almost all professions, preference continued to be given to graduates of Oxford and Cambridge. Though the Education Act of 1944 had put forward measures to increase the number of working-class students at British universities, many of the old attitudes persisted.

In a controversial award, the Beatles were appointed MBEs (Members of the British Empire) in 1965. Even more controversially, John Lennon commented in March of the following year that the group was "more popular than Jesus."

Ironically, it may have been a Conservative rather than a Labour government that challenged the old ethos most successfully. Margaret Thatcher (Prime Minister from 1979 to 1990), represented a very different brand of Conservatism from that of Winston Churchill and earlier Conservatives, much as she admired him and shared some of the old notions of Britain as a power in world affairs. A grocer's daughter, she stood in her own way as firmly against the restrictions of a hierarchical class structure as did her political opponents. But whereas Labour had sought to achieve equity by creating a welfare state, Thatcher aimed to do so by bringing the universities to heel, creating a sense of empowerment among the working class and lower middle class—and dismantling much of the welfare state in order to lower taxes. Thatcher succeeded in changing a great many British attitudes over the 11 years she held power, but in the course of doing so she fiercely divided the nation.

The eighteen years of Conservative party government in Britain from 1979 to 1997—for the most part under Thatcher as Prime Minister—was a period in which government support for culture was cut back. In a series of moves that paralleled developments in the United States under Ronald Reagan,

Thatcher attacked the foundations of the welfare state and conveyed a sense that Britain's cultural identity was to be expressed through fiercely defending the last remnants of Empire (she led a war against Argentina over the Falkland Islands in 1982) and in resisting integration with continental Europe rather than in fostering cultural expression through literature, music, and the visual arts. Ironically, this period saw perhaps the greatest flowering of British literature since the first decades of the twentieth century. Novelists were especially prominent, with Margaret Drabble, A.S. Byatt, Ian McEwan, Martin Amis, Graham Swift, and Jeannette Winterson all creating impressive bodies of work. Ironically, too, literature in Britain experienced a cultural broadening that stands in direct contrast to the narrowness of Thatcher's cultural focus. Britain itself was increasingly becoming a multicultural society with the continuing influx of immigrants from former British possessions; more and more, that diversity began to shape the British literary scene. Among the major figures of British literature during this period are Salman Rushdie, a novelist with a Pakistani family background whose works—from *Midnight's Children* (1980) and *Shame* (1983) to *Shalimar's Clown* (2005)—explore the cultures of India and Pakistan as much as they do that of Britain; Vikram Seth, another novelist whose major works (most notable among them *A Suitable Boy* [1993]) are set in India; Zadie Smith, who burst onto the literary scene in 2000 with a wide-ranging novel of post-colonial communities in England, *White Teeth*; and Nagasaki-born Kazuo Ishiguro, whose Japanese heritage informs much of his work but who has lived in Britain since the age of six.[1]

Ishiguro's best-known work, *The Remains of the Day* (1989), recounts the story of a British butler in a country house where collaborators with the Nazi regime are holding secret meetings; the novel has been widely acclaimed as among the most fully rounded fictional expressions of life under the old British class system, and of the stifling of human feeling under the sense of reserve that formed an integral part of that system. Much of Ishiguro's other work is set

---

[1]   In the first decade of the twenty-first century, five of the Man Booker literary prize winners have been from former British colonies: the Australian Peter Carey (2001), the Canadian Yann Martel (2002), the Australian/Mexican DBC Pierre (2003), the Indian Kiran Desai (2006), and the Indian Aravind Adiga (2008).

in the world of post-war Japan *(A Pale View of Hills* [1982]) and/or in dream-like worlds that resist identification with fixed geographical or temporal loca-tions *(The Unconsoled* [1995]). In his acclaimed novel *Never Let Me Go* (2005), young people are prepared for a mysterious fate at a boarding school in the English countryside where the precise geographical setting remains vague, and the temporal setting in an unspecified future even more so. Like the literatures of Canada and Australia, that of Britain in the late twentieth and early twenty-first centuries was often more difficult to place. The diversity of British writing also came to be expressed during this period through an unrestricted openness regarding sexual orientation. Whereas leading writers such as W.H. Auden in the 1930s and Thom Gunn in the 1950s had left Britain for America in large part because American cities such as New York and San Francisco were then far more accepting of homosexuality than was London (let alone any other part of the British Isles), in the 1980s and 1990s gay and lesbian writers such as Hanif Kureishi and Jeannette Winterson remained in Britain and became central fig-ures of London's literary culture. And in the twenty-first century, Carol Ann Duffy came to be acknowledged as a leading—arguably, *the* leading—poetic voice in Britain. The choice of Andrew Motion over Duffy as Poet Laureate in 1999 was controversial; the choice of Duffy for the post in 2009 was greeted with near-universal praise.[1]

Diversity of form and style also became increasingly characteristic of Brit-ish literature in the 1980s and 1990s. Poets such as Geoffrey Hill carried on something akin to the modernist tradition, while poets such as Tony Harrison infused their work with powerful political content; poets such as Alice Oswald revived and extended traditions of English nature poetry; and a range of other poets (including Grace Nichols, Moniza Alvi, and Linton Kwesi Johnson) gave full expression to the new Britain. Women poets came to the fore as never be-fore, in Ireland as well as in Britain, with Eavan Boland and Maedbh McGuck-ian particularly highly regarded.

The 1980s and 1990s may in some respects be characterized as the era of postmodernism in British literary culture; *postmodern* is a notoriously slip-pery term, however, and one worth pausing over. The most fruitful avenue

---

1   Duffy is the first woman, the first Scot, and the first openly gay or lesbian poet to be ap-pointed to the post of Poet Laureate.

of approach may be to look at Modernism and postmodernism side by side. In some ways postmodernism represents a reaction to Modernism, in others an extension of it—and in many ways the history of the one parallels that of the other. As Modernism had been the leading artistic and intellectual movement of the second and third decades of the twentieth century, so was postmodernism during the century's final two decades—at least in literature and the visual arts. Both Modernism and postmodernism may be said to have begun in France—Modernism with poets such as Arthur Rimbaud and Stephane Mallarmé and the Post-Impressionist and Cubist painters, postmodernism with philosophers such as Jacques Derrida and Michel Foucault. Modernism had at its core a rejection of traditional artistic forms and a tendency toward fragmentation of meaning as well as of form. The breaking down of the image in poetry and in painting was accompanied by extensive theorizing—by Mallarmé and the French Symbolists, by Ezra Pound and the Imagists, by the Italian Futurists, and by various others. Postmodernism was even more deeply colored by theory; indeed, it may be said to have begun at the "meta" level of theorizing rather than at the level of practice. It is notoriously resistant to definition—indeed, resistance to fixed definitions is itself a characteristic of postmodernism. Like Modernism, postmodernism

Graham Law's edition of Wilkie Collins's The Evil Genius, *one of the series-launching batch of four Broadview Literary Texts published in 1994. Even as English Studies focused to an unprecedented degree in the 1980s and 1990s on literary theory, the discipline was also becoming increasingly aware of the importance of historicizing literary works—understanding them first of all in the cultural context out of which they emerged. An important related publishing venture was the launch of the Broadview series (later renamed Broadview Editions), which includes within each volume appendices of relevant historical and cultural documents.*

embraces difficulty and distrusts the simple and straightforward. More broadly, postmodernism is characterized by a rejection of absolute truth or value, of closed systems, of grand unified narratives. As the French social philosopher Jean Baudrillard put it in 1987, "truth is what we should rid ourselves of as fast as possible and pass it on to somebody else. As with illnesses, it's the only way to be cured of it. He who hangs on to truth has lost."

As a style of discourse rather than a philosophical system, postmodernist theory dominated the academic study of literature in British and North American universities through much of the 1980s and 1990s. Postmodernism never came to dominate literature itself during that period to anything like the same degree, but the 1980s' and 1990s' fictions of Rushdie, Byatt, Ishiguro, Winterson, and Will Self, among others, often played with reality and illusion in ways that could be broadly characterized as postmodern. Works such as Byatt's novel *Possession* (1990) and Winterson's *Written on the Body* (1992), for example, display a willingness to combine different styles or forms in a single work—just as in architecture the postmodernist spirit embodies a willingness to borrow from seemingly disparate styles in designing a single structure.

One of the main thrusts of Modernism had been to apprehend consciousness directly in its often-chaotic progression. The main thrust of postmodernism, by contrast, was one of analysis more than of direct apprehension; the characteristic spirit of postmodernism is one of *self*-consciousness, of a highly attuned awareness to the problematized state of the writer, artist, or theorist as observer. Often that awareness encompasses a playfulness with regard to time—as famously expressed, for example, in the opening lines of Rushdie's Booker Prize-winning novel *Midnight's Children* (1980): "I was born in the city of Bombay ... once upon a time. No, that won't do, there's no getting away from the date."

British drama, which was influenced both by Modernism and by postmodernism, experienced great success throughout most of the second half of the twentieth century, and the beginning of the twenty-first. Major figures such as Harold Pinter and Tom Stoppard followed on from the work of Samuel Beckett in the attention that they paid to life's absurdity. In his most important plays, Pinter's focus was on personal and family relationships, whereas Stoppard's was on surprising conjunctions of circumstance and large ideas. In the groundbreaking *Rosencrantz and Guildenstern Are Dead* (1967), for example, he rewrote Shakespeare's *Hamlet* from the point of view of two of its most minor characters; in *Arcadia* (1993), which takes place both in the present and in the early years of the nineteenth century, he brought together ideas about eighteenth-century formal gardens, the science of Isaac Newton, and the life of Byron. Other leading dramatists of the period extended the frontiers of British drama in a variety of other directions. David Hare combined elements of realism with an often larger-than-life framework in plays such as *Plenty* (1978); Caryl Churchill experimented broadly with form in plays such as *Cloud Nine* (1979) and *Top Girls* (1982)—the latter informed both by an ear for dialogue closely attuned to the realities of contemporary Britain and by Churchill's strong feminist convictions; Alan Ayckbourn displayed a talent for farce in the extraordinary tour-de-force *The Norman Conquests* (1973), and a deep sense, as well, of the ways in which the apparently meaningless surface details of life relate to its sad undertones; and Michael Frayn created works ranging from farce as broad as that of Ayckbourn (as in *Noises Off* [1982]) to large-scale dramas of ideas (such as *Copenhagen* [1998]) as ambitious as those of Stoppard.

As British literature underwent these changes in the last few decades of the twentieth century, so too did it expand to embrace a range of new modes of expression. In the 1940s and 1950s, Graham Greene had been a rarity among major British writers in his willingness to write screenplays for films based on his works. By the end of the century, however, "crossover" writing of this sort had become common with Harold Pinter, Tom Stoppard, Hanif Kureishi, Neil Jordan, and Irvine Welsh among those who had written screenplays based on their novels or plays. Many also wrote for television; indeed, some of the finest drama of the era—including Stoppard's remarkable comedy *Professional Foul* (1977) on the conjunction of language philosophy and football (i.e., British soccer)—was written for the BBC. Some regularly scheduled British television programs may also lay claim to being among the more important works of the second half of the twentieth century. The comedy sketches of *Monty Python's Flying Circus* invented a new form of absurdist comedy in the early 1970s; the 12 episodes of *Fawlty Towers* (1975) set what some argued to be entirely new standards of farce; and the many episodes of *Yes, Minister* and its sequel *Yes, Prime Minister* introduced a new brand of cynical and yet warmly human comedy about the workings of British politics. Arguably, more recent television programs such as *The Office* (2001–02) have reached an equally high standard of comedy.[1]

Ireland, Scotland, Wales

The establishment of the Republic of Ireland in 1949 did not bring enduring peace to the island. With the six Ulster counties of Northern Ireland remaining a part of the United Kingdom of Great Britain and Northern Ireland, there was ongoing tension and, beginning in the late 1960s, almost recurrent violence over the status of Northern Ireland. The conflict came to be referred to as "The Troubles." A cycle of violence and repression continued, into the 1990s, as the Irish Republican Army (IRA) launched attacks on targets in England as well as in Northern Ireland, and the police and the British army launched repeated crackdowns, often involving considerable brutality. Staunchly Protestant Northern Irish politicians (the Reverend Ian Paisley most prominent among them) vowed "no surrender" to those who sought a compromise solution with Ireland and the Catholic minority in Northern Ireland.

In the late 1970s and early 1980s, a series of hunger strikes by IRA prisoners under British internment heightened tensions still further, and even after an Anglo-Irish agreement in 1985, periodic ceasefires brought only temporary cessations of conflict. In 1997, however, the IRA was persuaded to declare a ceasefire that showed promise of holding, and its political arm, Sinn Fein, joined in the multilateral Stormont talks aimed at finding a lasting solution. On 10 April 1998, an agreement was finally signed by the British and Irish governments. The Belfast Agreement (or "Good Friday Agreement") was endorsed by the major political parties of Ireland and of Northern Ireland, and in separate referendums by the electorates of both Ireland and Northern Ireland. Among the key provisions of the agreement were a commitment by all involved to an exclusively peaceful and democratic approach to change; abandonment by the Republic of its territorial claim to Northern Ireland; acceptance of the principle that the citizens of Northern Ireland had the right to determine by majority vote their constitutional future (in other words, partition was formally accepted, but so was the possibility that the Northern Irish could one day vote to join the Republic); and provision

---

1   *The Office* has been successfully adapted in a number of countries, including the US, where the series debuted in March 2005.

A gaping hole in front of the Grand Hotel in Brighton, site of the Conservative Party's conference in October 1980, was the result of an IRA bomb. Five were killed and many others injured; Prime Minister Thatcher was in her suite at the hotel when the explosion occurred, but was unharmed. An IRA statement acknowledged that Thatcher had been a target; "Today we were unlucky, but remember—we only have to be lucky once: you will have to be lucky always."

for a Northern Ireland Assembly to which additional power would devolve from the British government (still leaving Northern Ireland as part of the United Kingdom). Troubles of one sort or another remained in both Ireland and Northern Ireland, but "The Troubles" ended with the 1998 agreement; leaders on both sides were awarded the Nobel Peace Prize for their efforts.

Perhaps as important to the evolution of late twentieth- and early twenty-first-century Ireland as the coming of peace have been a precipitous decline of religious authority over Irish life and an extraordinary economic boom that has transformed the economy, particularly of the Irish Republic. Ireland has been slower than other Roman-Catholic-dominated societies of Europe (such as France, Italy, and Spain) to distance itself from the more socially conservative pronouncements of the papacy; not until 1995 was divorce permitted under Irish law, and it remains illegal to obtain an abortion in Ireland.[1] But over the past generation, Ireland has steadily become a more secular society. Over the course of a remarkably brief period in the 1980s and 1990s it also went from being one of the poorest countries in Europe to one of the wealthiest and most dynamic. Changed attitudes, a highly educated work-

---

1   A June 2007 poll found that 43 per cent of the Irish supported the legalization of abortion if a woman believed it to be in her best interest; 82 per cent of those polled supported legalizing abortion in those cases when the woman's life is in danger.

force, and programs to encourage particular sectors of high-tech industry wrought an extraordinary economic transformation.

Perhaps not surprisingly, given these circumstances, one of the most engaging literary treatments in all of English literature of the transformative effects of capitalism on the human psyche emerged from this period of economic and cultural change in Ireland. Dublin novelist Roddy Doyle's *The Van* (1991) deals with a variety of business start-up—a fish-and-chip van—that is at the opposite end of the economic spectrum from the high-tech businesses that were the well-publicized stars of Ireland's economic transformation. But in the tragicomic microcosm that Doyle creates, he captures with deep understanding the ways in which energy, imagination, and heartlessness fuse together in the heated environment in which businesses grow. (Doyle's distinguished body of work includes two trilogies, among them the Barrytown trilogy of which *The Van* forms a part, as well as his 1993 Booker Prize-winning novel of childhood, *Paddy Clarke Ha Ha Ha*).

The Irish contribution to the literature of the English-speaking world was scarcely less in the late twentieth century than it had been in the extraordinary period of 1890–1960—the period of Oscar Wilde, George Bernard Shaw, J.M. Synge, W.B. Yeats, James Joyce, and Samuel Beckett. Interestingly, a disproportionate number of the important Irish writers of the late twentieth and early twenty-first centuries are poets of Northern Irish background—among them Seamus Heaney, Derek Mahon, Medbh McGuckian, Paul Muldoon, and Tom Paulin. (It is important to note here that Heaney and others on this list self-identify as Irish, not as Northern Irish.) The list of important Irish writers in this period, however, includes writers in all genres and regions, from the short-story writer William Trevor, whose early years in a Protestant family in County Cork provided him with a unique perspective; to the acclaimed poet and Dubliner Eavan Boland; to the fiction-writer and film-maker Neil Jordan, a native of County Sligo in the northwest of Ireland, whose *The Crying Game* (1992) remains among the most memorable depictions of "The Troubles"; to the novelist Edna O'Brien, whose reaction against her childhood in what she later described as the "enclosed, fervid, and bigoted" atmosphere of the 1930s in a small village in County Clare colored much of her later fiction; to the novelist and Belfast native (in later life, Canadian citizen) Brian Moore; to the novelist, journalist, and Wexford native John Banville, whose *The Sea* (2005) was awarded the Booker Prize; and to Dublin dramatist and film-maker Conor McPherson, whose plays *The Weir* (1997) and *Shining City* (2004) explore the worlds of the living and the dead, and the ways in which Ireland continues to be possessed by its past. Writers who choose to write in Irish have also gained prominence—perhaps most notable among them the poet Nuala Ní Dhomhnaill, whose collections have often appeared with facing-page English translations.

Discontent with the dominant role played by England within Great Britain was a constant throughout the twentieth century in both Wales and Scotland, though in neither case was there a history of violence. In 1997, Tony Blair's Labour Party included in its election platform a commitment to devolution—a granting of power by the central government to proposed regional governments in Scotland and Wales. (Unlike the allocation of powers in a federal system, the granting of power under a system of devolution may be reversed; ultimate authority continues to reside with the central government.) Labour was elected with a solid majority, and devolution was approved in Scottish and Welsh referendums in the autumn of 1997; elections for the new Scottish Parliament and Welsh National assembly were held in May 1999, and since then the two regional governments have assumed a variety of responsibilities in such areas as health, housing, education, and culture.

A number of important British writers in the second half of the twentieth century were either Scottish or Welsh, including the Scottish novelist Muriel Spark, the Scottish poet Edwin Muir, and the Welsh poets Dylan Thomas and Gwyneth Lewis. Concern over the preservation of local language has been a constant both in Scotland and in Wales. The language known as Gaelic in Scotland, where it is the traditional language of the Highlands, is in its Irish variant referred to simply as Irish; on both sides of the Irish Sea it was long under pressure from English, but it was substantially revived in both Scotland and Ireland over the course of the twentieth century. In Ireland, both Irish and English are official languages, and approximately 100,000 are able to speak and 300,000 able to read the language; in Scotland, there were in the late twentieth century approximately 80,000 able to speak Gaelic. Lowland Scots, on the other hand, is a variant of English—a very substantially different dialect from that spoken by most in England, but still a related tongue. It, too, was considered to be threatened by "Standard English," but determined efforts were made in the twentieth century to maintain its vitality. In the early twentieth century, the poet and political activist Hugh MacDiarmid (1892–1978) played a leading role in such efforts. A founder in 1928 of the National Party of Scotland, MacDiarmid worked to revive many of the words he found in John Jamieson's 1808 *Etymological Dictionary of the Scottish Language*, and enjoyed considerable success in reviving Scots as a language of poetry. And in the late twentieth and early twenty-first centuries, Lowland Scots has remained very much alive, in literature as well as in speech. Such is the case, for example, with the Edinburgh dialect that is reproduced by the novelist and film-maker Irvine Welsh in *Trainspotting* (novel 1993; film screenplay 1996): "Johnny wis a junky as well as a dealer. Ye hud tae go a wee bit further up the ladder before ye found a dealer whae didnae use."

Like Gaelic/Irish, Welsh is a language quite distinct from English. From the time of Henry VIII until the second half of the twentieth century, the Welsh language had been in more or less steady decline. Henry VIII had united England and Wales and forbidden the use of Welsh for official purposes with the 1536 Statute of Wales and the 1542 Acts of Union. In 1962, however, as a central element in the budding Welsh nationalist movement, a Welsh Language Society (Cymdeithas yr Iaith Gymraeg) was formed, and in 1967 its protests prompted the British government to pass the Welsh Language Act, assigning equal status within Wales to Welsh and English—and declaring Wales to be no longer an official part of England. Since then the teaching of Welsh has been made an integral part of the educational system, and public agencies are obliged to offer bilingual service. It is now estimated that over 500,000 people in Wales are bilingual in Welsh and English, with the percentage of the population speaking the language increasing for the first time in over a century. In 2005, Gwyneth Lewis, who writes both in English and in Welsh, was named Wales's first Poet Laureate.

The New Millennium

Through the era of Conservative government under Thatcher and John Major, Britain remained deeply divided politically—over cultural politics and issues such as immigration policy; over to what extent Britain should be a free market economy or a social democratic one; and over foreign affairs. With the coming to power of Tony Blair and "New Labour," as the Labour Party began to style itself in 1994, a new era dawned in British politics. Blair had blunted the power of the unions within his own party, and the party now blended its long-standing commitment to social justice with a commitment to economic enterprise and to modernity that had been sorely lacking in the Labour Party for the previous generation or more. At century's end, long-divisive issues such as the racial composition of Britain and the conflict in Northern Ireland seemed well on the way to being resolved. Constitutional reforms had included not only the devolution of considerable power to new assemblies in Scotland and Wales but also a phasing-out of the hereditary peerage; no longer would one be able to inherit a seat in the House of Lords. Class divisions had receded, and Britons expressed a fresh confidence and a fresh sense of unity. The British seemed to have finally come to terms with their place in the world—a position of far less importance than that which they had held a century earlier, but one that no longer forced them to carry the economic and moral baggage of imperialism. It was also a position of surprising strength economically—particularly in the south of England, with London consolidating its position as one of the great financial centers of the world. Britain seemed to be in the forefront culturally, too. In the visual arts and in fashion, London held a central place, with publicity generating an annual furor over the awarding of the Turner Prize for best work by a British artist under the age of 50, and with brashly controversial artists such as Damien Hirst, Chris Ofili, and Gillian Wearing and celebrity collectors such as advertising mogul Charles Saatchi driving a culture of "Sensation" (to echo the name of the highly controversial 1997 and 2000 exhibitions from the Saatchi Collection in London and Brooklyn, respectively). London also laid claim to be the literary center of the world. "Rule, Britannia" had been Britain's defining song at its imperial zenith; "Cool Britannia" was the term now coined to define Britain. During the millennium celebrations of 2000, Britain was as confident, as united, and as prosperous as she had been at any time since the great celebrations over the Diamond Jubilee of Queen Victoria, 100 years before Tony Blair, New Labour, and "Cool Britannia."

The sky over Britain at the millennium was far from cloudless, however, and in the early years of the twenty-first century many have perceived Britain's problems as standing out in bolder relief than her triumphs. In the first few years of the twentieth century, the British people—the *English* people, especially— were stereotypically thought of as a people of civility and self-restraint, with an adherence to religion and religious propriety, and modesty that verged on prudery. In the first few years of the twenty-first century, the stereotype of the British—again, the *English*, especially—included the behavior of the "lager louts" that went on nightly rampages in city centers; the lowest rates of church atten-

dance in Europe; drunken hooliganism among soccer fans, displayed since the 1970s at matches across Europe as well as at home; and poverty-stricken and largely racially defined ghettos in post-industrial towns such as Leeds—areas which, as the suicide bombings on the London transport system in 2005 made painfully clear, could become breeding grounds for terrorism. According to social critics such as Theodore Dalrymple in works such as *Life at the Bottom* (2002), the lack of civility commonly associated with an alienated underclass was becoming more and more pervasive throughout all Britain, fueled by a "radical egotism" that had taken root in the new cultural freedom of the 1960s and that had become more and more strongly tainted during the late 1970s and the Thatcher years by materialism and uncaring individualism.

Grafted onto concern over these domestic issues was a broad concern over the place of a new Britain in a changed world. Was Britain's appropriate role that of aggressive ally of an increasingly bellicose United States? Could intervention in other

London's Millennium Bridge. The Bridge, the first new river crossing since the Tower Bridge opened in 1894, was designed jointly by Foster and Partners and Sir Anthony Caro. It opened on 10 June 2000 but had to be closed three days later due to unexpectedly strong swaying. Since its reopening on 22 February 2002 it has proved enormously popular. To the north is St. Paul's Cathedral, to the south the Tate Modern gallery. The Tate Modern opened on 12 May 2000 in a building that had previously served as the Battersea Power Station. It now houses the Tate's collection of twentieth- and twenty-first-century art; the original Tate Gallery in Chelsea, now renamed Tate Britain, houses the gallery's main collection.

nations' affairs, on either humanitarian or strategic grounds, be readily justified in a world in which concerns about terrorism, about human rights, and about the potential for a worldwide clash of cultures were coming to the fore? The participation by Prime Minister Tony Blair's government in the early twentieth-century wars in Afghanistan and Iraq provided powerful fuel for these debates. In 2007, Gordon Brown took over as Prime Minister. In 2008, Brown promised to hold an inquiry into the British involvement in the war in Iraq. A hard-hitting economic recession, beginning in 2008 and continuing into 2009 and 2010, has, however, brought an increased emphasis on domestic and economic issues.

These troubled aspects of British life are memorably represented in the literature of the late twentieth and early twenty-first centuries. The hooliganism that began to plague England in the late 1960s and 1970s was foreshadowed in Anthony Burgess's novel *A Clockwork Orange* (1962), in which the protagonist, 15-year-old Alex DeLarge, leads a gang that commits a variety of violent crimes purely for the "kick" it gives them. The early fiction of Ian McEwan—perhaps most notably his first novel, *The Cement Garden* (1978)—depicts the grim plight of young people fending for themselves in the bleakness of a post-industrial landscape. The occasion for Tony Harrison's wide-ranging long poem *v* (1985) was the graffiti left on gravestones by Leeds United soccer hooligans; in a cemetery above the ground where "Leeds United play but disappoint their fans week after week," the fans "spray words on tombstones, pissed on beer":

> Subsidence makes the obelisks all list.
> One leaning left's marked FUCK, one right's
> marked SHIT
> sprayed by some peeved supporter who was pissed....

In some cases the graffiti is football-related as well as foul-mouthed:

> Or, more expansively, there's LEEDS v.
> the opponent of last week, this week, or next,
> and a repertoire of blunt four-letter curses
> on the team or race that makes the sprayer vexed.

And, Harrison suggests, there is a wider resonance to these oppositions:

These Vs are all the versuses of life
From LEEDS v. DERBY, Black/White
and (as I've known to my cost) man v. wife,
Communist v. Fascist, Left v. Right,

Class v. class as bitter as before,
the unending violence of US and THEM ...

Hanif Kureishi's *My Son the Fanatic* (both a short story and a screenplay for a film [1997]) depicts the violent radicalization in Britain of Islamic youth as a reaction to what they see as the hypocrisy and decadence of their fathers' assimilated Britishness. Caryl Churchill's work—notably her short apocalyptic play *Far Away* (2000)—presents a world in which individuals abandon responsibility for one another, and in which the possibility of wider and wider conflict (not only nations or civilizations at war with one another, but also the human at war with the non-human environment) is beginning to seem increasingly real. And Ian McEwan's celebrated novel *Saturday* (2005) captures much of the sense of ambivalence toward violence that at the time was coming to seem a part of British life—violence both on the streets of Britain and overseas. That novel, which concerns a surgeon who becomes terrorized by violent criminals and is provoked to violent response, is set against a backdrop of looming military conflict in Iraq. Asked if he is "for the war," the beleaguered surgeon Henry Perowne replies, "I'm not for any war. But this one could be the lesser evil. In five years' time we'll know." Five years on, it was still being argued whether the war in Iraq (or that in Afghanistan) could be considered a "lesser evil;" most Britons thought not.[1]

In the space of a few hours in 2005, Britain experienced the extremes of jubilation and anguish as four coordinated terrorist attacks by suicide bombers (three of them British born) shook the London Transport system less than 24 hours after London had been announced as the surprise winner in the competition to host the 2012 Summer Olympics. Those experiences pointed in dramatically different directions. Would the lively spirit that animated Britain culturally and economically at the turn of the millennium continue to

---

1   In 2007, the novelist Martin Amis (son of Kingsley) made controversial remarks in an interview, when he described Islamists as "anti-Semites, psychotic misogynists and homophobes" and defended a proposal he had made previously to deport Muslims from Britain.

flourish and expand, with the 2012 London Olympics as a centerpiece? Or would the shadows that had been cast across modern Britain lengthen ...and darken?

Gordon Brown, Blair's successor as Prime Minister, struggled in the face of scandals, the worldwide recession of 2008-09, and a widespread perception that "New Labour" had gone stale. Meanwhile, Britain's Conservative Party, after years of indirection, began under David Cameron to find its way as a more modern and moderate party. The election of May 2010 gave the Conservatives the most seats—though as a minority looking for support to Britain's third party, Nick Clegg's Liberal Democrats. Many saw the rise of Cameron—like Clegg, an energetic and forward-looking young leader whose policies often cut across ideological lines—as signaling a return not to the spirit of the previous Conservative era dominated by Margaret Thatcher, but rather to that of the early days of Tony Blair and New Labour in the 1990s.

The 41-storey tower universally known as "The Gherkin," which houses offices of the insurance company Swiss Re, has quickly become one of London's most recognizable structures. Designed by the prominent British architect Sir Norman Foster, it officially opened on 27 April 2004. The previous day Foster chanced to discover that Sir Christopher Wren, designer of St. Paul's Cathedral, had sketched plans for a similar structure more than 300 years earlier.

No account of the cultural history of the first decade of the twenty-first century would be complete without some mention of J.K. Rowling's series of fantasy novels that began with the 1997 publication of *Harry Potter and the Philosopher's Stone*. The series became a phenomenon in popular culture; more than 500 million copies of the seven novels were sold, the film adaptations were massively successful—and the series was credited with engendering a love for reading in many young people in an era when many began to predict the demise of the book.

But popular fantasy has been only one of many directions that British literature has taken in recent years. Very much in vogue have been historical novels, ranging from McEwan's acclaimed 2007 short novel *On Chesil Beach*, set in the pre-Beatles 1960s, to Hilary Mantel's Booker Prize-winning 2009 novel *Wolf Hall*, set in the time of Henry VIII, Thomas Cromwell, and Sir Thomas More. Rhyme has become a more and more frequent presence in serious poetry, with young poets as diverse as Patience Agbabi and Sophie Hannah joining Duffy and others in using rhyme extensively; few in today's Britain associate a habit of rhyming in verse with stuffy attitudes or with political conservatism.

Literary currents in the world of "British" literature seem to become more and more international with each passing year. Aravind Adinga, for example, author of *The White Tiger*, the 2008 Booker Prize-winning novel of poverty, corruption, and religious conflict in India, was born and raised in India, and lives there again now, but has also lived for years at a time in Australia, New York, and Oxford. Kiran Desai, whose 2006 novel *The Inheritance of Loss* also won the Booker, is a citizen of India, too—but one who lived for some time in Britain after leaving India at the age of 14, and who is now a long-time resident of the United States. Even Hilary Mantel, who in 2009 became the first British citizen in five years to win the Booker Prize, spent more than a decade living in Botswana and in Saudi Arabia. If it has always been difficult to circumscribe "British literature," it is surely even more so today—as difficult, perhaps, as it is to draw any firm conclusions as to the future of Britain or of its place in the world. But of the continuing vitality of its literary traditions as we move further into the twenty-first century there can be little doubt.

The History of the English Language

Perhaps the most extraordinary feature of English language in the late twentieth and early twenty-first centuries has been the pace of its growth—growth in its size and communicative capacity, but also in the extent to which it is spoken around the world. The two phenomena are now closely linked. Linguist Paul Payack of Global Language Monitor has estimated that English likely passed the one million word mark in 2006. (By comparison, the number of words in

Old English was less than 60,000.) As in the first half of the twentieth century, much of that growth comes from new scientific coinages. But much of it is now also coming from "Chinglish" (Chinese-English) or "Hinglish" (Hindi-English) words, or other dual-language coinages. "Torunbusiness," for example, draws both on English and on the Mandarin word meaning *operating*; it means *open*, with reference to a business during opening hours.

In the 20-year period 1947–67, almost all of Britain's former colonies became independent. Recognizing the importance of English as a world-wide means of communication, most retained some official status for the English language. When India became independent in 1947, Hindi was declared the official language, English an "associate official language." In many new nations, English was accorded equal status with one or more other languages; thus in Malawi English and Chichewa are the official languages, in Swaziland, English and Swazi. In former colonies such as Nigeria and Zambia, where many local languages are spoken in different areas of the country, English was declared the *only* official language.

The speaking of English acquired a different coloring as it became the world's lingua franca, not only in the proliferation of accents but also in the timing of speech, and in the use of pitch rather than stress to mark "strong" syllables. English as it is spoken in Britain, the United States, Canada, Australia, and New Zealand remains a strongly inflected, stress-timed language; in other words, speakers typically stress certain syllables much more strongly than others, and vary the speed of speech in order to make the elapsed time between stresses more nearly equal. In other regions, however, where most people's first language is syllable- rather than stress-timed, and where pitch rather than stress marks "accented" syllables, those habits tend to be carried over into local habits of English pronunciation.

Inevitably, very substantial differences have arisen as well in the conventions of grammar and usage in different areas of the world. In the most extreme cases—as in Jamaica and several other Caribbean nations, pidgin and Creole forms of English that have become independent languages are more widely spoken than English itself. Elsewhere, conventions of spoken and of written English very different from those of "Standard English" have come to be broadly received as acceptable variants. In India "He is working here, isn't it?" or "I am not very much pleased" are generally regarded as entirely acceptable local usage. Indian Prime Minister Manmohan Singh put the matter clearly in a 2005 speech at Oxford University:

> Of course, people here may not recognise the language we speak, but let me assure you that it *is* English! In indigenising English, as so many people have done in so many nations across the world, we have made the language our own. Our choice of prepositions may not always be the Queen's English; we might occasionally split the infinitive; and we may drop an article here and add an extra one there. I am sure everyone will agree, however, that English has been enriched by Indian creativity....

Some of the most important changes in the English language in the second half of the twentieth century stemmed from the growing realization that the language had a systemic bias toward the male. In a landmark case referred to Britain by the Canadian courts, the Privy Council ruled in 1929 that the word *person* could not legally be taken to refer only to men. But could the word *man* be taken in an unbiased fashion to mean *human being*? To many, such usages seemed unproblematic—until they started to be brought up short by usages such as "the gestation period of the elephant is eleven months; that of man is nine months." From the 1970s onward it came to be more and more widely understood that *man* and *mankind* would always carry with them a whiff of malenesss, and thus could never fully and fairly represent all of humanity. Similarly the use of *he* to stand for both males and females has come to be widely criticised—and widely replaced, whether by "he or she" or simply by the use of plural constructions ("students ... they" rather than "a student ... he"); gender-specific nouns have largely been superceded by gender-neutral alternatives (*police officer* for *policeman, server* for *waitress*); and patronizing gender terms ("the girls in the office") have largely fallen into disuse. Such change did not occur without a struggle, however. For many decades, those who ventured to suggest gender-neutral alternatives to the general practice were subjected to the sort of ridicule that H.W. Fowler and F.G. Fowler (authors of *Modern English Usage* and for most of the twentieth century considered the leading arbiters of proper English usage) aimed at one S. Ferrier in *The King's English* (1906, 1931; issued without further revision in paperback, 1962). Existing habit or convention was in such cases often the only "argument" advanced against principles of fairness:

He, his, him may generally be allowed to stand for the common gender; the particular aversion to them shown by Miss Ferrier in the examples [quoted by the Fowlers] may be referred to her sex; and, ungallant as it may seem, we shall probably persist in refusing women their due here as stubbornly as Englishmen continue to offend the Scots by saying *England* instead of *Britain*.

One of the visible manifestations of changes in attitudes in the late twentieth century was the radical shift in the meaning of certain words and expressions relating to sexual behavior and sexual orientation. At mid-century, *queer* was both an adjective meaning strange and a "descriptive" term with derogatory implications, used casually and openly by heterosexuals to denote homosexuals; in the 1970s it had come to be acknowledged as an offensive word that should be avoided; in the 1980s and 1990s it was claimed by the gay and lesbian community, many of whom began to self-identify as queer. In the academic community queer theory grew up as a sub-discipline of literary theory and criticism. *Gay*, which until mid-century had meant *merry* or *given to merriment*, began in the 1970s to replace *queer* as a colloquial designator—but one that carried positive rather than negative connotations. (Toward the end of the century, however, those positive associations began to be eroded somewhat, as heterosexual youth began to use *gay* in a derogatory fashion.)

Terms relating to heterosexual relationships were often also unstable. A noteworthy example is *making love*, which until the 1950s referred to the process of courting, emphatically not including the act of sexual intercourse. In the early 1960s, the meaning of the phrase quickly shifted, so that by the 1970s, the *only* commonly used denotation of *to make love* was *to have sex*. That was one of many examples of an increasingly overt sexualization of the language. In the case of a number of words that in the early twentieth century could carry either a sexual or a non-sexual meaning (e.g., *intercourse*, *ejaculate*), the sexual meaning had completely crowded out the non-sexual one by the end of the 1960s.

The twentieth century also saw a great change in the use of obscenities. In 1914, the utterance on stage of the phrase "not bloody likely" caused an uproar during the first English performance of Bernard Shaw's *Pygmalion*. Over the first half of the century, other swear words gradually made their way into print ("d— it all," for example, eventually gave way to "damn it all"). As the Christian religion held less and less sway over Britain in the second half of the century, so the sharp shock of swear words with religious referents was rubbed smooth, and stronger and stronger sexual terms came to replace them. In the world of literary publishing the publication of Philip Larkin's "This Be The Verse" in 1974 ("They fuck you up, your mum and dad") was something of a watershed. For some time after that, most reputable newspapers and magazines resisted the appearance of "the f-word" in their pages, but in the last few years of the twentieth century and the early twenty-first that, too, has changed. In 2006, even the eminently respectable British newsmagazine *The Economist* found it acceptable to use such language in the course of quoting others; here is how their report in their 25–31 March 2006 issue on the state of Iraq three years after the 2003 invasion by American and British troops concluded: "On a toiletwall in an American airbase in Western Iraq an American soldier has scrawled his own summary analysis: 'We came, we wasted a year of our lives. At least we got the fuckers to vote.'" In 1903—even in 1953 or 1963—such language in a respectable publication would have been entirely unimaginable.

Monarchs and Prime Ministers of Great Britain

MONARCHS

House of Wessex

Egbert (Ecgberht)	829–39
Æthelwulf	839–58
Æthelbald	858–60
Æthelbert	860–66
Æthelred I	866–71
Alfred the Great	871–99
Edward the Elder	899–924
Athelstan	924–40
Edmund I	940–46
Edred (Eadred)	946–55
Edwy (Eadwig)	955–59
Edgar	959–75
Edward the Martyr	975–78
Æthelred II (the Unready)	978–1016
Edmund II (Ironside)	1016

Danish Line

Canute (Cnut)	1016–35
Harold I (Harefoot)	1035–40
Hardecanute	1040–42

Wessex Line, Restored

Edward the Confessor	1042–66
Harold II	1066

Norman Line

William I (the Conqueror)	1066–87
William II (Rufus)	1087–1100
Henry I (Beauclerc)	1100–35
Stephen	·1135–54

Harold II

William I

MONARCHS

Plantagenet, Angevin Line

Henry II	1154–89
Richard I (Coeur de Lion)	1189–99
John (Lackland)	1199–1216
Henry III	1216–72
Edward I (Longshanks)	1272–1307
Edward II	1307–27
Edward III	1327–77
Richard II	1377–99

Plantagenet, Lancastrian Line

Henry IV	1399–1413
Henry V	1413–22
Henry VI	1422–61

Plantagenet, Yorkist Line

Edward IV	1461–83
Edward V	1483
Richard III	1483–85

House of Tudor

Henry VII	1485–1509
Henry VIII	1509–47
Edward VI	1547–53
Mary I	1553–58
Elizabeth I	1558–1603

House of Stuart

James I	1603–25
Charles I	1625–49

(The Commonwealth)

(The Commonwealth)	1649–60
Oliver Cromwell	1649–58
Richard Cromwell	1658–59

House of Stuart, Restored

Charles II	1660–85
James II	1685–88

Henry VIII

Mary I

MONARCHS

House of Orange and Stuart

William III and Mary II	1689–94
William III	1694–1702

House of Stuart

Anne	1702–14

House of Brunswick, Hanover Line

George I	1714–27
George II	1727–60
George III	1760–1820

George III

George, Prince of Wales, Prince Regent	1811–20

PRIME MINISTERS

Sir Robert Walpole (Whig)	1721–42
Earl of Wilmington (Whig)	1742–43
Henry Pelham (Whig)	1743–54
Duke of Newcastle (Whig)	1754–56
Duke of Devonshire (Whig)	1756–57
Duke of Newcastle (Whig)	1757–62
Earl of Bute (Tory)	1762–63
George Grenville (Whig)	1763–65
Marquess of Rockingham (Whig)	1765–66
William Pitt the Elder (Earl of Chatham) (Whig)	1766–68
Duke of Grafton (Whig)	1768–70
Frederick North (Lord North) (Tory)	1770–82
Marquess of Rockingham (Whig)	1782
Earl of Shelburne (Whig)	1782–83
Duke of Portland	1783
William Pitt the Younger (Tory)	1783–1801
Henry Addington (Tory)	1801–04
William Pitt the Younger (Tory)	1804–06
William Wyndham Grenville (Baron Grenville) (Whig)	1806–07
Duke of Portland (Whig)	1807–09
Spencer Perceval (Tory)	1809–12
Earl of Liverpool (Tory)	1812–27

MONARCHS

George IV	1820–30
William IV	1830–37
Victoria	1837–1901

Victoria

House of
Saxe-Coburg-Gotha

Edward VII	1901–10

House of Windsor

George V	1910–36

PRIME MINISTERS

George Canning (Tory)	1827
Viscount Goderich (Tory)	1827–28
Duke of Wellington (Tory)	1828–30
Earl Grey (Whig)	1830–34
Viscount Melbourne (Whig)	1834
Sir Robert Peel (Tory)	1834–35
Viscount Melbourne (Whig)	1835–41
Sir Robert Peel (Tory)	1841–46
Lord John Russell (later Earl) (Liberal)	1846–52
Earl of Derby (Con.)	1852
Earl of Aberdeen (Tory)	1852–55
Viscount Palmerston (Lib.)	1855–58
Earl of Derby (Con.)	1858–59
Viscount Palmerston (Lib.)	1859–65
Earl Russell (Lib.)	1865–66
Earl of Derby (Con.)	1866–68
Benjamin Disraeli (Con.)	1868
William Gladstone (Lib.)	1868–74
Benjamin Disraeli (Con.)	1874–80
William Gladstone (Lib.)	1880–85
Marquess of Salisbury (Con.)	1885–86
William Gladstone (Lib.)	1886
Marquess of Salisbury (Con.)	1886–92
William Gladstone (Lib.)	1892–94
Earl of Rosebery (Lib.)	1894–95
Marquess of Salisbury (Con.)	1895–1902
Arthur Balfour (Con.)	1902–05
Sir Henry Campbell-Bannerman (Lib.)	1905–08
Herbert Asquith (Lib.)	1908–15
Herbert Asquith (Lib.)	1915–16
Andrew Bonar Law (Con.)	1922–23
Stanley Baldwin (Con.)	1923–24
James Ramsay MacDonald (Labour)	1924
Stanley Baldwin (Con.)	1924–29

MONARCHS

Edward VIII	1936
George VI	1936–52
Elizabeth II	1952–

Winston Churchill

PRIME MINISTERS

James Ramsay MacDonald (Labour)	1929–31
James Ramsay MacDonald (Labour)	1931–35
Stanley Baldwin (Con.)	1935–37
Neville Chamberlain (Con.)	1937–40
Winston Churchill (Con.)	1940–45
Winston Churchill (Con.)	1945
Clement Attlee (Labour)	1945–51
Sir Winston Churchill (Con.)	1951–55
Sir Anthony Eden (Con.)	1955–57
Harold Macmillan (Con.)	1957–63
Sir Alex Douglas-Home (Con.)	1963–64
Harold Wilson (Labour)	1964–70
Edward Heath (Con.)	1970–74
Harold Wilson (Labour)	1974–76
James Callaghan (Labour)	1976–79
Margaret Thatcher (Con.)	1979–90
John Major (Con.)	1990–97
Tony Blair (Labour)	1997–2007
Gordon Brown (Labour)	2007–2010

INDEX

Using 1832 lb. of Rolland Enviro100 Print instead
of virgin fibres paper reduces your ecological footprint of:

Trees: 16 ; 0.3 American football field
Solid waste: 990lb
Water: 9,340gal ; a shower of 2.0 days
Air emissions: 2,173lb ; emissions of 0.2 car per year